Scotland) Gladstone Club (Glasgow

Narrative of the Cretan war of independence, ed. from the

G?pomnymoneúmata of K. Kritovoulid?s by A. Ioannides

Scotland) Gladstone Club (Glasgow

Narrative of the Cretan war of independence, ed. from the G?pomnymoneúmata of K. Kritovoulid?s by A. Ioannides

ISBN/EAN: 9783741149597

Manufactured in Europe, USA, Canada, Australia, Japa

Cover: Foto ©Thomas Meinert / pixelio.de

Manufactured and distributed by brebook publishing software
(www.brebook.com)

Scotland) Gladstone Club (Glasgow

Narrative of the Cretan war of independence, ed. from the

G?pomnymoneúmata of K. Kritovoulid?s by A. Ioannides

NARRATIVE

OF THE

Cretan War of Independence.

EDITED BY

A. IOANNIDES, M.D., F.A.S.L.,

LICENTIATE OF THE LONDON ROYAL COLLEGE OF PHYSICIANS.

LONDON.

1864.

THE RIGHT HONOURABLE

W. E. GLADSTONE, M.P.,

THE ACCOMPLISHED HELLENIST

AND

ENLIGHTENED FRIEND OF THE GREEKS,

This Narrative

IS RESPECTFULLY DEDICATED BY

THE EDITOR.

PREFACE.

THE heroic contendings and direful sufferings of Cretan Patriots, both in Crete and elsewhere, during the Greek war of independence, as well as the social condition of that rich and interesting island at the present day, are very imperfectly known even to those who take a lively interest in the general progress of Greece.

The object of the following work, "*Narrative of the Cretan War of Independence,*" is to present to the English reader such authentic information as might help to guide the statesman, the scholar, the philanthropist, and the Christian, in forming a correct estimate of the condition and capabilities of one of the most important sections of the Panhellenium.

The editor, while confessing that he is proud of being not only a Greek, but a Cretan, and while he is not ashamed to avow his fond sympathies for everything connected with his native isle, ventures to believe that his residence in Western Europe, his acquaintance with its literature, and his intercourse with many of its literary and professional men of distinction, as well as his deep devotion to the general interests of Greece, have preserved him from any unpardonable prejudice, or perceptible want of historical impartiality, in treating of the special affairs of Crete.

To write a *History*, properly so called, of Greece during the last fifty years, would be a work beyond the editor's powers or pretensions, and a work that can only be executed at some subsequent period, when some gifted individual, possessing the requisite leisure, fortune, and attainments, shall deduce, from the examination of original documents and personal memoirs, materials for a performance aspiring to the dignity of a standard and enduring History of Hellenic affairs since the commencement of the nineteenth century.

The title of the present work is intended to indicate, that it is merely a simple and truthful statement of facts, supplying authentic information to readers interested in the subject, and fitted to serve as materials to be weighed and turned to account in the composition of a History of Greece.

Based on the excellent and conscientious "Apomne-moneumata of C. Critovulides," and, in fact, mainly an English paraphrase of that contribution to Cretan History, it will, it is hoped, be found to possess, even for those who are perfectly acquainted with the language in which M. C. Critovulides has written, much greater perspicuity and precision than the original work of that patriot.

A. IOANNIDES, M.D., F.A.S.L,

Licentiate of the London Royal College of Physicians.

8 Chepstow Place, Bayswater, W.

London.

NARRATIVE

OF THE

CRETAN WAR OF INDEPENDENCE.

CHAPTER I.

EVENTS IN CRETE FROM THE BEGINNING OF MAY TO THE 15TH OF SEPTEMBER, 1821.

THE Turks of Kydonia (Canea) selected as the first victims of their intended measures against the Christian inhabitants, the Bishop of Kisamos, Melchisedech, a native of Crete, and Kallinicos, teacher of a Lancastrian school in the town, and a native of Berea. They were exasperated against the Bishop on account of his resolute resistance to all their attempts to interfere with him in the faithful discharge of his duties; and they were incensed at the schoolmaster, whom they nicknamed Nizamzetitle (soldier-trainer), on account of his new system of instruction. Accordingly, about the middle of May they dragged the Bishop from Kisamos, and, simultaneously seizing Kallinicos, at the country seat of Konstantine Geracakes, in the village of Perivolia, tumultuously threw them both into the dungeons of the fortress, in spite of the remonstrances of Latiphes, then Pasha of the district of Kydonia.

They, from the same motives, surrounded without loss of time the Greek Grammar School of Kydonia for the purpose of seizing its teacher, Nicholas Phurakes. He, however, having been apprised of their intentions, succeeded in concealing himself in the humble abode of a poor woman, where he soon afterwards expired from the effects of fear.

Nearly on the same day the Turks of Rethymne, acting in concert with those of Kydonia, seized, in the environs, Georgios Buos, a native of Siphnos, who conducted a Lancastrian school recently established at Rethymne, and, in the same tumultuous manner, cast him into one of the dungeons of that town. The

Greeks of Rethymne succeeded in delivering Baos on paying a high ransom; but Geracakes was unable to accomplish the same thing in behalf of Kallinicos, although he earnestly offered for his liberty a large sum of money.

After these brief but necessary statements, we return to what was now taking place at Kydonia.

The Turks, having soon afterwards broken open the prison, dragged the Bishop and the Lancastrian teacher to the gallows on the day of our Saviour's Ascension. Kallinicos was half dead on reaching the place of execution; but the Bishop continued to the last to say to his torturers, who were dragging him naked amid blows and outrage: "Devour, ye wild beasts, my flesh; my soul, which I this day give back to my Maker, ye have no power to hurt. I die with the assurance that God will soon avenge the innocent Christian blood ye are now shedding!"

After hanging these, their first victims, the Turks directed their fury indiscriminately against the whole Christian population, and no longer heeded the commands of the local authorities.

Melchisedech was a native of one of the eastern provinces of Crete. Going abroad, as a simple ecclesiastic, while still a youth, he had passed the greatest part of his life in Bulgaria, where he attained the rank of Protosyngelos. In 1818, while still residing in Bulgaria, he was raised to the Bishopric of Kisamos in Crete, then vacant. Distinguished for courage and decision, he fearlessly defied all the outrageous threats and iniquitous demands of even the most powerful Turks; and employed the civil power, with which he was invested as a prelate of the church, to protect his flock from the cruel and brutal oppression, which at that time lay more heavily on the Christians of Crete than on any other Hellenic population. As, from his courageous bearing towards the Turks, he was exposed to the manifest danger of being murdered, it is to be regretted that he did not save himself by flight on the outbreak of the insurrection in Continental Greece, and reserve his valuable life for the service of his country during the war of independence.

The two Lancastrian teachers, mentioned above, had been trained at Iassy, in the school of Kleovulos, who first introduced into Greece from Western Europe the Lancastrian system of instruction. Being members of the Hetæria, they had initiated some of the most prominent Cretans. The deacon Kallinicos was a native of Berea in Macedonia, and was, when put to death, about 30 years of age. Blameless and courteous in his deportment, he was respected and beloved by all with whom he had intercourse. Having solemnly devoted himself to the service of his country, he was doomed to be offered up as one of the first victims on the altar of liberty.

Nicolaos Phurakes also fell a sacrifice to his devoted patriotism. Having studied under Konstantine Kumas at the celebrated Greek Gymnasium of Smyrna, he returned to Crete in 1818, a period at which it frequently happened that even youthful students were made acquainted with the plan of Greek emancipation. He was a native of the village of Alikianos in the province of Kydonia.

Shortly after the tumultuous proceedings we have just recorded, a ferocious Turk of Suda, called Hassan Reizes, the captain of a merchantman, happened to make a voyage from Kydonia (Canea)* to the island of Kimolos; and, having heard from some of the inhabitants the news of the Greek insurrection, suddenly left the place, alarmed for his own safety. On returning to Kydonia he related, with boundless indignation, what he had ascertained at Kimolos, and thus inflamed still more the exasperation of the Turkish mob, who continued, with increasing fanaticism, to wreak their fury on the unarmed Christian population.

The consternation of the Christians on each successive outburst of Turkish barbarity, was universal and indescribable. Accordingly, they sought by every possible contrivance to escape the impending danger. Such of them as found the means, fled from the fortresses and their environs, leaving warehouses, shops and houses full of property, to the discretion of the mob. It is but fair, however, to state, that the more enlightened of the Turks evinced, at this crisis, great moderation, and even encouraged and assisted their Christian acquaintances to effect their escape.

In fact, the Agas and the Pasha himself, desirous, it would appear, to control the fury of the mob, adopted for the pur-

---

* If the word Khania be not a corruption of Khthonia, an ancient designation of Crete, it is probable that Khania received its name from Khani, one of its Saracen conquerors, during their temporary ascendancy in Crete. Such, at least, is the local tradition

pose of preventing or postponing a fresh outbreak, an expedient which had proved of some use during the tumult raised by Captain Hassan, of Suda. They apprehended that the mob, if left unrestrained, would ultimately direct its fury against them. Accordingly, they represented the importance of suspending acts of violence against the Christian population, till they should ascertain the state of matters in other parts. The insular situation of Crete contributed to the adoption of this decision. All intercourse was in the meantime prohibited between Cretan and other Turkish ports, from the danger to which Turkish vessels were exposed from the Greek insurgent vessels, which almost every island of the Ægean had sent out to cruise in all parts of the Greek seas. In order to obtain the fullest information the Turkish authorities of Kydonia induced, by promises of ample recompense, Valestra, an old Frenchman, who had long resided among them, to proceed to Kythera (Cerigo) and elsewhere, for the purpose of procuring authentic intelligence about passing events.

Valestra returned from Kythera on the 9th of June, and informed the crowd, which surrounded him the moment he landed, that there was a general insurrection of the Greeks against Ottoman domination, and stated the progress of the insurgents both by sea and land. One of the insurgent flags, which he held up to satisfy the curiosity of the multitude, was snatched from his hand, dashed on the ground, and trod upon with every possible insult. The crowd instantly commenced a massacre of the Christian population, and from that moment threw off all restraint. The first victim of their ferocity was the well-known head of a guild, the father of Misael, Archbishop of Achaia and Elis, in Peloponnesus. The infuriated mob killed many other persons whom they happened to meet in the streets. A large body of Turks, issuing from the fortress with displayed banners, commenced an indiscriminate slaughter of the inhabitants of the environs, of such as, from ignorance of the state of affairs, were travelling towards the town, and of all others that came in their way.

On the 14th of June a cruel and ferocious Turk, called Tamburazes, putting himself at the head of sixty select followers, issued from the fortress, and proceeded to Kerameia,*

* A division of the province of Kydonia, consisting of several villages with respective names, and known collectively by the term Kerameia.

for the purpose of committing similar atrocities there. But Joannes Halles, Papadandreaa, and Mutsoyannes, happening to be there at the head of about forty armed followers, partly from Rhizac* and partly from Sphakia, attacked for the first time the oppressors, at a place called Lulos. The Turks, on meeting this unexpected resistance, took up a strong position, and with threats of vengeance defended themselves at first courageously. Their threats, however, and their resistance were equally vain. Henceforth the oppressors were to encounter bold warriors breathing righteous vengeance for the wrongs and slaughter of their helpless Christian brethren. On this occasion the Greeks displayed great gallantry, and the Turks, assailed with impetuosity, took to flight. So great, in fact, was the consternation of the Turks that, in their flight, they threw away their arms. The Greeks, emboldened by this success, pursued them as far as the plain below Nerocuron, situated at less than an hour's distance from the fortress. Eight Turks, including the ferocious leader, Tamburazes, fell in this engagement. The Greeks, without the loss of a man, felt for the first time the delight of making booty of Turkish arms of great value,

This victorious skirmish greatly encouraged the Greeks. and led to a series of more important victories. The Christians, hitherto unarmed and cowed by oppression, now conceived the hope of being able, with God's aid, to vanquish their gigantic enemy. The Turks, on the contrary, were now struck with corresponding despondency and dismay. Convinced that the subject population would, if once they got arms into their hands, no longer unresistingly submit to be slaughtered as their brethren had been when unarmed and unprepared, the Turks, as will by-and-by appear, now energetically endeavoured to prevent the impending danger. All their efforts, however, proved ineffectual.

Those who had been routed in the above-mentioned encounter were at great pains, in order to disguise the disgrace of defeat, to give out, on returning to the fortress, that they had seen the neighbouring hills covered with troops, consisting partly of Muscovites in the dress of Western Europe, and partly of Peloponnesian Greeks with white kilts.

* The designation Rhizac has been given to the more mountainous parts of Kydonia, situated at the foot of the White Mountains (Madarae). The inhabitants are called in Crete Rhizitae.

The exasperation of the Turks, in consequence of this occurrence, produced within the fortress, on the 15th of June, a fearful tragedy. Tumultuously closing the gates early in the morning, they first made an indiscriminate slaughter of all Christians found in the streets. Then rushing into the houses, inhabited by Christians, they killed or captured men, women, and children, and, at the same time, plundered the Christian houses, shops, and warehouses. A vast Turkish crowd surrounded with cries and uproar the residence of Kasimaga, a Mussulman of distinction, and dragged from it about 80 Christians, who had taken refuge there. All these were massacred before Kasimaga's door; and that kind and generous Mussulman was unable, with all his efforts, to save even one of them. After this, the leaders of the mob addressed Kasimaga himself with the greatest insolence, and outrageously demanded that Georgios Papadakes, Euthymios Psarudakes, and Joannes Kuvarites, persons who enjoyed his favour and confidence, and who had by his encouragement, a few days before, made their escape, should be delivered up to them.

Two young men, belonging to the distinguished family of the Levtheraci, were slaughtered in their mother's arms. The Pasha's interpreter Apostolakes and Stavrakes Sumarupas, persons of influence, were murdered, and their dead bodies were dragged through the streets, with every conceivable outrage. Kallinicos Sarpakes, Bishop of Kydonia, the abbots of the monasteries of Gonia and of Guvernetos, and a great number of others, clergymen and laymen, were thrown into prison naked and barefooted, and every thing within reach of the mob was plundered and profaned, whether sacred or secular. On that dreadful day about 300 persons perished within the fortress, in addition to the large number of Christians, who had been slaughtered on the preceding days in the environs.

The Greeks now began to retaliate; and the inhabitants of the large village Therison and those of Prassia and Bamia of Apocoronos, respectively put to death the resident Turkish Authorities (Subascs). The same thing occured also in many other places. This naturally made the Turks, residing in the country, repair for safety to the fortresses of Kydonia and Suda, abandoning their estates, houses, and most of their effects.

The anticipation of such occurrences had induced the leading
Greeks of the Western Provinces of Crete to assemble previously in the province of Sphakia. At this meeting had
been present all the influential Greeks both of Sphakia and
of the neighbouring province, who had been able to attend.
The object of the meeting had been to deliberate on the
means of averting impending dangers, and preparing for the
ensuing struggle, as it had now become manifest that the
oppressors aimed at a general extermination of the Christian
population.

The names of the individuals present at this assemblage, as
representatives of their respective towns and villages, were:—

From Sphakia: Hadji Joannes Poludakes, Andeas Krearas,
Anagnostes and Andreas Pannyotes, brothers, Anagnostes
Psarudakes, Nicolaos Andrulakes, Manusos Papadakes,
Andreas Phasules, Georgios Dascalakes, surnamed Tselepes,
Georgios, Protopapas of Sphakia, Joseph Kavcalakes, Rusos
Vurdumbas, Anagnostes Protopapadakes, Georgios Poloy-
annakes, Strates Pelivanes, Anagnostes and Konstantinos
Manusakes, Hadji Khionias, Petros Munuseles, Siphes Dasca-
lakes and the brothers Deliyannakes, Georgios, Joseph and
Strates, the most influential inhabitants of the mountainous
province of Sphakia.

From Kydonia: Vasilios and Joannes Halles of Therison;
the Proimidae, the Paraskevaei and the Plazii, from the
town of Lakki; Papadandreas from Kcramcia, Anthimos,
Abbot of Chrysopegé, Neophytos Œconomos, Konstantinos
Geracakes*, Euthymios Psarudakes, Joannes Kuvarites.

* This person was, with his brother Euthymios, a minor, and two females,
Anastasia and Elisabeth, a remaining descendant of the distinguished
family of the Hadji Nicollani, as they were called at Kydonia, and a son of
the murdered Manolakes Geracakes. Hadji Nicolos, the father of Manolakes,
had been the most opulent of the Cretans in landed and other property,
about the end of the last century, and had shown himself in various ways a
munificent benefactor of his country. He was the first who established at
Kydonia a Greek Grammar School, and that in spite of the danger to which
he was exposed, owing to the ruthless oppression which the Greeks of Crete
then endured. He erected an hospital for the sick, and bestowed large
sums in aiding the poor. After his death his Greek fellow-citizens, in token
of gratitude, hung up his portrait in the school of which he was the
founder.

His son Manolakes, a gentleman of elevated sentiments and dignified
bearing, was his worthy successor as patron of these philanthropic institutions. He was at great pains to raise the efficiency of the school, by
procuring for it the most learned teachers of the time. Manolakes, however,
was, at the instigation of a prominent Turk, called Yaya Aphentakes, who

From Apocoronos: Siphacas Konstantudakes, Joannes Sakires, of Kephaladae, Georgios Papadakes, Georgios Velicines of Halicampi, and the aged Yánnares of Prosneron.

From Lampo: Melchisedech, Abbot of Prevelo, Georgios and Joannes Suderos, brothers, and Georgios Sakkorraphos.

From Rethymne: Joannes Druliskos, G. Kallerges, Hadji Joannes Damverges, Zorzes and Gregorios Saunatsos, brothers, Stylianos and Michael Khionakes, brothers.

The two distinguished brothers, Kurmulidae,* Michael and

was onvious of his commercial success, assassinated by a Turkish ruffian. The assassin shot his victim on the 5th of August, 1804, in the crowded market-place of Kydonia, in open day.

Manolakes' son, Konstantinos, mentioned in the text, took part in the insurrection, and rendered, in a variety of ways, most effective services, devoting nearly the whole of his large patrimony to the cause. He died in 1855, in abject poverty, in free Athens. Such has been the lot of many luckless Cretans, who toiled and suffered to achieve national independence.

We hear with great pleasure that some of the most prominent Ottoman inhabitants of the Cretan towns, ashamed of their former ferocity, are exerting themselves for the moral improvement of the community, and that, besides exhibiting milder sentiments and a more social bearing towards the Christians, are causing their children to be instructed in Greek and French.

* The house of the Kurmulidae was an ancient and distinguished Christian family in Crete. At the beginning of the Revolution it consisted of about 80 members. The seat of the heads of the family was Kusé, a village in the province of Gortyna, containing about a hundred families, all Christian. The ancestors of the Kurmulidae, like many other families, were under the necessity, during the fearful period of the capture of Crete by the Turks, of submitting to an outward change of religion. They inwardly, however, and with great fervency, adhered to the Christian and orthodox religion, which was with great care and caution transmitted to their descendants. They had their concealed chapels, and secretly, but punctually and earnestly, observed all its rites.

This was the case with the two brothers still alive at the commencement of the war of independence. The elder of these bore ostensibly the Turkish name of Husein, while his real and Christian name was Michael. The younger, whose Christian name was Georgios, outwardly bore the Turkish name of Yusuphes. They were the most wealthy landed proprietors and owners of flocks and herds in Gortynia, and exercised in those parts very great influence.

Michael was the more gifted and energetic of the two. Though from time to time subjected, through the machinations of the enemies of his family, to charges of heterodoxy and other offences, he succeeded in evading them all, partly through various expedients, and partly by means of the friendly relations which he was at pains to cultivate with the Turkish authorities and the most powerful personages of the day. He was an undaunted adversary of the oppressors, and a fervid patron of his oppressed Christian brethren. When, in consequence of this, he was, in 1814, denounced to Hadji Osman Pasha as guilty of putting various Turks to death and of heterodoxy, he dexterously and successfully defended himself in the following manner: "I caused such Turks," he said, "to be put to death as set at naught the life, honour and property of our mighty Sultan's subjects,

Georgios, who had made their escape from Gortyna, and other leaders from other parts of Crete, were also present. These assembled patriots, solemnly invoking the Almighty, unanimously resolved to take up arms in order to avert the impending extermination of themselves, their Christian brethren and their children.

On the suggestion of N. Œconomos, a general fund was established, to which each person present contributed according to his means, towards defraying the first expenses of the war. The assembly, at the same time, elected a deputation, consisting of G. Papadakes, A. Panaoytes, and Stratos Pelivanakes, who immediately proceeded, with a portion of the money that had been collected, to Hydra, in order to procure ammunition and arms. Unfortunately there was a scarcity of these even there; but all they could then obtain they forthwith despatched to Crete.

It was an obvious necessity to appoint military leaders and range their followers under their respective standards. Accordingly the following arrangements were made. A. Panayotes, Georgios Dascalakes and A. Phasules were directed to take the command of the whole armed population of Anopolis,* and

whom he sent you to protect." Instead of being punished on this occasion, he was rewarded by the Pasha with a commission, which gave him an extension of authority in the district of Gortyna. The Pasha, at the same time, bestowed on him a mantle (binla), the usual gift of honour conferred on Turkish functionaries.

Michael Kurmules had become a member of the Hetaeria a few months before the outbreak of the war of independence. He had been initiated by the deacon Gregorios Kallonas, and had ardently hailed the *great idea*. Deliberately foregoing rank and influence among the Turks, he unhesitatingly quitted his splendid castle and vast property, avowing himself a fervid champion of his faith and country. During the war of independence he endured the greatest privations and hardships without a murmur. Having, as the war was just beginning, been invited as a faithful Mussulman by the Turkish inhabitants of Tympaklon and Pompelon, villages of Gortynia, to aid them in slaughtering the Christians of those parts, he acted with so much prudence of mind and judgment as to save from destruction about a thousand Christians, who, by his directions and aid, were, about the middle of May, safely conveyed to Sphakia in two Sphakian vessels. He, at the same time, effected his own escape from Zonari, a roadstead of Gortynia. We shall subsequently find Kurmules acting a prominent part as a gallant patriot warrior.

* The province of Sphakia was divided into two sections, one of which was that of Anopolis, comprehending all the villages situate on the western part of the province, on the coast of the Lybian sea. The modern name, Sphakia, is probably a corruption of Phœnix or Phœnikia, an ancient city, some of the ruins of which are still to be seen near port Lutron, and are still called Phœnikias. In ancient times it was a dependency of Lampe. Its

forming a junction with the corps under the Hallæ at Therison, and that of Siphacas at Melidoni, to make head against the Turks of Kydonia. A. Protopapadakes, commanding the Skyphiots and A. Manusoyannakes, commanding the Imbriots, were directed to act against Alidakes, at Prosneron, and other Turkish Chiefs in the province of Apocoronos, and have the co-operation of Joannes Sakires from Kephaladæ, Georgios Velizines from Halicampi, and Yannares from Prosneron. Georgios Deliyannakes and Petros Manuscles, at the head of the armed population of their villages, and Georgios Suderos at the head of the Lampæi, were to operate simultaneously against the Turks of Rethymne, and to have the assistance of Joannes Draliskos at the head of all such Greeks of Rethymne as were in possession of arms. Rusos Vurdumbas and Georgios Poloyannakes, who was afterwards surnamed Pologeorgakes, with the Prosyalitae,* the Komithiani and the Muriotae, and Michael Kurmules, with his followers, among whom was Antonios Melidones, undertook to watch the movements of the Turks of Gortyna, and of those, who from their head quarters at Heracleion‡ were making frequent incursions into the neighbouring districts. These last mentioned Greek leaders, however, were instructed to act, for some time, when necessary, in concert with those especially appointed to operate against the Rethymnian Turks. Such were the mutual arrangements adopted for the occasion by the commanders of the insurgents.

Before commencing an account of the military operations, it is necessary to premise a few remarks regarding the preparations and resources of the Cretan Greeks, at the moment they took up arms against their Turkish oppressors, so numerous, powerful, possessing great resources, trained to

citadel was, undoubtedly, what is now called Anopolis. It is mentioned by St. Luke, in the Acts of the Apostles, under the name of Phœnika, whence commenced the dangerous part of Paul's voyage to Rome. Under the Byzantine emperors Phœnikia had, on account of its ancient celebrity, a separate bishop

* The town of Prosyalos, considered the chief town of the Sphakians, and of which Vurdumbas is a native, is situated on the coast opposite and to the east of port Lutron.

‡ Heracleion was the ancient naval station of the great city of Knossos. Here was subsequently erected Khandax (whence the name Candia), a place of great strength on account of its remarkable fortifications, built at vast expense by the Venetians. It is situated on the north coast, and is at the present day the ecclesiastical metropolis of Crete.

arms, and bent on the utter extermination of their Christian subjects.

To enter on so unequal a contest, the Greeks of Creto would have required a considerable supply of arms and warlike stores; but their position under the Turks rendered such a supply impossible. The most rigorous measures had been employed to take from them any arms they happened to possess for the protection of their flocks, for killing game, or for any other lawful purpose. The Turks had especially used every means to disarm the mountaineers of Sphakia, as they were more apprehensive of them than of any other portion of the Greek population. The Sphakians, however, under various plausible pretexts, evaded compliance with all orders to deliver up their arms.

The Cretans had previously applied on various occasions to the inhabitants of Hydra and Spezzia for a supply of arms and ammunition, as well as for the aid of a naval force. M. Tricoupi is, therefore, mistaken in saying that the Cretans regarded with indifference the preparations made in other parts of Greece for the ensuing war of independence. In fact, the preparations for the national contest were common to every section of the Panhellenion; and the songs of Ferraeos in praise of liberty—and these constituted the main preparations for an appeal to arms—were known and cherished all over Greece. Stephanos Halles, celebrated for his sweet voice and musical skill, had long been accustomed to sing these to his lyre at Therison, kindling thereby the patriotism and military ardour of his countrymen.

The sagacious Hydriota, aware of the precarious position of the Christian population of Crete, had, in reply to all applications for assistance, judiciously urged on the Cretans the necessity of caution and patience till the expected moment should arrive.

When at length the Turkish mob, regardless alike of the commands of the authorities and the entreaties of individuals, evinced their determination to exterminate the Christian subjects, the Greeks felt there was no alternative, but either to submit unresistingly to destruction, or to take up arms in defence of themselves and their families, notwithstanding the meagreness of their resources. Unaided and alone, therefore, they entered on the contest, and the God of battles strengthened the feeble against the mighty.

The whole amount of warlike stores, possessed by the insurgents at the moment of the outbreak, was insignificant in the extreme. They obtained from Andreas Phasules forty small barrels of powder (about 360 okas), being part of a miscellaneous cargo, with which he was proceeding to Alexandria; they further procured a small quantity of powder from ten Sphakian vessels, which happened at that time to have touched at Lutron. In addition to this many Sphakians and other Cretans, who had been able to preserve their fire-arms, had a small supply of cartridges. Kurmules had also from time to time secretly sent from Heracleion some small quantities of ammunition to places of security. Finally, V. Halles of Therison had, simultaneously with the commencement of the insurrection in other parts of Greece, had the foresight to commence collecting ammunition. The Cretans, however, were in almost total want both of lead and of paper to make cartridges. The books of the churches, leaden weights and whatever else could be obtained that was of any use in making cartridges, were turned to account. For many months the Cretan insurgent continued to purchase powder at his own expense, paying for it at the rate of four or even five Spanish dollars an oka to fight in defence of his faith and country.

The number of muskets at this time in the insurgent army was exceedingly small, certainly not more than 1200. Of these about 800 belonged to Sphakians, the remainder belonging to such persons from the more mountainous parts of the provinces of Kydonia, Lampe, Apocorono and Re-thymne, as had been able to conceal their arms, when, as above mentioned, the Turks had endeavoured to disarm the Christian population. Such then was, at this period, the amount of the whole armed force of the Greeks in Crete.

The circumstances already detailed, sufficiently justify the leading men among the Sphakians, who, from apprehension of the possible consequences, hesitated at first to call their brethren to arms. The other Christians of Crete were natur-ally guided by the example of the Sphakians, whose position was more advantageous than their own, in regard both to the possession of arms and natural strength of their country. It is an undoubted fact, however, that the Sphakians shared in the general aspirations of the Greeks, and had eagerly hailed the plan of insurrection, which had been communicated to them on the spot by various persons, and, in particular, by Nicolaos Barelzoglos, surnamed Karazzas, a native of Crete. Their sentiments had been evinced by their persevering refusal to give up their arms, notwithstanding the frequent and rigorous demands of the Turks to obtain them as a security for their fidelity. Their sympathies had been further manifested by their cordially affording an asylum among their mountains to many armed Greeks, who had repaired thither from Peloponnesus after previous insurrections.

The object of these details is to refute the unjust charges brought against the Cretans by M. Tricoupi. In book I. of his history (Chap. 12, page 226) that writer expresses himself as follows: " Though the insurrection continued to spread all over Greece and had extended to all the islands of the Ægean; and though armed vessels under the Greek flag frequently made their appearance on the coast of Crete, the inhabitants both of the lowlands and of the highlands of that island remained entirely unconcerned."

The Cretans to a man felt the most lively interest in the general movement, and prepared for the contest the moment the din of Grecian arms reached their ears. M. Tricoupi, however, seems to have forgotten that the Turks of Crete were a daring and warlike race, and the most cruel of all the oppressors of Greece. The Cretans, thirsting for emancipation, had caught the patriotic flame on every occasion on which their brethren in other parts of Greece had taken up arms to assert their liberty. In proof of this it is sufficient to revert to the disasters incurred by the Cretans in 1770, during the insurrection of Peloponnesus and other parts of Greece, in the war between Russia and Turkey.

So early as the beginning of May, 1821, armed insurgents from other parts of Greece began to arrive in Sphakia. Among these were Georgios Dascalakes, Nicolaos and Vasilios Lakiotm, Stavros Andrakos, Joannes Mutsakes, Antonios Melidones, Nicolaos Zavolas, Panayes Suliotes, and Nicolaos Zervos, all intrepid warriors and declared enemies of the oppressors. Most of these patriots had been previously residing in Asia Minor. By the enthusiastic accounts they gave of the triumphs and progress of the insurrection in other parts of Greece, they inflamed the warlike ardour of the Cretans, and inspired them with confident hopes of victory. All the above-mentioned individuals were natives of Crete except the

two last, Zervos from Eleusis, in Attica, and Suliotes from
Constantinople. They possessed great warlike skill and
experience, having distinguished themselves in numerous engagements in Peloponnesus, whither they had accompanied
their friend Nicolaos Kriziotes of Euboea. From Peloponnesus they passed over to Crete, to aid also in the emancipation
of their native island.

After the victorious skirmish at Lulos, and the fearful
massacre of Christians in Kydonia, which followed that event,
a body of Turks marched out of the fortress (on the 17th
of the month). Part of them proceeded to the village of
Murios, in the district of Kydonia, while another division,
consisting of about 700 men, under Ali Sophtas and Tsuranes,
occupied a village of Apocoronos, called Kalyvæ, opposite
Suda. A detachment of about eighty men were sent to
Alidakes to aid him in occupying, as an outpost, the strong
tower of Prosneron,* to keep the Sphakians in check, whom
the Turks dreaded more than any other section of the Cretans, on account of the strength of their country, as well as of
their suspicious conduct in affording an asylum to those who
had refused to give up their arms. These movements rendered it indispensable that the patriots should, with all possible
speed, attack the Turks who had occupied Kalyvæ.

As soon as these movements of the Turks became known
in Sphakia, Georgios Dascalakes, with a portion of Anopolitæ, was the first to unfurl the flag of independence. At
Melidoni, a village of Apocoronos, he joined Siphacas. These
united drove the Turkish inhabitants from Pemonia, Neokhori,
Fre, and other neighbouring villages, killing some of them,
and burning their fortified houses.

On the same day, Protopapadakes also appeared at Prosneron with displayed banner, and attacked the Turks under
Alidakes, who at first made a resolute stand, but were at
length compelled to shut themselves up in the tower. Protopapadakes, having appointed a detachment to besiege the tower,
proceeded at the head of the Halicampitæ, of such of the Apo-

* The village of Prosneron is situated at the commencement of the road
leading up to Krapo, and belongs to the province of Apocoronos. Here
stood the strongly fortified tower, serving as an important outpost, which
was demolished by the Sphakians when it was abandoned by the besieged.
The proprietor of this tower, an Ottoman of the name of Alidakes, was a
great landed proprietor, and owner of numerous flocks. Between him and
the mountaineers of Sphakia, and especially the neighbouring Skyphiots,
there existed perpetual and destructive feuds.

coronites as had procured arms, of a party of insurgents from Kephaladao under Sakires, and of his own Sphakian followers, towards the village of Syvara or Tzivara, where a body of Turks from Kalyvae had advanced to meet him. An engagement ensued in the vicinity. The combat was maintained on both sides with vigour and obstinacy, the Greeks frequently rushing on the Turks, while the Turks, on their part, impetuously charged the Greeks, and evinced a resolute determination to overpower adversaries, whom they had so recently regarded with contempt. After a conflict of several hours, the Turks obtained the advantage. In fact, Protopapadakes was on the point of commencing a retreat, when Dascalakes and Siphakas, rapidly advancing from Makhoerae, where they were stationed, unexpectedly attacked the Turks in the rear, and threw them into confusion. The enemy, now attacked both in front and in rear, and vigorously pressed, took to flight. Some of them, rushing towards the sea, leaped into boats, lying at anchor near the shore, in the hope of making their escape to Suda, while others fled in the direction of Kydonia. Thus terminated the second conflict between the insurgents and their oppressors.

In this engagement thirty-six Turks were killed, besides those who were drowned in the sea in attempting to escape. The Greeks lost only two men. The Turks left behind them ammunition and arms.* The real loss on the part of the enemy was indeed small, but the moral effect of the victory greatly contributed to animate the insurgents and to discourage their opponents.

Without loss of time Dascalakes and Siphacas occupied the village of Malaxa, a position of great strength, situated on a table-land to the south east of Kydonia, and at more than an hour's distance from that place. Protopapadakes, immediately repairing to the small fortress of Almyros on the coast of Apocoronos, opposite and to the west of Rethymne, killed part of the garrison, and drove out the rest. He then dismantled the strongest parts of the fortifications, and transported to Prosneron two guns of large calibre, to cannonade the besieged tower.

* During the early period of the war of independence, the armed insurgents were actually accompanied by a retinue of unarmed Greeks, carrying clubs on their shoulders for want of muskets, for the purpose of striking terror into the enemy from a distance. These gradually became part of the armed force by eagerly purchasing, at a high price, such Turkish muskets and other arms, as fell into the hands of their victorious brethren.

At the same time V. Halles and A. Phasules occupied Hayia Kyriake, situated to the south-west of Almyros, and built on the site of an ancient city, nearly at the same distance as Malaxa. A. Panayotes, with part of the insurgents from Rhizae and Anopolis, occupied the military position called Apopegadi, situated opposite to the provinces of Selinon and Kisamos eastward. This position was very convenient for watching and checking the movements of the warlike Turkish inhabitants of those parts.

On the same day on which the engagement took place at Kalyvae, the Turks of Murniae also hastened to proceed by Digene to Kerameia. They were, however, vigorously attacked by the detachment under V. Halles and A. Phasules, and, at the same time, by the Greek inhabitants of Kerameia under the leadership of Joannes Halles and Papadandreas, and speedily put to flight, leaving a considerable number of dead and of arms on the field.

On the 20th of the month a large body of Turks proceeded towards Malaxa for the purpose of dislodging Dascalakes, but met a vigorous resistance. After an obstinate conflict of three hours, in which they displayed great courage, they were compelled to retreat, and, being pursued to a great distance along the plain, lost about 15 men in the retreat.

Such encounters continued to take place almost daily. Sometimes they attacked at Barypetros the insurgents of Lakki and other villages of Rhizae under A. Panayotes, and made frequent attacks on Halles, sometimes at Kusunaria, sometimes at Hayia Marina, and sometimes at Keratide, above Murniae, as they were very desirous of occupying all these positions, convenient for harassing the insurgents. Worsted, however, after obstinate skirmishes, in all their attempts to get possession of these positions, they retired invariably with loss, mortified in the extreme at their failures. The victorious Greeks, on the contrary, thus gradually learned to despise their oppressors. They were now daily procuring supplies of arms in the spoils of the vanquished. They began, in consequence of their frequent success, to be convinced of their superiority to their opponents; and they unhesitatingly exposed themselves to dangers and toil, animated by the assurance that the day of vengeance was now come for all the outrages and atrocities which the Turks had recklessly and with impunity inflicted on them and theirs.

The reader will naturally be desirous of knowing what was going on in other parts of Crete during these terrible events. We shall first describe what took place in the districts around Rethymne.

The Turks of those parts, on hearing of the massacres and plunderings which had taken place in the province of Kydonia on the 15th of the month, broke forth into similar excesses, and perpetrated equal atrocities. Within the town they slaughtered more than a hundred unarmed and inoffensive Greeks, including Kh. Kallerges and Joannes Deligeorges. They then rushed with unbridled fury to the houses of Greeks, whether the owners were still in the town or had previously effected their escape.* Entering the shops and stores of the Greeks, they plundered whatever they found there. All the adult males that fell into their hands were murdered, and all the women and children were made captives. Gerasimos Perdicares, Bishop of Rethymne, the Abbots of several monasteries, Joannes,† teacher of the Grammar School, and others, of whom some were clergymen and some laymen, were dragged to prison. For three days bodies of armed and infuriated Turks, with displayed banners, continued to over-run the surrounding villages, plundering, capturing, or killing all Christians that had not been able to conceal themselves or flee to the mountains.

At Perivolia, a village at a small distance from the fortress, about sixty were put to death; and at the villages of Marula and Magula a great number of others, including Georgios, the venerable clergyman. Three young females, of singular beauty, were also slaughtered, a contention about the possession of whom had occasioned the death of two of the Turkish plunderers. Similar barbarities were perpetrated in other villages of the districts around Rethymne. The whole

---

* Many of the more prominent Greeks had, from time to time, absconded, and particularly during Passion Week, under the pretext of attending to their religious duties in connexion with the Easter festivals, thus escaping with their lives, but leaving behind them, as some of the Kydonian Greeks also had done, their effects.

† The Greeks of Rethymne also had displayed great patriotism in maintaining both a Grammar and a Lancastrian School, as has been mentioned above. To give greater efficiency to these institutions, they had procured the services of Joannes, previously connected with the celebrated Gymnasium of Kydonia (Haivali.) Joannes was a nephew of the Bishop of Aulopotamos, who in 1827 became also Bishop of Rethymne.

c

number of victims in those parts, during this fearful crisis, was reckoned at about five hundred, besides the women and children who were made captives. One savage and relentless Turk alone, called Hadjalakes, had slaughtered a large proportion of the victims with his own hand, rushing like a tiger against all Christians within his reach. After these terrible scenes, the Turks retired to the fortress of Rethymne, while many Christians, who had escaped slaughter, found a safe retreat in Sphakia and the neighbouring mountains.

On the 17th of the month, when the Turks of Kydonia had issued from the fortress to over-run the surrounding districts, those also of Rethymne had collected in large numbers at Hayios Konstantinos and Rustica, villages situated to the south-west of Rethymne, and at about an hour's distance, for the purpose of attacking and dispersing the insurgents who were mustering at the foot of the mountains. A plan for simultaneously invading Sphakia had been concerted between the Turks of Kydonia and those of Rethymne, the former of whom were to proceed from Apocoronos, and the latter to advance from Rethymne. This intended expedition, however, was baffled by the vigilance and vigour of the insurgents. Protopapadakes, Siphacas, and Dascalakes defeated a body of Turks at Kalyvae. Petros Manaselea, commanding the insurgents from Kallicrates, Georgios Deliyannakes at the head of his usual followers, Joannes Druliskos, and Manoles Rustikianos, leaders of the Rethymnian Greeks, had previously attacked a Turkish force in the neighbourhood of Rethymne, and compelled the enemy to return in disorder to the fortress. On this occasion seven Turks were killed, while the Greeks did not sustain any loss whatever.

Simultaneously Ismael Kundures and Glymides, two Turkish leaders, famed for their courage and daring, proceeded at the head of about two hundred followers, by another route, animated with the persuasion that they would be able of themselves to spread consternation amongst the Sphakians, and exterminate the insurgents of Lampe (Hayios Vasilios) and Rethymne. At Hayios Joannes, a village in the province of Lampe, and surnamed Kaymenon, they made a vigorous attack on Rusos Vurdumbas, M. Kurmules, G. Suderos, Poloycorgakes and Melidones, whom they found waiting to receive them. The engagement, which ensued, continued for several hours, and was maintained on both sides with great bravery and obstinacy, both parties contending with a spirit of heroic rivalry for superiority. The Turks frequently rushed, like lions, on the insurgents, whom they had expected to find contemptible opponents, and would have actually gained the day, had not the haughty Kundures been killed, while storming the position of the insurgents, who at the same moment advanced to meet him. Twenty-two Turks, one of whom was Glymides, fell by his side. Two Turkish flags were captured by the followers of Vurdumbas and Melidones. On the Greek side three were killed and seven wounded. The Turks, discouraged by the loss of their leader, immediately retired; and the victorious Greeks, not deeming it expedient to pursue them, satisfied themselves in the meantime with having destroyed the far-famed Kundures.

Thus ended the first formidable expedition of the Turks. Returning to the fortress they lamented the loss of their leader.

The Turks, both of Rethymno and Kydonia, were now convinced that it was out of the question to think of exterminating at pleasure their adversaries, as they had a short time before massacred the Christian population while unarmed and helpless. The insurgents, with arms in their hands, were now resolved to defend their lives and avenge the treatment they had previously endured.

The Greeks now succeeded, by continual skirmishes and ambuscades, in shutting up within the fortress the Rethymnian Turks, who had hitherto made frequent incursions into the surrounding districts to harass the insurgents.

After this account of events in the province of Rethymne, we resume our narrative of hostilities in the province of Kydonia.

The Turks, resenting their defeat at Digene, plundered and burnt the monasteries of Chrysopege, Hayios Eleutherios, Hayia Mone, etc., situated on the plain, and every Christian house in the same district. After the engagement at Malaxa, Kusunaria, and Hayia Marina, Nicolaos Lakkiotes, A. Phasales, Stamates Synetakes of Kephaladne, with several other leaders, descending into the plain by night, burnt and demolished a great number of Turkish mansions, including the magnificent edifice, called *Sersebilia*, belonging to a prominent Turk of the name of Hussein Sophtas, which had been erected at great expense, or rather by means of extorted gratuitous labours of the Christian population.

The Turks now began to give up the idea of distant incursions, and confine themselves to maintaining as outposts of the fortress the Grange of Ibraïm Sophta (called Kokkinon), that of Ali Sophta (called Barbu), and the strong tower of Tarazzos. The Greeks, however, by frequent ambuscades, continued to harass the Turks occupying these positions.

In the meantime, a Turkish detachment, consisting of about a hundred and fifty men, issuing from Suda, proceeded with great caution towards Kalyvœ, to assist about a hundred Turks besieged in the tower of Alidakes, and reduced to great extremities. The detachment, however, was encountered above the village of Armeni by a body of insurgents from Skyphos and Apocoronos, and compelled, after a short resistance, to return to Suda. In their retreat they lost five men and some arms. Three Greeks, too, were killed on this occasion. The besieged were now left to their fate. The moment the insurgents, stationed at Malaxa, had heard the firing at Armeni, Joannes Sakires, with about fifty insurgents of that place, hastened to the aid of the Greeks; and, if this leader had succeeded in occupying Kalyvœ in time, it would have been scarcely possible for the retreating Turks to have reached their boats. At the commencement of the war the Cretan insurgent did not wait for orders from a superior officer, but putting his musket on his shoulder, and bread into his scrip, he eagerly hastened wherever his country required his presence.

Early in the morning of the 23rd of June the scouts of Dascalakes and Halles announced the advance of a large body of Turks from the fortress. Of these about five hundred took the direction of Malaxa, while the main body, about 2,000 strong, proceeded to attack the mountaineers under Phasales and Halles. The plan of the Turks was to make such a diversion, as to prevent Dascalakes from coming to the assistance of the other Greek leaders. By these means they hoped to throw into confusion the insurgents occupying Hayia Kyriake and other advantageous positions, and thus advance farther into the interior, as they had long been especially eager to destroy Therison and Lakki, important towns in the district of Rhizae.

Their enterprise, however, entirely failed. The Greeks, though aware of the courage and strength of the enemy, had now acquired that confidence in themselves, which leads to victory. As soon as the Turks reached Yerolakkos in the district of Keramcia, A. Phasules and his followers attacked them with impetuosity and success, preventing their advance till the arrival of I. Halles with his followers from Kemmein, V. Halles with insurgents of Therison, and A. Panayotes with his followers from Lakki and other parts of Rhizae. The Turks, now vigorously attacked on all sides, made a brave, but unavailing resistance. Unable to hold their positions, owing to the impetuous and destructive fire of the Greeks, they took to flight, proceeding along a declivity, and were pursued to a great distance.

About a hundred Turks fell in this engagement. Many of the fugitives threw away their arms to facilitate their escape. Hassan Bey Tukmezes,* a Turk notorious for his murders and his iniquities of every description, was killed in the pursuit, having being found concealed under a bush. Not one of the Greeks fell in this affair, and only seven were wounded, including Joannes Strongylos of Therison.

Dascalakes, at the head of eighty select followers, had hastened from Malaxa to aid the insurgents in the engagement at Yerolakkos. On his arrival, however, he found the Turks completely routed, and had not an opportunity of sharing in the action. The defeat of the Turks at Yerolakkos now gave them a still higher idea of the courage of the insurgents. Siphaens had proceeded from Malaxa at the head of a considerable body of Sphakians and Apocoronites to attack at Nerocuron the above mentioned Turkish detachment of 500 men. These, however, on learning, it would appear, the defeat of the main body at Yerolakkos, had previously retreated.

All these events inspired the insurgents with increasing confidence, and prepared them for success in every future encounter. Such was now the courage of the Greeks, that about 300 of them from Malaxa, passing unobserved by night the Turkish sentinels at the grangest we mentioned above,

* Besides slaughtering, on various occasions, many other Christians, he killed five, all at once, at Aavestopelon (lime kiln) in the district of Acroterion, previously to 1812, a period at which the lives of the Greeks were at the mercy of the lowest and most insignificant of the Turks. One of the five, murdered in the district of Acroterion, was Adames Andredakes, a landed proprietor of the village Khordaki, who happened to be there on a visit at the time.

† Metokhia is the name given by the Cretans to granges or farms, and their cultivators are designated Metokhari, elsewhere named Collega.

advanced to the very fortress of Kydonia, and, in the immediate vicinity of the wall, set fire to a number of small buildings, situated outside the gate and used as provision shops. This daring and unexpected exploit threw the Turks in the fortress into the greatest consternation, as they supposed it to be the commencement of a concerted attempt to storm the place. Touching cries and lamentations of women and children were now heard; and, during the whole night, indescribable confusion continued, the whole of the inhabitants evidently giving themselves up for lost! Till daylight armed Turks continued to crowd the ramparts, and to fire off guns without intermission in the dark to repel the supposed assailants. The Greeks, after setting fire to the above mentioned buildings, retired amid showers of bullets. Only one Greek, however, a native of Murion in Sphakia, was killed by a ball. His dead body was conveyed by his comrades to Malaxa and buried there.

After the Turks had sustained numerous defeats, the Greek, now provided with arms to assert his liberty, was able to set his former oppressors at defiance. These now directed their fury against the unarmed and helpless portions of the Christian population. About the end of June large bodies of Turks suddenly spread over the whole district of Acroterion,* capturing or massacring all the old men, children and women that fell into their hands. Multitudes of such helpless creatures, as were able to save themselves by flight, continued to wander like hunted hares on the mountains and in the ravines, and would have all perished, had it not been for the arrival of seven Kassian vessels, which happened to be cruising on that part of the coast. The Kassians received on board a great number of them, who with loud lamentations were imploring their aid along the shore, and conveyed part of them to Apocoronos, now in the hands of the Greeks, and the rest to Kassos.

At this crisis twelve armed insurgents of Acroterion, including Gregorios Daminos, Stephanos Lerus, and N. Tambares, succeeded in saving many of the fugitives. Evading the efforts of the bloody pursuers, and conducting the fugitives

* Acroterion, situated to the east of the fortified town of Kydonia, is now called Melekhas, probably the ancient Kyamon, and forms part of the province of Kydonia. It contained 18 flourishing villages and two magnificent monasteries, that of the Holy Trinity and that of Guvernetos.

under their protection by unfrequented and rugged paths, during moonless nights, they brought them in safety to Malaxa.

The Turks, immediately after this, pillaged and burnt all the villages of Acroterion, and the rich monasteries of the Holy Trinity and Guvernetos.

We return to the state of affairs in the province of Rethymne. After the engagement at Kaymenon, G. Deliyannakes, P. Mannseles, Protopapadakes, J. Draliskos, and Kustikianos, blockaded, as we have already mentioned, the Turks in the fortress of Rethymne, gallantly repulsing their frequent sallies. Rusos, Suderos, Kurmules, Poloyorgakes and Melidones proceeded on the 20th of June to the province of Panacron or Amarion, whose inhabitants had taken part in the national struggle from the very commencement, purchasing, at a very high price, all the arms they could procure. The Greeks of Crete generally were eager to separate themselves from the Turks, among whom they had previously lived, and this desire naturally increased with the progress of the insurrection, and the increasing danger to which they were exposed from outbursts of Turkish ferocity. This was peculiarly the case with the inhabitants of Amarion, who had always been subjected in a pre-eminent degree to Turkish outrage and oppression, as nearly the whole landed property in the province was in the hands of the Turks.

The Turks of Amarion, like those of Selinon, were brave and warlike. They were, however, unpolished and uncivilized, and, owing to this, they oppressed the Christian population with peculiar harshness. With their exception the Turkish inhabitants of Crete are of a fair complexion, generally, with ruddy cheeks, and, on the whole, a very handsome race, like the Greeks, from whose ancestors they are unquestionably descended. Consequently, they have preserved the Greek language and Greek manners, and differ from the Christian inhabitants merely in religion and moral culture. It is little more than a century since the ancestors of the present Turks of Selinon embraced the Moslem religion, driven by intolerable oppression to apostasy. The Turks of Amarion, on the contrary, are of a dark complexion, and, for the most part, of small stature, their accent resembling the Arabic.
* From all these circumstances, it would appear that they are the descendants of Saracens who remained in the island, when

the greater part of the Saracen invaders were expelled by the Emperor Phokas in the 9th century. When the other Turks of Crete wish to represent a Moslem as remarkably uncouth and ugly, they call him an Ambadiot, Ambadia being the chief town of the province of Amarion.

Such, then, were the adversaries whom the above mentioned insurgent leaders proceeded to assail. The Ambadiots, on ascertaining that an insurrection of the Greeks had taken place, and was spreading towards their province, conveyed, without loss of time, their families and portable effects to Heracleion; but remained themselves concentrated at Vathyacon, the centre of their settlement, and kept themselves in readiness to defend themselves by arms. Their commander Delimustaphas, a chief renowned for his valour, occupied a strong position with about a hundred chosen men, and, with unremitting vigilance waited for the approach of the insurgents.

This detachment was at length attacked by the Greeks, and an obstinate engagement was kept up without intermission for nearly two days and two nights. On the second day the Turks, rushing from their position, charged the Greeks in the hope of putting them to flight. The Greeks, however, retiring to stronger positions, at a small distance, maintained a vigorous conflict for nearly four hours. Perceiving, after this, that Delimustaphas had been wounded in the hand by the bursting of his musket, Vurdumbas and his followers rushed forward, and surrounded a considerable number of Turks in a detached position. These, along with their leader, Delimustaphas were all cut to pieces. The rest of the Turks offered no further resistance, as other parties of Greeks, and in particular, Melidones and his followers, attacked all the other positions with great impetuosity. Besides, the enemy had been completely discouraged by the death of their commander. Bravo as the Ambadiots were, they now took to flight.

Part of them, pursued to the mountains by Greek insurgents of Amarion, were nearly all overtaken and killed. In this engagement near Vathyacon the Greeks had seven killed and nine wounded. The victorious insurgents, after pillaging and burning the Turkish villages, continued for several days to deliberate whether it would be most expedient to proceed first to Aulopotamos or to Gortyna, the Turks of which latter province, after the loss of their outpost Ampadia, were waiting

for the advance of Karmales and other insurgent leaders.
In the meantime about 1500 Turks, issuing from Rethymne
about the beginning of July, proceeded in a body to attack the
insurgents of Kallicrates. Their intention, it is said, was
immediately on the expected discomfiture of these, to proceed
to Lampe and overpower the insurgents there. The Lampæi,
inhabiting a rather mountainous district, were as formidable
to the Moslems of Rethymne as the Sphakian or Kydonian
mountaineers were to those of Kydonia.

But Manuseles with the Kallicratiani, Suderos with the
Lampæi, Siphodascalakes with the Asphodiots, G. Deliyannakes
and Protopapadakes with the Skyphiots, Druliskos with the
Rethymnian insurgents and Frangules Karianos, supported
by Poloyorgakes, Melidones and several other leaders, who
had returned from Ampadia, presented a bold front to the
enemy.

For three days the conflict was maintained with great gallantry on both sides. Early in the morning of the following
day a detachment of the Turks, advancing unobserved, set fire
to several quarters of the village of Kallicrates. The greater
part of the village was burnt down, but, as it had been deserted by the inhabitants, there was no loss of life. The detachment returned with great despatch and unhurt to their previous
positions, where they remained for the three following days.
Vigorous resistance, frequent skirmishes, and constant ambuscades on the part of the Greeks, frustrated on this occasion,
too, the plan of the Turks, who were at length obliged to
return to the fortress with the loss of about thirty of their
number, after having burnt down monasteries and Christian
houses, and desolated entire villages. In all these encounters
the Greeks lost nine men, of whom three were Lampæi, two
Rethymnians, the rest belonging to other corps, besides
thirteen wounded. The Greeks, in retaliation, burnt many
Turkish houses and demolished the mosque at Rustica, the
lead of the roof of which served for making musket balls.

As the Lakkiots and Therisiani were, on account of their
pre-eminent valour, objects of the special antipathy of the
Kydonian Turks, so the neighbouring Kallicratiani and the
Christians inhabiting the foot of the mountains of Lampe and
Rethymne, were, for the same reason, peculiarly detested by
their Rethymnian oppressors. Consequently, the Moslems were
determined to spare no effort towards accomplishing the

destruction of the Christian population of these parts. During the above mentioned movements of the Rethymnian Turks, those of Kydonia were preparing to take the field, agreeably to the concerted plan of operation. On the 1st of July three Christian females made their escape from the fortress, and, evading the vigilance of the Turkish posts in the plain, reached Malaxa in safety. They informed Dascalakes that the Turks were with great energy preparing an expedition of 5,000 men against the Christians, and were bringing with them guns, mortars, ropes, and chains; and that their intention was to proceed first to Rhizae, and thence to Sphakia, slaughtering every Christian able to bear arms, and dragging to the fortress as captives, all the women, children and old men that might fall into their hands.

Dascalakes, alarmed at this important intelligence, instantly gave notice to Halles and Phasules at Hayia Kyriake, and A. Panayotes at Apopegadi, to muster their followers without a moment's delay, and, watching the enemy's movements, hasten to his assistance, leaving only the necessary force to occupy indispensable posts. He himself made every suitable arrangement at Malaxa, appointing Joseph Kavcalakes and J. Sakires with the requisite number of Apocoronites and Sphakinns to garrison the place. He further directed Siphacas, N. Zervos, P. Suliotes, G. Daminos, Mutsoyannes, Leras and other leaders of distinguished bravery, together with a select body of Anopolitæ, to hold themselves in readiness to follow him wherever circumstances might require their presence. The Turks, according to expectation, issued from the fortress in the afternoon of the 4th of July, about 5,000 strong, and carrying with them all the above mentioned preparations. They encamped at Hayia, a short distance from the fortress. Next day, about sunrise, they started under the usual salute from the fortress, and advanced in a close column with the intention of proceeding to Therison, Latiph Pasha accompanying the expedition. On reaching a valley near Campia they were heroically attacked by V. Halles and A. Phasules at the head of about 300 followers. J. Halles arriving simultaneously with the Keramiani, and various bodies of insurgents eagerly hastening from different quarters to share in the action, the Greeks succeeded in preventing for the space of three hours the advance of an enemy incomparably superior in numbers.

During the engagement Dascalakes arrived at the spot in

great haste, at the head of about 150 followers, and joined the
small but gallant body of patriots. Without loss of time, he
flew successively to the positions of the Greeks, enthusiastically
exhorting them to continue resistance : " Let us, my dear
brethren," he exclaimed, " let us quit ourselves like men, and
with God's aid gain at present, as on every former encounter,
the victory, taming the presumption of our oppressors, who
advanced with the expectation of accomplishing our total
destruction. If we now gain the day, we shall have nothing
to fear for ever afterwards. Fight then, dear friends, with an
unshrinking valour ;and see ! the brave Lakkiots are hastening
to our assistance, and will soon be here." Dascalakes' brief
address, as might have been expected, greatly animated the
Christian combatants, and the arrival of fresh assistance
confirmed still farther their determination to maintain their
ground. As the day advanced, however, the enemy, so superior
in numbers, succeeded in occupying more advantageous
positions, and for a time the victory, to all appearance, was
to be on their side.

It was now about mid-day. At this critical moment the
approach of eighty-four Lakkiots, headed by the Proïmidæ,
and Paraskeviani, was announced by discharges of musketry.
Halting for a moment at the ruined church of Hayios Antonios,
situated to the west of the scene of action, to deliberate on
the most advantageous mode of attacking the now advancing
enemy, they were addressed by one of their number, the
gallant Saridantones, as follows :—" If we are Christian men,
let us instantly fall upon the enemy, let us resolve to conquer
or to perish with our brethren at this moment in danger. If
they be destroyed, who are now fighting against such odds,
our children, our wives, and ourselves are undone." The heroic
band, taking off their bonnets, and, according to a Cretan
usage preceding an impetuous charge, holding them with
their teeth, attacked the enemy in flank, who were now resolutely advancing in spite of all opposition. The heroism of
the Lakkiots on this occasion, though so remarkable as almost
to exceed belief, is an unquestionable fact, and saved the insurgent army from destruction. Had the Turks continued to
advance but for a few minutes longer, the Greeks, notwithstanding their heroic resistance, would have been entirely
discomfited and exposed to the fury of merciless victors.
The Cretans, whether Christians or Moslems, born and brought

up on the same soil, have the same natural courage. They have, moreover, the same arms and the same mode of fighting. Placing themselves behind stones, they use their pre-eminently long muskets, which carry to a surprising distance, with deadly effect. They had not, however, as yet adopted the system of *tamburia*, hastily erected dykes, which had long been in use among the warlike Rumeliots. In consequence of this, it happened that among the Cretans, those who were acting on the defensive, were at the mercy of assailants sufficiently resolute to storm their position.

Perceiving the impetuous advance of the Lakkiots, those of the Turks against whom the charge was more immediately directed, instantly quitted their positions, under the persuasion that, owing to the rugged surface of the country in their rear, they would be able to retreat unmolested; but the mountaineers, by whom they were now assailed, had been trained to bound over ¦the most rugged ground with ease. The movement we have now described, decided the fortune of the day. Triumphant acclamations and thundering shouts raised by all the rest of the Greeks, who now simultaneously advanced from their positions, threw the enemy into confusion, and compelled them to imitate the example of those who had already taken to flight. The whole Turkish army was now completely routed, and the spectacle that ensued was truly wonderful. About 800 Greeks had discomfited and were pursuing nearly 5,000 Turks. The pursuit continued along a declivity as far as Sycolia, a position in the plain. Parties of the fugitives repeatedly turned on their pursuers, and made a gallant stand. These encounters were often sanguinary and obstinate, but all terminated in favour of the Greeks. At length the Turks, completely disheartened, ceased to offer any further resistance. Great numbers of them threw away their arms to facilitate their escape. The victors, in numerous instances, slew fugitives with the very weapons they snatched from them. Flags, animals, ammunition, and spoils of every description, in great abundance, fell into the hands of the victors. Among the spoils were the very ropes and chains with which the enemy had expected to drag to the fortress the Rhizitæ and Sphakians. The Pasha, who, during the main engagement, had stood at a distance on horseback, and had seasonably taken to flight, escaped to the fortress. In the rout, Turks, habituated to every luxury, outran fleet-footed and hardy mountaineers, amid the burning heat of a summer day.

More than 500 Turks fell in the engagement and pursuit, besides those who, parched with thirst in their flight, rushed in desperation to brooks on the way, and, drinking inordinately, instantly expired. On the part of the Greeks there were killed 13 of the followers of V. Halles and Phasules, 7 of those of Dascalakes, and 8 men belonging to Koramcia and other places, besides, about 40 were wounded. Not one of the daring Lakkiots fell, and Saridantones alone was wounded, and that but slightly. It is said that this heroic Lakkiot, who continued the pursuit to the last, killed with his own hand about 14 of the enemy. Another Lakkiot, George Nicoludakes, the rival of Saridantones in daring as well as in fleetness of foot, distinguished himself pre-eminently. Pressing on in advance of his followers, he too killed a considerable number of the fugitives, and disarmed others whom he allowed to escape.

The slaughter of fugitives on this occasion was no difficult matter. Had the victors vigorously continued the pursuit, the number of killed on the part of the Turks would have been much greater than it was. Many of the Greeks, however, in consequence of a very improper custom, too common, not only in Crete, but in all parts of Greece, gave up the pursuit of the fugitives, in order to plunder the slain.

This victory supplied the Greeks with ammunition, furnished arms to a large number of insurgents previously unarmed, greatly dispirited the Turks, and, in a corresponding degree, raised the courage and hopes of the patriots. This important victory was mainly owing to the valour and spirit of Halles and Phasules, to the exhortations and example of Dascalakes, and to the chivalrous courage of the Lakkiots.*

M. Tricoupi erroneously represents the scene of this engagement as in Sphakia (vol I. page 235). In another passage he speaks of the Cretans in the following manner, in connection with the inroad of the Turks into Sphakia, on the 29th of August:—"Those," he says, "who had shunned encountering the enemy, now returned, and spreading themselves over various parts, began to plunder, in the most shameless and reckless manner, their countrymen and fellow-christians, the Khians (Sciots), living in the vicinity." But when, we ask, were Khians living in any part of Crete?—Never! It is a melancholy truth that in Crete, among Cretans, disorders occurred and excesses were committed when, on the 29th of August, part of

Kaüres, the same day on which the engagement we have
described took place, marched at the head of such Turks of
Kisamos and Selinon as had remained in these districts,
when most of the Turkish inhabitants of those parts had
proceeded with the expedition against Campia. Kaüres was
one of the most distinguished leaders in the Moslem army,
and commanded the brave Seliniot Turks. He now hastened
with the reserve to promote the object of the general
expedition by effecting a diversion. But A. Panayotes, with
a detachment of Kydonians and Anopolitæ, and Andreas
Papapolakes at the head of the Livanians and Hayio-
ramelites, and also Stamatios Anoyanos at the head of some
non-Cretan Greeks stationed at Trypete, a strong position
in the province of Selinon, to the west of the glen of Hayia
Raméle, bravely kept the enemy in check, and prevented
his advance, till night came, and put an end to a conflict
that had been gallantly maintained on both sides, and in
which 12 of Kaüres' followers were killed. The Greeks
lost 3 men belonging to the corps of Papapolakes, and 1 at
Apopegadi. About 9 also were wounded.

We now proceed, for the first time, to direct the reader's
attention to the state of matters in the Eastern parts of
Crete, having to narrate the tragic events which occurred in
Heraklcion and the surrounding districts.

The Greeks of those parts did not take up arms at the
same time as their brethren of Rethymne and Kydonia. The
cause of their inaction was not merely the want of arms and
ammunition, but their distance from Sphakia, the centre of
the insurrection, though the patriotic cause required the
co-operation of the whole Greek population, and particularly
of the Greeks who inhabited this portion of the island, the
largest and most fertile in Crete. A movement here, however, was hopeless, both for want of money and for want of
strong position, to which the Greek inhabitants might flee
as places of refuge. The Christians of those parts,
accordingly, continued to endure a more galling oppression
than that to which their brethren elsewhere were exposed,
and patiently waited the moment that might enable them to
join the general insurrection. Though eager to join their
insurgent brethren, with whom they were in correspondence,

the population went over from Sphakia to Gandos. Similar disorders, unfortunately, took place occasionally in every other part of Greece.

and to whom they had earnestly applied for arms and aid, they were compelled from their position to endure the yoke.

The whole population of Crete had at all times cherished in their hearts the love of liberty. In proof of this we may refer to the numerous traces of the free institutions of Minos, still preserved in the manners and customs of the Cretans. This innate love of freedom was never effaced, by all the attempts of successive oppressors to destroy whatever knowledge and self-respect remained among them, and thus obliterate their national character.

The inherent love of liberty among the Cretans has been further testified by their strong disaffection to the Roman yoke; by their persevering efforts to throw it off; by their determined resistance to other powerful invaders; by their incessant revolts against Venetian domination during a long series of ages; and lastly, by the frequently armed protests which they made from time to time against their last and worst oppressors, the Turks. Towards a successful insurrection against Ottoman rule it would have been requisite that there should be a simultaneous rising of the whole Christian population, and that the insurgents should be provided, to some extent, with military resources. Notwithstanding, however, their meagre means at the commencement of the present struggle, the gallant efforts of the Cretan patriots achieved in all parts of the island brilliant success.

Previously to the late war of independence the simple suspicion of an approaching war between Russia and Turkey sufficed to make the Turks assume the most threatening attitude towards their Christian subjects. They were under the erroneous impression that every war of the Russians against Turkey was undertaken for the sole purpose of emancipating their fellow Christians, who were under the Turkish yoke. The alarm of the Turks, however, at the beginning of 1821, arose, not from the expectation of a Russian war, but from indications of an internal movement among the Greeks themselves.

Before the events, then taking place in other parts of the Ottoman Empire, were distinctly known in Crete, the Cretan Turks broke out into the most atrocious excesses, and slaughtered great numbers of Christians in every part of the island. At Heracleion, Hassan Tzelepes, of Khaseké, a Turk of great ferocity, put himself at the head of a miscellaneous Mussulman multitude, and, after committing numberless atrocities within that town, overran the provinces around, for the purpose of disarming the Christian population, putting numbers of Christians to death with the utmost barbarity.

When news of the events, which took place at Kydonia and Rethyme in the beginning of May, reached Heracleion, Serif Pasha, the governor of that district, gave his consent to the general arming of the Turks, a measure he had hitherto opposed. From this moment nothing was heard, day or night, but such incessant firing as takes place during a long and sanguinary conflict. The anxiety and consternation of the Greeks, in the meantime, were beyond description, as they felt their lives and honour, as well as their property, were at the mercy of every infuriated ruffian.

The Turkish authorities enjoined the Metropolitan and other Bishops to issue pastoral letters and solemn comminations,* warning and exhorting their respective flocks to be faithful to the Ottoman Government. The Metropolitan was further commanded to direct his suffragans, the Abbotts of Monasteries, and all prominent individuals as had previously absconded, to repair immediately to Heracleion, on pain of having their property confiscated, and themselves declared rebels in case of disobedience. At the same time the Pasha brought into the town about 3,000 of the Christian population of the neighbourhood, and employed them along with the Christians already in the town, in repairing the fortifications.

During this period of uproar and consternation a Moslem Cretan, called Billal Pulakos, sailed from Halicarnassus on the night of the 23rd and 24th June, and, evading the vigilance of the Greek cruisers, arrived in the harbour of Hera-

* M. Tricoupi speaks of this with disapprobation in the following manner: "These prelates used every endeavour to maintain tranquility, publishing circulars, in which they extolled the boundless beneficence of the Sultan, and warned their flocks against being misled by fallacious representations, as the ungrateful Peloponnesians had been, forsaking the salutary path of obedience to the Sublime Porte. These efforts of the prelates were perfectly sincere (vol. I. chap. xli. p. 225)." M. Tricoupi forgets that under similar circumstances the Patriarch Gregorios issued dreadful comminations against the Insurgents, and added these words: ' I write this on the altar.' What, we ask, could the prelates do while the axe of the oppressor lay on their necks? Their apparent efforts and exhortations were not sincere and spontaneous, but extorted by necessity. All these venerable men soon after laid down their lives for their flocks, though it was in their power to effect their escape. M. Tricoupi should remember the proverb, " the Bishop wrote and signed under the gallows."

cleion. He brought with him a tatar, or imperial courier, dispatched from Constantinople with imperial instructions, and also a dervish. Scarcely had the captain of the vessel and the dervish spread the intelligence that there had been general massacres at Constantinople, Smyrna, and other parts of Turkey, and that everywhere the Christians were plotting against Moslem rule, when the Turkish mob threw aside all restraint. Running furiously through the streets they continued to slaughter, without distinction and without mercy, every Greek they could lay their hands on. They pillaged at the same time all the Christian houses, and made captives of such women and children as they did not instantly put to death. Assailing in great numbers the metropolitan palace, they there killed about one hundred persons, who, after having attended divine service, were about to proceed to work at the fortifications, in the hope of softening, by their apparent obedience and zeal, their cruel oppressors; these, however, relentlessly perpetrated every conceivable atrocity, and continued to outrage whatever the Greeks held most sacred.

On this occasion were assembled in the streets and around the church a large number of prominent Christians, including Gerasimos Pardales, the Metropolitan, Neophytos Phinticakes, Bishop of Knossos, Ioakim Ierotheos, Bishop of Lampe, Zaccharias, Bishop of Sitcia, Kallinicos, Bishop of Diospolis, many Abbots of Monasteries, and Joannes Lentheraos, the well-known and worthy physician.

The whole Christian population remained entirely at the mercy of the infuriated Turkish mob. The strong remonstrances of the French and English Vice-Consuls, Domenicos and Vase, were utterly disregarded. Not only did atrocities and carnage continue unabated, but the mob proceeded to threaten the Pasha himself, and peremptorily demanded that he should deliver up to them his interpreter Lazarakes Iordanes, who, by the Pasha's connivance and aid, had made his escape, and subsequently found refuge in the house of Kurmules.

The Vice-Consuls having ascertained that two British subjects, natives of Malta, had been massacred, protested and threatened the Pasha in the strongest terms. In consequence of this the massacre somewhat abated towards afternoon, otherwise many thousand Christians would have perished on that memorable day. The number of Christians put to death on this occasion, within the fortress of Heradeion, amounted to about 800.

On the following day a large body of Turks, issuing from the fortress, overran the neighbouring districts, and perpetrated such atrocities as one shudders to record in detail. Every Greek that fell into their hands was put to death. Twenty-eight persons were slaughtered at Veneralon, a village in the province of Knossos, besides large numbers in other villages. The Bishops of Petra and Arcadia were slain at their respective places of residence. A very prominent and notorious Turk, called Aphentakakes, of the province of Sitoia, having on various pretexts collected about 300 unarmed Greeks in the courtyard of his castle, massacred them to a man with the assistance of his ferocious followers. Such was the barbarity exhibited at this period by the Turks! and yet at this crisis the Christians of Crete, who, escaping the sword, gallantly, and often triumphantly, asserted their freedom with arms in their hands, were finally compelled by the Christian powers of Europe to submit again to the yoke of their treacherous and bloody oppression!

Hitherto the Turks of the Eastern provinces continued to slaughter unarmed Greeks with impunity, and entertained the persuasion that the defeat of the insurgents would be a matter of no difficulty. Accordingly, Kaünes, a Turk of great influence on account of his acknowledged valour, marched from Heracleion without delay at the head of about 3,000 men. He was reinforced on his way by 500 Rethymnian Turks. As the insurgents in those parts were enabled to make head against so large a force, Kaünes suddenly advanced on the 16th of July from Daphnomadaræ, at the foot of the White Mountains, and above Kurna, a village in the province of Apocoronos, and encamped at Skyphos, the most mountainous and most populous village in Sphakia. The Greeks in those parts were, owing to the sudden appearance of the enemy, unable to make a stand, and therefore retired to the surrounding hills, to which they had conveyed their families in safety. A body of 500 Sphakians, however, under the command of A. Protopapadakes, R. Vurdumbas, and Poloyoryakes, was soon collected in the vicinity. The Turks remained two days in Skyphos, and became alarmed at the perilous position in which they had unreflectingly placed themselves. The appearance of a Greek force, ready to offer resistance, was something they had not anticipated. Their stay at Skyphos was, according to reports, owing to their expectation that reinforcements from Heracleion would arrive and enable them to proceed forward with fuller confidence.

On the 18th about 30 Greeks, advancing to Lenos, where the Turks were stationed, offered them battle. For about two hours a sharp fire was kept up on both sides, but apparently without effect. The result, however, proved unexpectedly very important. The firing from all the Turkish positions soon became general, and was replied to by the Greeks, who, at the moment they expected a general attack, perceived the enemy preparing to turn their backs. The Turks, commencing a lusty retreat without offering any further opposition, attempted to retire through the deep glen of Katreus. The Sphakians, stationed in the vicinity immediately followed them, and, overtaking them at the narrow pass of Katreus, attacked them, but without much success.

While the enemy were in the most impassable part of the glen, and were just about to enter the open plain of Krape, Dascalakes suddenly made his appearance with about 120 followers from Malaxa. These attacked them in front, while the Sphakians assailed them in the rear. In a very short space of time, about 300 of the enemy were killed, but the remainder effected their escape. Leaving behind them their colours, a large number of animals, arms, and all their baggage, the Turks continued their flight over the plain of Krape till they reached Prosneron. Here, after being joined by the Turkish detachment, besieged, and in great extremities in the tower, under Alidakes, started the same day for Rethymne. In this rash expedition, prompted by blind animosity against the mountaineers of Sphakia, the Turks, by advancing into a rugged country, and venturing into dangerous defiles at a distance from any of their fortresses, and beyond the reach of assistance, afforded the insurgents an opportunity, if duly turned to account, of destroying the whole invading army. On perceiving, however, the rashness of their enterprise, they at once hastened to escape from the perilous situation in which they had inconsiderately placed themselves.

The position of Katreus was much more favorable for the Greeks than that of Kampia, where they achieved the complete victory we have already recorded. The former is a precipitous and narrow defile among lofty mountains, at a distance from any plain or fortress ; the latter is more level, and in the vicinity of a plain and a fortress. Had the Greeks displayed greater vigour at Krateus they might have cut off to a man the invaders of Sphakia, who had come from so great a distance as Heracleion for the purpose of desolating the hated province, exterminating the formidable Sphakians, and leading away captives their wives and children.

In the encounters at Katreus only one Greek, Georgios Tatinapes, of Halepa, a village in Kydonia, was killed. He was distinguished for valour, judgment, and courtesy, and had great skill and experience in the use of arms.

The victors of Krape returned to the places they had previously occupied, the illustrious Dascalakes, with his followers, to Malaxa, and the rest elsewhere, exulting in the victory and the spoils they had obtained. Two days afterwards, however, Omer Ephendes, commander of the corps of Yerlis, suddenly made his appearance at Ampelos, a sequestered quarter of Skyphos, at the head of about 400 men, who, ignorant of the defeat of their friends, were hastening by another route to reinforce Kaünes.

Poloyoryakes, happening at this time to be stationed with his followers at Imbros, a village at a short distance southward of Skyphos, immediately hastened to attack the Turks, who at first mistook this body of Greeks for a Turkish detachment, taking it for granted that Kaünes had already made himself master of those parts. About fifty of the foremost of the Turks were killed at Ampelos. The remainder, on learning what had befallen their friends at Krape, took to flight. Dispersing themselves in different directions, they were pursued into mountains with which they were unacquainted. Some of them remained concealed, and a few escaped to the fortresses, but a large proportion of them perished among the mountains.

Kaünes and his followers, on returning to Heracleion after their defeat, vented their fury on whatever was Christian, whether animate or inanimate. No longer daring to meet armed insurgents in the field, they attacked the unprotected

and unarmed, pillaged and desolated churches and Christian
property, and vowed they would put every surviving Christian to death.

It is said that, on this occasion, the female relatives of
the Turks, that had been slain in the late expedition, upbraided those who had returned, on perceiving the cowardly
excesses they were now perpetrating. Amid their lamentations they indignantly exclaimed, " Why did you not display
your courage in fighting the Sphakians and others who opposed you with arms in their hands, instead of now slaugh
tering the unarmed Rayas, like unresisting sheep ?" " Where,"
said one mourner, " where is my son ? " " Where," said
another, " is my husband ? " " Where," said a third, " is
my brother ? "

Thus the expedition of the Heracleiot Turks proved as
disastrous to their cause as the expedition of the Kydonian
and Rethymnian Turks had been.

The Greeks, elated by this series of victories, now displayed increasing vigour in assailing the enemy, and, by frequent skirmishes and ambuscades, confined the Turks more
and more stringently to the fortresses of Rethymne, Suda,
Kydonia, and other Turkish strongholds.

On the 25th of July a large body of Turks, issuing from
the fortress of Kydonia, ventured to attack V. Halles and
A. Phasules, at Garypa, a village at a considerable distance
to the south-west of the fortress. On the speedy arrival,
however, of Dascalakes from Malaxa, Siphakos, and J. Halles from Kerameia, and A. Panayotes with Lakkiots, to the
assistance of the insurgents, the Turks were compelled, after
a brief resistance, to return to the fortress.

The Greeks, on gaining possession, as they did at this
early period of the struggle, of the provinces of Apocoronos,
Kydonia, Lampo, Rethymno, and Amarion, should have had
the foresight to gather in and lay up in places of safety for
future exigencies, the abundant crops that had belonged to the
vanquished Turks. We are compelled, however, to confess
that the insurgent leaders displayed no such foresight. The
neglect of suitable measures on this occasion on the part of the
Greeks proved, as we shall afterwards see, of immense advantage to their opponents.

At the outbreak of the insurrection in Crete, the fortresses were almost entirely destitute of provisions. The slender supplies in the public storehouses were quickly consumed by the inhabitants and the multitudes that flocked for security from the surrounding districts. The Turks, as we have already stated, were unable to transport the provisions they had in their possession at the moment of the outbreak, and the subsequent crops remained in the power of the insurgents.

Under such circumstances the Greeks, with due foresight and vigour, might have achieved the conquest of the island. The Turkish fortresses in the Peloponnesus were in a similar state of destitution, when the insurrection commenced there, but Greek armed vessels from the neighbouring islands instantly established a blockade of the ports held by the Turks, and, in consequence, the fortresses of Epidaurus Limera (Monemvasia), Pylos (Navarino) and Nauplia were, from famine, successively compelled to surrender.

A similar result would have been achieved in Crete, had the insurgents there been supplied from the commencement with a naval force. The Cretans had, indeed, as we have already mentioned, applied forthwith to the Naval Islands for assistance. The time, too, at which application was made, was favourable, as the events at Lesbos and Samos had frightened the Turkish fleet, and the Greeks had the command of the Ægean.

The presence of an adequate Greek naval force in Crete might have prevented, to a great extent, the fearful massacres which we have recorded. A few Cassian vessels, that cruised for a time on the Cretan coast, were able to prevent communication between the fortresses, and captured or destroyed coasting Turkish vessels that ventured to put to sea. This fact proves that the permanent presence of a blockading force would have had a decisive influence on the progress of the Cretan insurrection, and, in particular, might have prevented the combined Turkish expedition in August following, in which the insurgents suffered so severely. Unfortunately, however, the central Greek Government failed to adopt at the commencement suitable measures in regard to Crete, the strongest bulwark of Greece, though the Cretan insurrection, as a most formidable diversion, very effectively promoted the general cause of Greek independence, as well as secured from immediate aggression Peloponnesus, the islands of the Ægean and other Grecian coasts.

The assembly, we have already mentioned as having met in Sphakia, and as consisting of deputies from various provinces, appointed a political commission, which was styled "The Sphakian Board," with a seal bearing the image of the Panayia, and the superscription, "Panayia of Lutros," from the church of Saint Mary in that place. It thus happened that the Insurgent Government in Crete assumed a local rather than a general character; in other words, it was rather Sphakian than Cretan.

This Board should have consisted of the most prominent individuals, not merely of Sphakia, but of all the provinces of Crete, and should have been styled "The Cretan Board." As the whole of Crete was now in a state of insurrection, justice and expediency required that the provisional Government of Crete should, as fairly and fully as under the circumstances it was possible, represent the whole Christian population of the island, without any preposterous Sphakian preponderance. Members of the Sphakian Board, as it was called, were Kh. J. Poludakes, A. Krearas, P. Polides, A. Psarndakes, St. Vurdumbakes, G. Protopapas of Sphakia. Demetrios Flamburiales, of Heracleion, was appointed secretary. The Board at first acted as circumstances might permit or require, without having very definite functions assigned it.

It is perfectly true that Sphakia was from the commencement regarded as the centre of the insurrection, both on account of its strong natural situation and of its harbour, Lutros, which for some time was the centre of all the trade of insurgent Crete; and the Cretans generally accorded to the Sphakians due consideration in regard to these accidental advantages. It is, however, equally true that the leading men among the Sphakians would have but acted in accordance with wisdom and patriotism, had they duly respected the rights and feelings of all their brethren and fellow-insurgents. Without righteousness no great enterprise can ever prosper.

The Sphakian Board sent a deputation, consisting of N. Oeconomos, and A. Panayotes to Demotrios Hypsilantes, who had sometime previously arrived in Greece from the Danubian Principalities, where the Greek insurrection had commenced. Demetrios Hypsilantes styled himself "Plenipotentiary of the General Commissioner of the Arché," his brother Alexander. The object of the deputation was to request support from the National Government, and the appointment of a competent individual to administer the affairs of Crete. Unfortunately, however, Demetrios had arrived in Greece with the title of Plenipotentiary of the General Commissioner, and with patriotic zeal for the national cause, but without resources or effective power.

When the Cretan deputation arrived in Peloponnesus, the speedy surrender of the fortress of Monemvasia was expected, as it was strictly blockaded both by sea and land, and both the garrison and the inhabitants were in great extremities. The Turkish authorities in the fortress were actually negotiating a capitulation with Alexander Kantacuzenos, which was carried into effect on the 23rd of July, 1821. To him D. Hypsilantes sent the Cretan deputation, and directed him to furnish them with a supply of arms and ammunition from the stores, expected to be found in the fortress. Great, however, was the disappointment, when all the supplies, thus obtained, proved to be an inconsiderable number of old arms, and a small quantity of almost useless powder. The deputation immediately forwarded these supplies to Crete, but they were found to be of no use whatever.

D. Hypsilantes had also promised to send as Governor of Crete, at the special request of the deputation, A. Kantacuzenos, as soon as that gentleman had arranged matters in Monemvasia. Kantacuzenos, however, did not accept the invitation, though supported by the exhortations of many prominent persons in Peloponnesus, and alleged private affairs as the cause of his refusal to proceed to Crete. In consequence of this, Michael Aphentules, an officer, who had accompanied Kantacuzenos from Russia, but who was then altogether unknown, both in Crete and in Peloponnesus, contrived to obtain for himself the appointment, which, by common consent had been offered to Kantacuzenos. The Cretan deputation, refusing at first to accept Aphentules, remained in the island of Spezzia till the following November, using their efforts to promote the cause of the insurrection in Crete.

Acting in concert with G. Papadakes and other Cretans, they urged the primates of Hydra and Spezzia to furnish a naval force, sufficient to blockade the coasts of Crete. They represented, in the strongest terms, the importance of supporting the common cause in Crete, assuring the Hydriots and Spezziots of the speedy triumph of the insurrection there, if they would vigorously co-operate with the Cretans now, as they had previously done with the insurgents of Peloponnesus. They added, with great force of reason, that the appointment of a political leader in Crete, could not have great and permanent results, unless he was supported by an adequate naval force. Unfortunately the urgent applications of the Cretans were fruitless, owing partly to the want of funds, and partly to other difficulties. Nicolaos Orlof of Spezzia, who professed a great interest in the Cretan cause, was at length induced to promise his services, and, accompanied by two other naval captains, proceeded, in January, 1822, to Lutros, where Aphentules had already entered on his functions. The Spezziot captains proposed that their ships, well armed, should, in concert with such Cassian or Sphakian vessels* as might be required, maintain a strict blockade of the coast of Crete, and stipulated that, for defraying the expenses of the squadron, including the pay of the crews, and in acknowledgment of their own services, they should receive certain assignments on the produce of Crete, and obtain, after the emancipation of the island, certain Turkish estates distinctly specified.

The Cretan authorities at Lutros accepted the proposed conditions, and eagerly looked for the arrival of the promised squadron. The agreement, however, was not carried into effect, and, consequently, no blockade of the Cretan coasts was established. It is necessary to add, that, owing to the neglect of those to whom the management of the Cretan affairs was entrusted, this important measure was at no subsequent period carried into effect.

The Turks of Heracleion as we have shown, had been defeated at Krape and Ampelos, and those of Rethymne and Kydonia had sustained numerous defeats. Their only possible plan of continuing the war, was to undertake a combined expedition against the earliest insurgents, that is, the Sphaki-

* The Sphakians at this time had about 20 vessels, consisting of brigs and golettes, some of which were fit to assist in maintaining a blockade. The Sphakian sailors, however, preferred the land service to the naval.

ans and the Greeks of the districts surrounding Kydonia and
Rethymne. Accordingly, they vigorously prepared themselves for the enterprise, corresponding with each other by sea,
and transporting troops in vessels without molestation where-
over they might find it necessary.

About the end of July Serif Pasha, of Heracleion, took the
field at the head of the whole Turkish population of the
town and neighbourhood, able to bear and accustomed to
arms. Having been reinforced on his march by the Rethymnian Turks under Osman Pasha, he encamped at the village
Episcopé in Rethymne. He was provided with guns, mortars,
and cavalry, and threatened an inroad into Apocorono.

About 2,000 Greeks had occupied positions around the
village of Kurna, Kastellon, and Patema, prepared to attack
the enemy. They were commanded by A. Protopapadakes,
R. Vurdumbna, G. Suderos, P. Manuseles, G. Deliyannakes,
Siphacas, A. Molidones, Kavkalosiphes, I. Halles, Rustikianos,
Poloyoryakes and others. By successive arrivals of detachments from various quarters the Greek army soon amounted
to about 3,000 men.

The two hostile armies remained inactive, and in face of
each other, for two days, as the Turks waited for the arrival of
reinforcements from Kydonia and Suda, with the intention
of entering Apocoronos from the west, and apprehensive of
being repulsed, should they attempt to proceed through the
defile of Halmyros, where the main force of the insurgents
was concentrated. Dascalakes and V. Halles, however, having
a considerable force at Garypas and Malaxa, drove back the
Kydonian Turks, while Sakires, at the head of a body of
Apocoronites and Sphakians, kept in check the Turks of
Suda.

On the 1st of August, Papa Joannes of Murion, in Sphakia, a person of distinguished bravery, crossed a stream called
Melana, that flowed between the two armies, and commenced
an attack on the enemy's positions. About 1000 Greeks
having joined him in the attack, a vigorous combat was
maintained during the greater part of the day. The Greeks
were unable to dislodge the enemy, who continued to fire on
them with guns and mortars. Before sunset the brave Papa
Joannes, who led the attack, was suddenly surrounded by
cavalry and killed, along with seven other Sphakians, his flag

also falling into the hands of the enemy. The Greeks deeply lamented the loss of this brave and enterprising warrior. The same day many fell also on the side of the Turks.

Early next morning the Turks, about 3000 strong, attacked the Greeks in their advantageous positions around Patema and Kastellon. An obstinate engagement was kept up during the whole day, and great gallantry displayed on both sides. Night put an end to the combat. The Greeks had nine killed and a few wounded. Of the enemy about sixty were killed, and a large number wounded. During the ensuing night the Pashas removed their camp to Dramia, a village on a plain in the district of Kurna,* and were joined there by many Turks, who had proceeded from Suda and Kydonia by sea, after they had vainly attempted to repulse Daacalakes at Malaxa, and Sakires at Kalyvæ.

On the 3rd of August a body of about 800 Turks attacked the positions of the Greeks, who received them with great gallantry, and showed they had now learned to despise the enemy's artillery. A very obstinate engagement was kept up during the whole of the day, both parties displaying most determined valour. Towards evening the Turks returned to Dramia, with great loss. The Greeks also had a considerable number killed.

On the two following days both armies remained inactive in their positions. In the meantime, an Ottoman deserter informed the Greeks that the Pashas were determined to advance in spite of all opposition. This communication may have been a stratagem intended to alarm the Greeks, but it may also have been a friendly warning. Accordingly, the Greeks began to calculate their strength, so inferior to the enemy in numbers and resources, and came to the conclusion that it would be inexpedient and perilous to continue to maintain their present positions, especially as their supply of ammunition was very nearly exhausted. The gunpowder, which had just arrived from Monemvasia, had from its bad quality not merely proved useless, but had rather done harm.‡

* What is now commonly called Kurnopatemata, is a division of the province of Apocoronos, and contains a number of villages with respective names. It lies between Rethymno and Halmyros. It has a large lake, called the lake of Kurna, at the foot of Daphnomadara.

‡ Through it many muskets burst. The Cretans, both Greeks and

46

pass of Halmyros, driving away the Greeks stationed there, and the whole of the Turkish infantry attacked the main body of the Greeks in their positions. An obstinate combat was

On the 6th of August, very early in the morning, the Turkish cavalry rapidly advanced and occupied the narrow kept up till midday with corresponding loss on both sides. In vain the Greeks endeavoured to drive the cavalry from the advantageous position of Halmyros, which commanded all the remaining Greek positions. They, accordingly, were compelled to give way before incomparably superior numbers, and retired to positions in which they might more reasonably hope to make a stand. The Turks, taking advantage of this movement, suddenly entered Apocoronos.

It is painful to narrate the disasters that followed this sudden inroad of the enemy. The Turks, now spreading themselves over the whole of the province, burnt down for the first time beautiful villages, and slaughtering or making captives great numbers of the inhabitants. About 70 aged, infirm and un-armed Greeks were dragged before the Pashas at Kalyvæ, and by their order, slaughtered there. Many of these were urged to save their lives by changing their religion, but they all, without a single exception, heroically preferred death to apostasy. The same day about 116 men, women and children, were dragged from a subterraneous grotto, situated at Kokkina by the seaside, in which they had taken refuge, and all put to death. Papa Manoles, the clergyman of the village, was literally cut in pieces, and portions of his flesh were hung upon the flags, the Turks regarding this savage device as an omen of victory over the Sphakians. Three young men, who had been found armed in the grotto, were impaled.

The following day the cavern of Orneros, which had been resolutely defended by thirty-eight Kephaliani, was taken by storm; thirty-six of the defenders were instantly slaughtered, but two of them, reaching the sea, which was close by, swam to Halmyros in safety. A cavern, situated above the village of Vapheus, in which 130 men, women and children had taken shelter, was gallantly defended for three days, and was at length only captured by the use of combustibles, which suf.

Turks, always made a point of procuring the very best sort of English or Dutch powder.

focated every living creature within it. The most desperate attempts had been made by fathers, sons, relatives and friends to rescue the besieged, but in vain. About 3,000 persons perished throughout Apocoronos in a similar manner, having concealed themselves for a time, under the persuasion that the Turkish occupation of the province was merely transient. A cavern called Kalavaté, in a rock on the sea shore, behind and to the north of the village of Kephalædæ, made a protracted resistance. Gregorios Daminos had selected this cavern as a place of refuge, and the number of men, women and children sheltered there, was about 80, including twelve armed men, besides Daminos. The Turks repeatedly attempted to get possession of the cavern, the Pasha sometimes threatening and cannonading, and sometimes offering rewards, to induce the besieged to surrender. The small body of armed Greeks in the cavern, repelled, from advantageous positions, repeated charges of the besiegers. Kaûres of Selinon, having haughtily sworn he would exterminate the besieged without mercy, Daminos fearlessly replied, " I will remain here and shoot the first Turk that enters, even should he be the Sultan himself."

The Greeks had previously laid up a considerable quantity of provisions in this almost inaccessible cavern, which the neighbouring Kephaliani used in times of danger as a place of refuge and a storehouse. As the place contained likewise a copious fountain of very sweet water, the besieged were provided with all necessaries. They were thus enabled to remain in the place from the 6th of August to the 14th of September, when it was again invested by Osman Pasha on his return from his expedition to Sphakia, of which we shall by and by give an account. Daminos (*) defied the renewed threats of Osman, and by his heroic determination saved himself and all who had taken refuge in the cavern.

The Pashas, after perpetrating the above mentioned atrocities in Apocoronos, removed their camp to Halykæ, at the top of the Amphimallic gulf (Suda), and were here joined by the Pasha of Kydonia, who had encountered no opposition in his march, as, after the occupation of Apocoronos, neither the

* This devoted Cretan patriot, Gregorios Daminos, after a series of similar achievements during the war of independence, died at Athens, in February, 1856 in the Municipal Infirmary of that place.

Halbe, nor Dascalakes and Siphakns, were able to resume their previous positions, and the Turks of Kydonia had now the command of the environs of that fortress.

The Turks of Heracleion, on this occasion, taunted those of Kydonia with their cowardice in having been defeated and ignominiously blockaded by rayas. These taunts, and in particular satirical verses to the same purport, gave rise to great animosity, and very nearly led to an open rupture and mutual slaughter. On this occasion, however, the most judicious of the Kydonian Turks, in reply to the jeers and satirical verses of the Heracleians, pointed to Therison saying, "Friends, there is Therison, and yonder are the Lakkiot mountaineers! Display against them your valour, if you please."

It is perfectly true that at the commencement of the in-surrection the Turks of Rethymne and Kydonia had sustained more numerous and more ignominious defeats than those of the Eastern provinces; as the former were exposed to the attacks of the Greek inhabitants of the White Mountains and the neighbourhood, that is, the warlike mountaineers of Kydonia, Apocoronos, Lampe, and Rethymne, etc. Accordingly, the Kydonian Turks very appropriately replied to the sneers and satires of their friends by pointing to Therison and Lakki, where, as we shall soon see, the taunters experienced disasters themselves.

At this time an anonymous letter was found in the Turkish camp at Halykae, expressing thanks on the part of the in-surgents to certain Kydonian Turks, mentioned by name, for communications made to them. Either such communications had been really made, or the individuals named had been denounced by the Pasha of Kydonia as insubordinate and riotous, and the Pasha of Heracleion, in his capacity of superior Governor of Crete, employed this device to justify his conduct in reference to the powerful Tsaruncs and two other prominent leaders, whom he caused to be hanged in the sight of the whole army. We subjoin the following state-ments, which, as we afterwards ascertained, were current among the Turks at this period.

Many lawless and sanguinary Turks, at the commence-ment of the Greek war of independence, relentlessly perse-cuted many of their milder and more humane brethren, charging them with indifference and even treason. It was asserted that the individualsi neriminated had, bytheir machinations, caused the death or banishment of many faithful and blameless Mussulmans in the time of Hadji Osman Pasha. The facts they misrepresented, were, however, simply the following:—Hadji Osman, on becoming, in September 1812, Pasha of Kydonia, prevented by his energy the execution of a plot to massacre the Greeks, without exception, and many Turks. To check the prevailing licentiousness and anarchy of the Mussulmans, Hadji Osman found it necessary to put to death many of the leaders, and to banish others, thus affording theChristian population some degree of protection from reckless and wanton oppression. Such considerations, among others, had induced the Pasha of Kydonia to denounce the individuals above mentioned.

Thus great excitement and open altercation prevailed for some time in the Turkish camp at Halykae. At length, 3,000 Heracleiots declared they were ready to attack without any assistance Therison and Lakki, and discomfit the Greek mountaineers, so terrible to the Moslems of Kydonia. The command of this select body was given to Kaïmes, famous for his valour, but previously defeated by the Greeks at Krápe. Advancing, on the 19th of August, by Hayia Kyriaké, they reached Therison without opposition, and burnt that place as well as the neighbouring Lakki, which had been left almost defenceless, and proceeded as far as Haliakae. In such inroads of the Turks, the Greeks first of all thought of securing their families and most valuable effects. On the present occasion the Therisians, aided by some other insurgents, made a long stand against infinitely superior numbers.*

Meanwhile, the brave Lakkiots under A. Panayotes, Anopolitae under Dascalakes, with other bodies of Rhizitae, arriving at the spot, impetuously attacked the Turks, and after an obstinate combat compelled them to commence a retreat from Haliakae. Vigorously pursued by the Greeks over rugged ground, the Turks had more than 200 killed,

* A woman of Therison, with a small basket of grapes in the one hand, and a pitcher of water on her shoulder, ventured to the scene of action, to present them to her husband and brother for their refreshment, which they greatly required owing to the burning sun. A bullet having knocked the pitcher to pieces, the heroine fearlessly advancing, gave her husband and brother the grapes, expressing her regret that the hated Turkish bullet had prevented her from giving them the intended supply of water.

whose arms fell into the hands of the victors. In this engagement Kaünes himself was killed. It is said that the Kydonian Turks, distant spectators of this engagement, could not conceal their delight at the defeat of the boasters, by whose jeers and taunts they had been so bitterly annoyed. In this action at Haliakae the Greeks lost about twenty men, including Stephanos Halles, who died of a wound in the forehead. The death of this patriot, a younger brother of the heroic leaders Hallae, so frequently mentioned in the preceding part of our narrative, was deeply lamented, not only by his kindred and acquaintances, but by the whole Christian population of Crete. Hardly 25 years of age, remarkable for manly beauty of form, engaging manners, and melodious voice, he was a general favourite; while his ardent patriotism, his gravity of character, and precocious practical wisdom, promised a brilliant and useful career.

During their temporary occupation of Apocoronos the Turks, who had previously taken refuge in the fortresses of Kydonia, Suda* and Rethymne, availed themselves of the opportunity of collecting and transporting with the greatest despatch all sorts of provisions, the scarcity of which they had begun to feel. Burning all the crops and supplies which they had not time to convey to the fortresses, they converted the fertile Apocoronos into a desert; so that the inhabitants and other Greeks, who afterwards flocked to this province, as a place of comparative safety, were long obliged to live on wild herbs, acorns, and the fruit of the carob tree (keratia). After the engagement at Therison, the Turks had made preparations to invade Sphakia. Before entering, however, on the details of this expedition, we shall submit to our readers a brief description of that province.

It is of an oblong form, and is situated on the southern coast of Crete, fronting the Libyan sea. On the north it is

* This fortress was strongly fortified by the Venetians. It is built on a small and precipitous island, situated at the entrance of the Amphimallio gulf. It is nearly at an equal distance from Cape Melekhae and the northern coast of Crete; and the adjoining harbour, now called the bay of Suda, is the most capacious in Crete. It was anciently called the Amphimallic bay, from Amphimallion, an ancient city of Crete, situated on the coast, and probably the ruins at Hayia Paraskevé point out its site. When the Turks, after a most destructive war of 28 years, took Crete from the Venetians, the latter by treaty retained for many years Suda, Spina Longa or Macracanthos and Grambusa.

bounded by the White Mountains, and the adjacent parts of
Kydonia, Apocoronos and Rethymne. The whole of its
frontier, from Selinon on the west to Rethymne on the east,
is rugged and mountainous.

The most practicable road between Sphakia and the adjacent
provinces, is that from Prosneron to Krapo. There is a
continuation of it from Krape to Katrena, thence to Skyphos,
and thence through the glen of Imbros. By this route the
Turks, in 1770, invaded Sphakia after the conclusion of the war
between Russia and Turkey, and encamping at Hayios Joannes
and Aradæna, in the district of Anopolia, desolated the whole
province.

To the west of the road we have described, and on the
opposite side, is a road which has received, as a propitious
designation, the name of Angelostrata (Angel-way), leading
through a very rugged glen. From Therison there is a
narrow pass, called Monopati (foot path). Both these lead
to Anopolis. The defile above Kurna, called the defile of
Apocoronos or Daphnomadaræ, leads up to Skyphos.

To the west of Sphakia is the equally mountainous province of Selinon. Between these provinces there is a very
rugged glen, called the glen of Hayia Ruméle, which
receives its name from a church situated there. In this glen
thousands of Christians found a refuge on various occasions
during the war of independence. It has three narrow outlets ;
one to Sphakia, called Saint Paul ; another to the north,
named Kaké Skala, at a tableland, of the name of Homalos ;
and a third on the west, leading up from the glen to Tripeté
at a place called Kustoyerakon in Selinon. All these defiles
are so narrow and rugged, that in many places only a single
person can at the same time pass through them.

To the east of Sphakia is the province of Lampe (Hayios
Vasiles). From Lampe Sphakia can be entered only by one
of three defiles, Skaloté, Rodakinon and Kakoskali. The
last is called also Khalara of Hayios Antonios, where
Mustapha Pasha, in his expedition against Frangocastellon,
was for a time in danger of being cut off with his whole
army

The inhabitants of the mountainous and rugged province
of Sphakia, of the population of which we shall afterwards
speak, were at all times inured to arms. Their valour and
skill in war rendered them formidable to the successive con-

E

querors of Crete. They maintained a sort of aristocratic government, their local leaders, who were elective and not hereditary, being called Primates or Captains.

Sphakia was under the immediate protection of the Sultana, and the inhabitants, instead of the capitation tax (haratch) imposed on the rest of the Cretans, paid a small fixed sum of money, and received, instead of the *haratzokhartion*, a simple receipt called *teskerés*. The tax, thus paid by the Sphakians, was collected on the spot by an Ottoman sent from Heracleion, who, though a regular Turkish functionary, found a strict respect for the manners and customs of the mountaineers indispensable for the success of his mission.

Into this, almost inaccessible country, the Turks, as we have mentioned above, ventured to penetrate, notwithstanding their recent defeat at Therison, and their previous discomfiture at Krape. The whole Turkish force at Halykæ marched from that place, under the command of Osman Pasha of Rethymne, and encamped at Prosneron, whence, on the 29th of August, they proceeded to Sphakia. In passing Krape they were struck with dread on beholding the scattered bones of their brethren, who had been here slain in the preceding July. Their fears increased as they reached Katreus, and entered the dangerous glen of Imbros, where they looked every moment for the appearance of assailants. Contrary to their expectation, however, they met no opposition in those parts, where it would have been very easy for the insurgents, particularly at Skyphos, to have impeded their advance. Had the Greeks vigorously harassed the invaders by incessant skirmishes at the most advantageous points of the defiles, the whole Turkish force might have been entirely destroyed, or, at least, compelled to abandon the hope of penetrating into Sphakia, especially as the Turks had not yet recovered from the dismay produced by their recent disasters at Krape and Ampelos.

Entering Sphakia they burnt Skyphos, Imbros, Prosyalos, Cometadæ, and Murion, all very populous villages, sparing no Christian habitation or property within their reach. Encamping near Anopolis they destroyed that place, and desolated the whole surrounding district.

Some of the inhabitants of each of the villages reached in safety the surrounding mountains, which were inaccessible to the Turks. Others, embarking in the vessels which were lying at Lutron, found a refuge in the opposite island of Clauda or Gaudos, abandoning to the mercy of the enemy thousands of their helpless brethren, and without striking a blow in defence of Sphakia, which the whole Christian population regarded as their surest place of refuge.

The Turks, in their advance, had captured and slaughtered near Murion about 20 persons, some of whom were Sphakians. On this occasion a young girl of great beauty, a daughter of Kh. Theodoros of Murion, on being made captive, conducted her captor, at his request, to a well to drink, and, while in the act of drawing water, resolutely jumped into the well, preferring death to slavery and dishonour.

It is beyond all question that the Sphakians are brave, daring and warlike, and that, during the war of independence, Sphakians have performed in every part of Crete the most brilliant achievements, and that, wherever, in other parts of Greece, Cretans displayed pre-eminent valour and enterprise, the most distinguished among them were usually Sphakians.

The conduct of the Sphakians, however, appears to us strange and inexplicable not only on the present occasion, but during a subsequent invasion of their country in February, 1824, when the Sphakians permitted the Albanian Khusein to overrun their rugged country, more inaccessible in fact than even the wildest part of Laconia, without offering the slightest resistance, and without evincing any concern for their warlike and patriotic reputation. At both periods they sadly disappointed the whole Greek nation, and exhibited a striking contrast to the Rhizitæ in Kydonia, who, fighting under far greater disadvantages, had routed and pursued almost the identical Turkish army which invaded Sphakia unopposed.

Let us for a moment compare the conduct of the Sphakians with that of the Laconian mountaineers (Maniats). Both Sphakians and Maniats are hardy mountaineers, trained to the use of arms. The Sphakians, when beyond the bounds of their native mountains, always display warlike ardour and enterprise. The Maniats, on the contrary, prefer to every spot on earth their native mountains, where they have at all times maintained their freedom, always ready to sacrifice themselves to a man, rather than allow their mountain home to be profaned by the presence of an invader. Their conduct, on the attempt of Ibraim to invade their country, is a striking

illustration of the spirit of independence that has always
existed among the Maniats.

The inferiority of the Sphakians in this comparison is not
to be attributed to any inferiority of the Sphakian people,
either in valour or in love of freedom, but to the fact, that
while the Sphakians were under the leadership of numerous
chiefs, jealous of each other, the Maniats had one acknowledged ruler, whom in all cases of common danger they
cheerfully obeyed. If the Sphakians had been cordially
united under the direction of a single commander-in-chief,
they would have triumphantly repulsed Osman Pasha, and
frustrated his attempt in August 1821, to enter their territory.
Aware of his inroad into Apocorono on the 6th of the month,
and of his preparations to invade Sphakia, they had time
to convey their families and effects to Gaudos, the inaccessible
glen of Hayia Rumelo, or elsewhere, and then, unincumbered,
assail the invaders in defiles, where the nature of the ground
would have given the Sphakians such advantage over any
superiority in numbers. Had they, on this occasion, acted
as their interest and honour required, they would undoubtedly
have received the support and co-operation of the insurgents
of the neighbouring provinces, so that the triumph of the
cause of independence, and perhaps the entire destruction
of the invading army, would have been achieved.

It cannot be said that the want of warlike stores prevented
the Sphakians from attempting to make head against the
enemy. The Cretan insurgents in general had commenced
the struggle unprepared, and with the most meagre resources,
yet the vanquished enemy supplied them with arms and
ammunition. Much more, then, might the Sphakians have
hoped at this period of the war to maintain a successful
resistance, had they acted with vigour and union. They
would, there can be no doubt, have obtained assistance from
the insurgents of other parts, as the Sphakians had frequently given assistance to them. The contest for liberty
was the common cause of the Greeks, and victory ever
crowns the persevering efforts of those who seasonably and
resolutely strike the first blow.

Many helpless inhabitants of the surrounding provinces
were seized with consternation and despair, when having,
as already mentioned, repaired to Sphakia, as the surest refuge, they saw the enemy enter and overrun the province

unopposed. The refugees, now giving vent to their dismay in heartrending lamentations, knew not which way to turn. The vessels which then happened to be at Lutros, could only take a small part of them on board at a time. In this crisis the most vigorous of the fugitives, who could not instantly embark, fled with precipitation to the neighbouring mountains, till the immediate danger should be over, leaving the rest to shift for themselves. A large multitude of men, women, and children repaired to the glen of Hayia Rumele.

A body of Turks, having attempted to enter this strong position through the pass of Saint Paul, were killed. The Turks, who had encamped at Anopolis, were astonished at the solitude of the surrounding country, and at their being allowed to overrun Sphakia without encountering opposition. An aged woman, who had been unable, from want of bodily strength, to follow the rest of the fugitives, fell into the hands of the Turks, and was brought before the Pasha, who, having given directions to supply her with refreshment, afterwards asked her why the Sphakians had made no stand, and what they intended to do. "All these mountains you see, my son" said the old woman "are full of Sphakians and other armed insurgents. Another portion of the Sphakians have conveyed their families to Gaudos, and will return forthwith, and then, all united, will fall upon you in concert."

While this conversation was going on, several vessels appeared in sight, proceeding from Gaudos, towards Hayia Rumele, for the purpose of transporting fugitives from the latter place to that island. The Pasha, receiving the old woman's statement as perfectly true, instantly commenced a retreat, proceeding along the coast of Francocastellon to Lampe, and thence to Rethymne. From Rethymne he returned to Vrysæ in Apocoronos, where he disbanded his army, and wrote to Constantinople that he had entirely extinguished the Cretan insurrection.

CHAPTER II.

Through the force of circumstances the Cretan insurrection was suspended, and even seemed to be at an end. A part of the insurgents retired to more inaccessible situations, while the rest professed submission, but all retained the flame of freedom unextinguished. Uncowed by the disasters they had suffered, they cherished the determination of renewing the struggle, whenever circumstances might permit; and in the meantime they employed, with great energy, though with great caution, every possible means of obtaining from other parts necessary supplies for renewing the war.

Immediately after disbanding the Turkish forces at Apocoronos, on their return from the Sphakian expedition, bodies of armed Greeks made their appearance in different parts both of the Rethymnian and of the Kydonian districts, and reawakened the hopes of the Christian population of Crete. The Turks no longer ventured to remain scattered in the country, where their presence had been considered necessary to overawe the Christians, but immediately repaired for safety to the fortresses, convinced that the apparent submission of the Greeks had been entirely feigned.

The blockade of the cavern of Katavaté was now raised. Gregorios Daminos, whose heroic defence of the place we have already recorded, had, with his armed followers, previously evaded the vigilance of a body of Turks quartered in the neighbouring villages for the purpose of continuing the blockade of the cavern, and repaired to Halicampos and Prosneron, situated at the foot of the White Mountains. Here he found assembled a considerable number of Sphakians and Apocoronites, including I. Sakires, Manusos Protopapadakes, Frangias also a Skyphiot, Stavros Lycakes, called also Lycostavrianos, Antonios Peneses of Vaphous, K. Prinoles, and D. Vorinos of Kephaladæ, the two Theodores of Prosneron, and other warlike leaders. All

these immediately concerted a plan with Siphacas at Melidonion, I. Mitsakes, Panayotes Myias, of Kampi in Kydonia,
Papadandreas, and G. Pipos, of Kerameia, for renewing the
war of independence.

The first to recommence hostilities were Gregorios Daminos
and M. Protopapadakes with their followers. These, lying
in ambuscade at the village of Karydion on the 6th of October,
killed seven Turks, who were proceeding to Kydonia. The
same body of insurgents subsequently attacked the Turks
still quartered at Kephaladæ, some of whom they killed,
and dispersed the rest. At the same time Siphacas with
his followers suddenly attacked and dispersed the Turks
quartered in the villages of Makhœræ, Armeni and Kalyva.
Thus the whole province of Apocoronoa, as well as Malaxa,
the most important military position in the district of
Kydonia, were again in the possession of the insurgents.

The example of the Greeks of these parts was followed by
those of Rethymne. Andreas Manuselcs, with other Kallicratiani, Frankules Kariotes, J. Druliskos from Franceskiana,
a village in Rethymne, M. Rustikianos, and the Deliyannakœ,
spreading themselves over the Rethymnian districts, created
alarm among the Turks by daily ambuscades and other
incessant hostile demonstrations, and thus obliged the Turks
to abandon the open country, and repair for safety to the
fortress of Rethymne and its immediate environs.

Georgios Nicoludes, with other Lakkiots, accompanied also
by Anopolitæ, I. Khudales, and J. Malekhutes of Perivolia in
Kydonia, Georgios Pipos with other Keramiani, and a considerable body of Acroteriani, under Stephanos Leras,[*] committed daily such acts of hostility as compelled the Turks of
Kydonia to abandon the plain, and retire into the fortress.

Scarcely had the Turks retired, when a vessel from Hydra
arrived at Lutros, and landed about 70 armed insurgents
there, among whom were persons distinguished for bravery
and military experience, such as Alexios Maurothalassites,
Lucas Livadeus, M. Kotes, G. Kapasakales, Andreas Pakhynakes of Heracleion, J. Hules, called also Huloyannes, from
the village of Pompeia, in Gortyna, and G. Sares from Siva
in Knossos, all natives of Crete except the first three.

(*) Leras was hanged by Mustaphas Pasha at the village of Murniæ, in
1833, along with 38 others, on the occasion of a large meeting of Greeks
there. Leras displayed great courage and military talent throughout the
war of independence, and distinguished himself in numerous engagements.

A short time after this, another vessel arrived at Lutros, bringing about 200 armed insurgents from Samos. They had been raised by Panuyotes Zervudakes and Theokhares Agathakes, natives of Eastern Crete, but settled in Asia Minor. Along with these came Zorzes and several other Cypriots, Panayes and Maggioros of Mitylene, Spyros Dracakes of Cephalonia, Frangias Tsiskakes of Selinon, and Hadji Georgios of Murion in Sphakia, celebrated for his exploits in Samos. The arrival of these reinforcements in Crete, and of others afterwards, greatly encouraged the Cretan insurgents.

We remark here, incidentally, that Samos, from its vicinity to Asia, afforded refuge at the commencement of the war of independence to large numbers of Greeks from the main land, who fled from the sword of the oppressor. A large proportion of these refugees were Cretans, who, owing to the cruel oppression to which they were exposed, had, though reluctantly, abandoned their native island, and emigrated to Asia Minor to live in comparative security there. The Cretan settlers in Asia Minor had been made acquainted with the intended national movement by their countrymen A. Melidones, who, as we shall have occasion to state afterwards, prepared many other Greeks of other parts for the impending insurrection. On this account there happened to be many Cretans in Samos, when in June 1821, the Turkish fleet attempted to land a body of troops on the coast of that island, opposite Mycale. On this occasion, the above mentioned Hadji Georgios of Murion, by his example, and with the co-operation of the Cretan and other refugees, greatly contributed to the success of the Samians in triumphantly repulsing the enemy.

The service thus rendered to the cause of independence in Samos is entirely overlooked by M. Tricoupi, when speaking of the events which then took place in that island. (See vol. 2, chap. I., page 21.) This omission is the more remarkable, as the gallant bearing of Hadji Georgios of Murion made his name at that period famous all over Greece. At that time all Greeks, from whatever part of Greece, whether Cretans, Asiatics, natives of the Ionian Islands, of Thrace, of Bulgaria, of Continental Greece, or of the Ægean, along with friends of the Greek cause from Western Europe, all rivalled each other in heroically maintaining the common

59

cause of Greek independence in Peloponnesus, Continental
Greece, and every other part, where a Turkish army presented itself; and what is now Liberated Greece, is the result
of the general contendings and sufferings of the Greeks and
their adherents during the national struggle.

Neophytos Œconomos and other Cretans, who had been
sent as a deputation to Peloponnesus, returned from the
island of Spezzia about the middle of October, 1821.* Touching at Æyilcia (Cerigotto), they were joined by a number of
Cretans, who had found a refuge there. Among these were
the Hallæ, Vasilios and Joannes, who were mourning the
recent death of their brother Stephanos.

These circumstances, and the intelligence brought by
Œconomos, that a Governor of Crete, appointed by the central Greek government, would arrive in that island forthwith,
greatly animated the patriotic zeal of the military leaders of
Crete. Dascalakes and Siphacas immediately occupied Malaxa, while the Hallæ occupied Garypas and Varypetros,
and A. Panayotes and his followers quartered themselves in
other important positions. The Deliyannakæ, with Drulis-
skos and Rustikianos, and the Manuscho at the head of
Kallicratiani, stationed themselves at various places in Rethymne, from which they could conveniently harass the
enemy. Vurdumbas, Sideros, and Protopapadakes, with
their followers, meanwhile proceeded wherever the common
cause might require their presence.

The Turks, in consequence of these measures of the
insurgents, were now more closely confined to the fortresses
of Rethymno, Suda and Kydonia. Though frequently
attempting inroads in the surrounding districts, they were
invariably driven back by the insurgents with loss.

About the beginning of November, Aphentules at length
arrived at Lutros, from Spezzia, on board a vessel belonging
to Joannes Vlakhos, an Ionian. The vessel brought also about
ten thousand okas of corn for sale, there being then great
scarcity in most parts of the island. Aphentules, who was

(*) N. Œconomos and A. Panayotes, and not Nicolaos Zervos and
Antonios Melidones, as M. Tricoupi state (vol. II. Chap. IV. page 105.)
had been sent as a deputation to D. Hypsilantes by the Cretan insurgents.
After the disasters in Sphakia, they remained in Peloponnesus as private
individuals. Zervos, with many other Cretans, who happened to be there,
took part in the unsuccessful attack on the fortress of Nauplia during the
night of 3rd—4th of September 1821, under the command of D. Hypsilantes.

accompanied by such armed Cretans as he had found in
Hydra and Spezzia, was received in Crete with great respect
and joy.   The military leaders hastened from all parts to
present their services to him as Governor General, notwithstanding the irregularity of his appointment. He was dressed
in a European military uniform, with epaulets, and wore the
insignia of the order of the Knights of Malta. All these
circumstances produced a great impression on the Cretan
population. He lost no time in calling a counsel of the
principal military chiefs to deliberate regarding the measures
to be adopted for the future conduct of the war.

The first proclamations issued by Aphentules greatly
encouraged the Christians of Crete. He expatiated on the
glory that would attend the Cretan movement, if all the
Greeks in Crete would support it with unanimity and vigour.
He announced to them the exploits of the insurgents in other
parts of Greece, such as the capture of the fortresses of
Monemvasia, Navarinos, Tripolis, and the brilliant naval
victory of Miaule at Patras. He added, that the almost
impregnable fortresses of Nauplia would soon be in the hands
of the insurgents, who were determined either to throw off the
Ottoman yoke, or to die with arms in their hands in the
glorious struggle for liberty. These proclamations were read
by the Cretans with great interest, and awakened the greatest
enthusiasm.

He addressed, at the same time, a proclamation to all
foreigners that might be trading with Crete, announcing
Lutros as the emporium of insurgent Crete, and inviting all
friends and neutrals to trade with it under the protection of
the Greek flag. In a short time vessels arrived in that harbour
from all parts, and abundantly supplied the insurgents with
provisions and ammunition.

In order to call forth military merit, he began to confer
military commissions, the highest of which was that of
Pentacosiarkhos, (Major.)   This rank was at first bestowed
on R. Vurdumbas, G. Dascalakes, A. Panayotes, and A. Protopapadakes. Aphentules appointed a counsel to aid him in
the administration. It consisted of the persons forming the
Sphakian Board, already mentioned, and now called coun-
cillors. Soon afterwards the rank of Pentacosiarkhos was
conferred also on G. Suderos of Lampe, M. Kurmules of
Gortyna, G. Deliyannakes the Sphakian, V. Halles of Kydonia, and P. Manuscles of Kallicrates.

On the recommendations of these superior officers, an immense number of subordinate commissions were conferred, and from this time promotion was awarded to every person who distinguished himself in action. The Cretan insurgent highly valued military rank, and was animated by the hope of obtaining it to deeds of enterprise and heroism.

Aphentules in all public documents styled himself at first " Michael Komnenos Aphentulief, Governor of Crete." To this he soon after began to add " Commander in chief of the Cretan army." He made use of two different seals. The one had the superscription, "Sphakian Board." The other was his own arms, which he always impressed on wax. On the recommendation of many Cretans, he appointed N. Œconomos his Secretary and Privy Counsellor.

On the establishment of the new administration, many skirmishes forthwith took place in different parts of Rethymno and Kydonia; and in December a battle was fought at Varypetros, to which place a large body of Turks had advanced against the Lakkiots. A. Panayotes, at the head of Kydonian mountaineers, having attacked the enemy, an engagement was maintained with great vigour on both sides for several hours. In this action some of the recently arrived auxiliaries took part, and many displayed remarkable gallantry. Among these were Zervudakes, at the head of natives of Eastern Crete, and Alexios Mavrothalassites, leading about 120 Greeks from other parts of Greece. The enemy continued to make a very gallant defence, till A. Mavrothalassites, G. Nicoludakes, the Lakkiot, and Zorzes the Cypriot, all of whom greatly distinguished themselves, charged the Turks, and put them to flight. The enemy, pursued by the whole Greek army, had a great number killed, and left a large quantity of arms to the victors. In this engagement about 30 Greeks were killed or wounded.

Shortly after this action, the Turks proceeded in greater strength as far as the village Tsicalaria with the intention of assailing Dascalakes, stationed at Malaxa. They were attacked, however, by the Greeks, and compelled after some resistance to abandon their intended enterprise, and return to the fortress. The Greeks now overran the whole plain, and, having captured a number of Turkish ladies of distinction at a Turkish country house, exchanged them for captive Greek females. After this the Turks were more strictly confined to the fortress.

Soon after this, in January 1822, Aphentules directed G. Dascalakes and A. Panayotes to clear the whole of Selinon of the Turks that still remained there, and might continue to harass the neighbouring districts. Accordingly, these leaders collected a body of 1,500 men, consisting of Sphakians, Kydonians, and of such Seliniots as had hitherto taken up arms under the leadership of Frangias Tsiscakes, and entering Selinon through the glen of Hayia Rumele, overran a great part of the province. The Turks dispersed over the country, were slain; the rest fled to the strong fortresses of Kandanos.[*] From 80 to 100 Turks of distinguished bravery, under Kaures, commander of the Seliniot Turks, a chief renowned for his valour and military skill, took possession of several strong buildings near the village of Stavros, having previously fortified them for defence in case of an inroad of the Greeks. V. Halles was directed to occupy a position near the village of Rhumata with a body of Kydonians and insurgent Kisamitae, to prevent the Turks that were still in Kisamos from coming to the assistance of the Seliniots, or effecting a diversion in their favour. The Seliniots, whose ancestors, as we have already mentioned, had become Moslems only about a century before this, were the bravest of all the Mussulman inhabitants of Crete, as well as the most robust, the most fleet-footed, and the most skilful in war. Like the Sphakians and the mountaineers of Kydonia, they inhabited a mountainous and rugged country, easily defended against invaders. Possessing all these natural advantages they were regarded by the insurgent Greeks as formidable opponents.

G. Dascalakes, having lost no time in proceeding with a large detachment to Stavros, attacked the Turks who had taken refuge there. He might easily have compelled them to surrender, if he had had the patience to maintain a strict blockade of the position for four or five days at most. He might even have destroyed the besieged with stones, had other means been wanting, as the buildings, in which the Turks had sheltered themselves, were small and low. Unfortunately, however,

(*) Kandanos is the principal town (or large village) in the province of Selinon. It consists of detached quarters at a short distance from each other, each quarter having a strong tower. It is situated in a small plain, bounded on the east and south by lofty mountains, and on the west by hills covered with olive and chesnut trees. The Turks have a mosque at Kandanos. In the time of the Byzantine emperors, Kandanos was a city of considerable size, having a Bishop of its own, styled the Bishop of Kandanos.

Dascalakes, instead of waiting to carry the position without any risk, was prompted by an inconsiderate bravery, unpardonable in a leader, to expose himself without necessity. Dascalakes, heedless of personal danger, leapt upon one of the small buildings, his followers eagerly followed his example, and attempted to destroy the besieged, or compelled them to surrender by opening a hole, and throwing in combustibles; the besieged, however, fired on Dascalakes through a loop-hole, and hit him in the forehead. He instantly expired, and his dead body was immediately carried off by followers.

The death of the Greek leader discouraged the Greeks, and frustrated the expedition. Had A. Panayotes at once assumed the command, as the troops under Dascalakes are said to have requested him to do, the object of the expedition might have been accomplished, and the death of the beloved leader avenged; but Panayotes, overwhelmed with grief for the loss of his kinsman, and eager to show his respect for his memory, accompanied the remains of Dascalakes to Lutros, along with the greatest part of the forces. The lamented leader was buried there, with all honours. In consequence of the departure of Panayotes, V. Halles was obliged to quit his position at Rhumata, and the Turks, who had been on the very point of destruction, were delivered from their perilous situation.

Georgios Dascalakes was a native of Anopolis in Sphakia. He was a lineal descendant of the famous Dascaloyannes, who, in concert with the Greeks of Peloponnesus, rose in arms, and was killed, in 1770. In his descendant Dascalakes glowed the same patriotic ardour, and the same desire to attain warlike renown. No sooner did he hear from afar the sound of Grecian arms, than he rose in defence of his oppressed country. He showed himself throughout an energetic and high-spirited leader, and the fame of his victories will be preserved among his countrymen to all generations. He was remarkable for fleetness of foot and unwearied activity, and during an engagement was always to be found at the post of greatest danger. His dignified and courteous bearing, combined with his towering stature, acquired for him in his native district the title of *Tselepés*, that is, "the Gentleman."

The death of Dascalakes, which took place in the 30th

year of his age, was deeply lamented by the whole Christian
population of Crete, and was a very severe loss to the cause
of Cretan independence.

The Seliniot Turks now became more intolerant than ever
towards the Greeks still remaining among them. This compelled the latter to seek refuge wherever they might hope to
find it. Frangias Tsiscakes, having displayed the flag of
independence on a hill in the eastern part of the province,
was joined by members of Seliniot Greeks, who had not
families to provide for. Among those who now repaired to
his standard, were Siphes Dracakes of Kakodike, Joannes
Pentares, called also Pentaroyannes, of the village of Hayia
Irene, and Joannes Papadakes, called also Papadoyannes of
Pelecanos, all men of courage and warlike experience. These
were subsequently followed by many others. Jacovos Kumes
also soon afterwards effected his escape from the village of
Stavros, when a party of Turks, suddenly entering it, killed
his mother-in-law, his wife, and an infant child in its mother's
arms. The insurgents under Frangias, thus daily increasing,
were soon able, in the rugged districts of Selinon, to make
an effective stand, so as to check the fury of their savage
oppressors.

The Turks had previously killed about seventy men,
women and children, in the village of Kakodike, and a body
of them, about 300 strong, were advancing on the village
Sclavopula to commit similar atrocities there. Papadoyannes,
however, happening to be near with a few followers, attacked
this body, and after a lengthened and obstinate engagement,
compelled the Turks to return with great loss, to their castles.
Kumes, whom we have just mentioned, remarkable for skill
and enterprise in conducting ambuscades, continued for a considerable time to harass the Turks by frequent and successful
stratagems, executed in the vicinity of the Turkish castles.

The Turks in Kisamos continued to be harassed in a
similar manner by the insurgents there. Georgios Draconianos, at the head of a considerable force, consisting partly of
Kisamitæ, and partly of Phizitæ, was the constant terror of
the enemy. In consequence of this, the Moslems were induced
to treat the Christians, still remaining among them, with
greater moderation, for fear of driving them to despair, and
compelling them to join the insurgents.

We now revert to the state of matters at this period in

Rethymne. The Kydonian and Rethymnian Greeks continued to harass the enemy by incessant skirmishes and ambuscades, but these undauntedly continued to make frequent raids into the surrounding country. It is but fair to admit that the Rethymnian Turks had been at all times milder than any of the other Turkish inhabitants of Crete, and they had neither the sternness of their Heracleiot nor the ferocity of their Kydonian brethren. In consequence of this the Christian inhabitants of Rethymne were numerous, and they enjoyed comparative freedom from oppression. The mitigated ferocity of the Rethymnian Moslems was owing to their having engaged in trade and other branches of industry. They too, however, during the war of independence, frequently committed great atrocities towards the Christian population.

M. Kurmules and A. Melidones now hastened to make inroads respectively into Gortyna and Aulopotamos for the emancipation of their native provinces. The latter was joined by A. Mavrothalassites and his followers from other parts of Greece, who were attached to Melidones from their previous acquaintance with him in Asia Minor, and their obligations to him for having apprised them of the impending insurrection, and enabled them to effect their escape from the subsequent massacres. All these reinforced by such armed insurgents from the eastern provinces, as were on the spot, eagerly prepared to promote the object of the expedition.

Yetimales, a Turk famed for his courage and enterprise, suddenly occupied, at the head of 55 chosen men, the monastery of Arcadi, situated to the east of the province and at more than an hour's distance from the town of Rethymne. This position was of great importance towards impeding the expected inroad of insurgents either into Aulopotamos or Gortyna. The Greek forces were, in the meantime, stationed in the villages of Amarion, Meron and Klesidi.

Georgios Deliyannakes, with the consent of the other leaders, put himself at the head of sixty of his followers, and on the night of 17th January, 1822, entered the monastery by surprise, and took possession of several strong buildings. Poloyoryakes, A. Melidones, and A. Mavrothalassites simultaneously surrounded the monastery, and early in the morning opened a fire on the Turks, who had occupied strong position. The enemy, astonished to perceive they were attacked by a party within the precincts of the monastery, were thrown into consternation, but continued to make a desperate resistance. Finally, the building in which they were posted was set on fire, and all perished in the flames, except one, who escaped to Rethymne. The Greeks on this occasion had fifteen killed or wounded. Among the former was a brother of Dellyannakes.

On the fifteenth of the same month a considerable body of Greeks formed an ambuscade in the vicinity of the town of Rethymne. The Turks, however, sallied forth in large numbers, and an obstinate engagement was maintained for several hours. At length the Greeks put the enemy to flight. The Turks had more than 100 killed, including one of the brothers Glymida, a leader of renowned valour. Musuragas, a Turk of distinction, was captured with his flag, as well as two other Turks. All these were sent to Aphentules, then at Latros.

Soon after this the Deliyannakes (Strates and Siphes) in concert with the insurgents of Amarion and Aulopotamos, executed a formidable ambuscade near Anoya, a village near Rethymne. Their object was to draw the Turks, stationed at Platancas, into an engagement on ground more favourable to the Greeks. In this they succeeded. Strates and his followers, having suddenly occupied positions near Perivolia and Peronzecula, an engagement ensued, which was kept up with great determination on both sides till night, the contending party frequently coming to close quarters. At length the Greeks were victorious. The enemy, pursued as far as the fortress, narrowly escaped being driven into the sea. Many Turks fell in this engagement. The Greeks had about thirty killed and many wounded, including N. Damberges, who afterwards, contrary to expectation, was cured of a wound he received in the eye.

Aphentules now promoted A. Melidones to the rank of Pentacosiarkhos in consideration of his numerous exploits, and daily increasing power from reinforcements he daily received of fresh Aulopotamite insurgent, and of Greeks, not natives of Crete. The victory, gained near the town of Rethymne, on the 23rd of January, was attributed by public opinion to his gallantry and enterprise. This promotion, though fully merited, appears to have given great offence to Vurdumbas.

About the same time the same rank was conferred also on Siphacas, the worthy successor, at Malaxa, of Dascalakes, with whom he had been accustomed to act, and often performed with him heroic achievements.

Soon afterwards Aphentules addressed from Lutros the following proclamation to the Turks, in the hope of inducing them to treat the Christian population with greater humanity.

" Ottomans of Crete !

" The Greeks have everywhere taken up arms, not for the purpose of slaughtering the unarmed and helpless, but of procuring to themselves justice, and delivering themselves once for all from cruel oppression. We regret that you do the very opposite. Reckless of the rules of humanity, you put to death unarmed old men, as well as women and children, and that, too, more wantonly than if they were brute beasts. You persist in your cruelties in a manner unequalled, except in the most barbarous ages and among the most barbarous nations, outraging both man and his Maker.

" The rights and usages of war between nations pretending to any degree of civilization, are well known. Men with arms in their hands, and persisting in resistance, are put to death while the combat lasts; but when the battle is over, slaughter ceases, and those who were previously engaged as enemies, often enter into courteous intercourse as friends. Whom have you been slaughtering so relentlessly, Ottomans ? Those who were born, who have lived, on the same soil with yourselves, — those, who have been your neighbours and acquaintances, with the same social interests as yourselves.

" On being invited to assume the government of this island, we directed the Greek force to abstain from all wanton bloodshed, to respect their fellow-creatures whenever, through the fortune of war, any of them should fall into their hands, and we are resolved to enforce these instructions. In proof of our determination we may mention the case of Musuragas of Rethymne, who, when a few days ago he and two others were made prisoners in battle, was with them safely conveyed to Lutros, where all three continue to be treated with kindness and courtesy. We call upon you to act with similar humanity in similar circumstances, and cease from slaughtering the helpless and unarmed. The fortune of war is uncertain, and none of us can tell to-day what may befall him to-morrow.

" You are, of course, already aware that, in Peloponnesus, the fortresses of Nonemvasia, Navarinos and Tripolis, have fallen into the hands of the Greeks ; that the fortresses of Nauplia are on the point of surrendering; and that all your brethren who have submitted to the Greeks, have been safely and comfortably conveyed to Asia, or wherever else they desired.

" We have been strictly enjoined by the Central Government to protect the life, property, and honour of all who submit to the Greek forces. The war in which we are engaged is not, as you erroneously suppose, a partial and lawless rising, but a general war of independence, already recognized as such by the whole civilized world. The Greeks are determined to live henceforth as freemen, establishing and maintaining, at the risk of their lives, such laws as shall effectively protect the rights of every individual."

Such was the tenour of the proclamation Aphentules addressed to the Ottomans. We are sorry we have not the original either of it or of any of his previous proclamations.

The Turks, in reply, denounced him to the Greeks as an impostor, who, dressed out in uniform with epaulets, had come to Crete to cheat the Cretans out of their oil. Notwithstanding the proclamation, the Turks continued to treat with the same atrocity as before, the Christians still living among them, as well as those who happened to fall into their power.

We may here appropriately mention a proceeding of Aphentules which was justly and generally condemned, as both unwise and unjustifiable. It proved highly injurious to Aphentules, as it occured at a time when that person; either for his own sake, or that of the cause, should have been careful to recommend himself by circumspection and righteousness to public approbation.

About the end of December, about 150 armed Greeks, partly natives of Crete, arrived at Lutros. They had been collected in Samos and other islands by Demetrios Khrysaphopulos and Michael Semirtsakes, the former a native of Kisamos, and the other of Knossos. Semerstakes had been accused, but whether justly or unjustly we have not evidence to determine, of having extorted sums of money in various parts of the Ægean. Aphentules, without reflecting on the consequences, sent Semertsakes back to the Aegean islands, giving him instructions to collect spontaneous contributions to the national cause in Crete. But this mission, so far as Semertsakes was concerned, was only a pretext, as Aphentules sent with him a Cypriot of the name of Cypriacos, and two Cretans, with secret instructions to assassinate Semertsakes on arriving at the first island they were to visit. Semertsakes was, consequently, assassinated immediately on landing in the island of Thera. We have never been able to ascertain what object Aphentules had in view in effecting this assassination. It has been said, however, that he wished to rid himself of a demagogue whose restless ambition and popular influence he dreaded. But whatever were Aphentules' motives, his conduct in this matter was severely and universally condemned, and contributed greatly to destroy his influence. Semertsakes had numerous friends, and in particular was a great favorite among the Sphakian merchants and traders who frequented Alexandria, where he was established before the commencement of the war. His murder excited general indignation, not only in his native district, but all over Crete, as his distinguished valour and enterprise had given great promise of his being pre-eminently useful to his country in the war of independence.

The Heracleiot Turks, after the events of the general expedition in August, were stationed in great force, partly at Tympakion in Gortyna, and partly in the province of Aulopotamos. These localities, respectively to the north and the south of the lofty Ida, were deemed important positions for checking the eastward progress of the insurrection, greatly apprehended by the Turks in consequence of the success of the insurgents in the western parts of the island. The Greeks, however, made every effort, at the same time, to get possession of the localities in question, considering them of extreme importance to their own cause.

A Turkish army 4,000 strong marched under the command of Tsilivotambases, a man of great notoriety at the time, and, about the end of January, occupied Furfura and Vizari, villages in the province of Amarion. Simultaneously about 2,000 Greeks, consisting of Sphakians, Rethymnians, Lampæi, Amariots and insurgents from other provinces, besides the auxiliaries under Mavrothalassites, occupied the villages of Merona, Monasterakion and Amarion in the same province. The Greek army, now in sight of the enemy and prepared for action, was commanded by Vurdumbas, Suderos, Poloyoryakes, Protopapadakes, Kurmules, Deliyannakes, Melidones, and Zervudakes.

On the 9th of February the Turks were the first to commence a fire, and a few Greeks were killed. Next day the enemy began to act on the offensive, and a general engagement took place, which ended in their defeat. Early in the morning, the Turks, crossing the stream that separated the two armies, opened a fire on the Greeks, who made a gallant resistance, notwithstanding the immense disparity of numbers. Repeated advances and charges were made, and the engagement was kept up with great obstinacy on both sides during the whole of the day. Sometimes the Greeks were driven back, and sometimes the Turks were compelled to retire to some distance. Sometimes the Greeks withdrew to more advantageous positions, from which they drove back the advancing Turks with great slaughter, and compelled them to recross the stream, in which about fifteen Turks in their flight were drowned. In this battle the enemy had more than 300 killed and a great number wounded. On the side of the Greeks about fifty were killed and thirteen wounded, including Kh. G. Muriotes, who had formerly distinguished himself in the island of Samos. The Turks and Greeks next day respectively resumed the positions they held previously to the engagement.

Four or five days after this engagement, Melidones, without the knowledge of the other Greek leaders, put himself at the head of about eighty chosen men, and proceeded by night to Vathyacon, a village in the same province, where the provisions and ammunition of the Turkish army, now at Furfura, were guarded in a mosque by eighteen Turks. A small number more were quartered in the houses of the village, to aid, if necessary, in guarding the mosque, but were not on the alert, as they suspected no danger. Some of Melidones' followers surrounded the houses in which these were quartered, and pretended to be a Turkish reinforcement from Heracleion on their way to join the army. In the meantime Melidones, with the rest of his followers, proceeded to the door of the mosque, and knocked for admission. When asked who was there, he replied in Turkish phraseology, and the Turks within immediately opened the door to receive, as they thought, a party of friends. The Greeks, suddenly falling upon the Turks in the mosque, put them all to death, and instantly destroyed all the stores, except what they were able to carry away. Next morning, Melidones was reinforced by the arrival of additional followers at Vathyacon. Of the Turks blockaded in various houses of the village, some were killed, and some effected their escape. Melidones and his followers the same day returned to Monasterakion with the ammunition and spoils they had captured.

In the Greek army generally this exploit of Melidones excited great joy; but Vurdumbas, A. Protopapadakes, and G. Saccorrhaphos, vehemently complained of the conduct of Melidones, as having recklessly risked the lives of so many followers, and maintained that the object of his rash enterprise would have been accomplished effectively and without danger, if Melidones had previously communicated his plan to them and the other Greek leaders. Notwithstanding this, Melidones related with great satisfaction the details of his adventure, adding that he was going to send a report of the whole affair directly to Aphentules. On this, Vurdumbas told him in great wrath, that he, as the commanding officer, and not Melidones, was the proper person to send a report. He further upbraided Melidones for having, after the engagement near Rethymne, on the 23rd of January, directly communicated with Aphentules and sent him Musuragas and the other two Turkish prisoners. After this altercation Melidones withdrew, full of indignation, but was overtaken by Saccorrhaphos, sent, it was said, by Protopapadakes, and persuaded to return, in order to accept a reconciliation with Vurdumbas. Saccorrhaphos had succeeded in bringing back Melidones, by representing to him the fatal consequences of a quarrel amongst the leaders, while the army was in the immediate vicinity of a Turkish force so superior in numbers. Scarcely, however, had Melidones entered the apartment where Vurdumbas and Protopapadakes were waiting for his return, when Vurdumbas instantly renewed the quarrel, and, after some outrageous language, inflicted on Melidones a wound with a dagger, of which he immediately expired.

The cause of Crete thus lost Melidones, a patriot from whose courage and enterprise the greatest services were expected, and who had been of incalculable use to his countrymen before the commencement of the war. By his judgment and energy in Asia Minor he had saved from the impending massacre a great number of his countrymen, having, at the risk of his own life, warned them of coming events. Not a few Greeks, saved through the patriotic solicitude of Melidones, lived to perform exploits during the war of independence, both in Crete and in other parts of Greece.

Melidones was a native of the village of Melidoni, in the province of Aulopotamos. He was a person of great courage and energy. Most of the non-Cretan Greeks who took part in the Cretan insurrection, had gone to that island through the persuasion of Melidones, to whom they remained remarkably attached. His death produced vehement indignation among these and all his followers, and almost led to a fatal outbreak in the Greek army. Though a collision was prevented, about 150 experienced and valiant warriors immediately left Crete in disgust. The only failing of Melidones was his hastiness of temperament, which sometimes led him to speak and act with indiscretion. His death was lamented by the whole Christian population of Crete. Aphentules immediately deprived Russos Vurdumbas of his military rank. The untimely end of Melidones and its immediate consequences occasioned the dispersion of the Greek army. The enemy manifested their joy by discharges of musketry when informed of Melidones' death, and when, after the dispersion of the Greek army, they got possession of Monasterakion, they disinterred his dead body, and treated it with every possible outrage.

After these events, and about the middle of February, Aphentules left Lutros for Argyropolis,[*] and thence proceeded to Hayios Konstantinos, both villages in the province of Rethymne. He was accompanied by N. Œconomos, G. Papadakes, Em. Antoniades, and other prominent patriots, and the object of their visit was to adopt on the spot measures for the more vigorous prosecution of the war. A series of important skirmishes and ambuscades were now executed with great spirit and success by G. Deliyannakes, at the head of a considerable Rethymnian force, with the co-operation of Rustikianos and Draliskos, and of the Kallicratiani and Sphediatæ under the command of P. Manuseles, Anagnostes Siphodascalakes and Suderos.

Aphentules and his above mentioned advisers, after giving

(*) At this village are ruins of an ancient city. Many antiquities have been found in tombs here, and walls of some height are still standing, which probably were those of a Mint.

a fresh impulse to the warlike operations of the insurgents in Rethymne, visited the military positions of the Greeks in Kydonia. They first repaired to Hayios Georgios in Kydonia, and thence to Armeni. At the latter village they were induced to remain a considerable time, owing to the security it offered them. Siphacas had removed his victorious banners from the mountainous Malaxa to the lowland villages of Tsicalaria and Nerocuron, and had thus the command of the whole plain of Kydonia, the Turks having been defeated in many encounters by A. Pannyotos and Halos.

A resolution was now adopted to dig an entrenchment to the east of the defile of Halmyros. From the earth collected in digging the entrenchment, was formed a mound, on which guns were planted. This work extended from the village of Kurna to the seashore, and its object was to provide a place of refuge in case of danger from Turkish inroads from the eastern parts of Crete. Phasules was appointed superintendant of the undertaking, and carried it into effect with great energy and despatch. The expediency, however, of this undertaking, to the neglect of offensive movements at a distance, was, to say the least, very doubtful.

At this time Valestras, a son of old Valestras the Frenchman, who for many years resided in Crete, arrived in the island. He had been trained to regular military service in France, and had served as a captain under Napoleon, but in 1814 retired from the service and returned to Crete.

On the outbreak of the Greek insurrection he lost no time in repairing to the theatre of war from Western Europe, where he had been for some time residing. At Kalamæ in Peloponnesus he organized the nucleus of a regular Greek army, and received from D. Hypsilantes the rank of Colonel. Various old Cretan acquaintances of his, and in particular J. Papadakes, then in Peloponnesus, induced Valestras to join the cause of independence in Crete, giving up his position in Peloponnesus. The Cretan insurgents welcomed with open arms an officer personally known to many of them, and possessing distinguished military skill and experience.

Valestras, arriving in Crete about the middle of March, immediately paid his respects to Aphentules at Hayios Georgios, and communicated to him his object in repairing to Crete, expressing his ardent desire to be serviceable to the cause of Cretan independence. He congratulated Aphentules,

at the same time, on the success which had already attended
his efforts in the direction of affairs, and offered him his
cordial co-operation in the military department, hoping by
his zealous services to be instrumental in promoting the
public cause as well as the individual reputation of Aphentules. Having visited the military positions of the insurgents
in Kydonia, and paid high compliments to the patriot leaders,
he repaired, without loss of time, to Kydonia, where the
Greek forces were preparing for an engagement. Under
the eye of Valestras, a Greek detachment, not exceeding 700
men, attacked about the end of March, and, after an obstinate
conflict, which lasted three hours, routed a Turkish force
about five times their number. The Turks were pursued
almost to the very gates of the fortress, and sustained a very
severe loss. The Greeks in this affair had only three killed
and seven wounded.

This achievement, of which Valestras was an eye-witness,
filled him with enthusiasm, and convinced him that with
such gallant troops he could easily make himself master of
the fortress of Rethymne, an object he deemed of the greatest
importance towards the success of the Cretan cause. His
military skill and judgment enabled him to perceive that
the possession of a fortress as a military depot and centre of
military operations, was indispensible to the success of the
insurrection. His experience in Peloponnesus had confirmed
this conviction. He clearly saw that the Cretan administration could not be consolidated, if its members were
compelled to perambulate from place to place, and especially
without being supported by a permanent military force, and
that Lutros was too remote a position for conveniently directing warlike operations and transmitting military supplies to
all parts of Crete.

Valestras was greatly aided and encouraged in the details
of his enterprise by the suggestions of some of the Greek
leaders, accurately acquainted with the localities and the
state of matters in Rethymne. He ascertained that the
Rethymnian Turks made frequent sorties from the fortress,
and on these occasions usually left only such of their troops
as were least efficient for service to defend the place. Communicating his plan to Aphentules he requested him to give
orders that as large a Greek force as possible should be
collected at a specified time and place to carry it into effect.

Accustomed to the discipline of a regular army, Valestras seems to have forgotten that he had to make use of undisciplined insurgents, and that their combined action in executing a complex plan was a matter of great difficulty, not to say of impossibility.

A Greek force mustered with the greatest alacrity. A position called Petalon, near a hill in the vicinity of the village of Vrysinon, was occupied by Suderos, Poloyoryakes, Joannes Moskhovites, Frangios Kariotes, P. Zervudakes, at the head of their followers, consisting of insurgents from the eastern provinces, Lampæi, Amariots, Anlopotamites, as well as of Rethymnians and others. A Protopapadakes at the head of the Skyphiots, and a portion of Apocoronites who served under Martuseles along with the Kallicratiani, and Siphodascalakes, commanding the Sphediots, occupied the village of Kastellon, where they were re-inforced by the auxiliaries under A. Mavrothalassites. The rest of the Rethymnians under G. Deliyannakes, Rustikianos and Druiscos, a large number of Apocoronites and Kydonians, led by J. Hales and N. Konstantudakes, brother of Siphacas, mustered at the villages of Upper and Lower Varsamoneron, under the immediate command of Valestras, who had repaired thither from Hayios Konstantinos, exulting, and, as it is said, singing, during the whole night of 13—14th of April, patriotic songs, in the persuasion that the troops under his leadership, more than 9,000 strong, would not fail to storm Rethymne sword in hand. Such were his enthusiasm and confidence, that he deliberately left behind him at Hayios Konstantinos the horse which he had been strongly urged by friends to make use of owing to the feeble state of his health.

Protopapadakes, commanding the centre at the head of the most warlike portion of the troops, was instructed to offer battle to the Turks. He was then to retire in order to draw the enemy to a distance from the fortress. When this had been accomplished, Poloyoryakes and Suderos were to attack the Turks in the flank, and Valestras was then to advance on the opposite side to the vicinity of the fortress. It was expected that the enemy, thus placed in the midst of three fires, would be overpowered, and in that case Valestras was instantly to commence the storming of the town. Had all the details of the plan been cordially and exactly executed, its object would, in all probability, have been accomplished. But the enterprise proved a complete failure, owing to a want of concert and cordiality in the execution.

On the day before the engagement, about fifty Turks, advancing towards Kastellon, either to reconnoitre, or for some other purpose, were attacked by the Skyphiots, who killed fourteen of them, and carried away their valuable arms. The Kallicratiani having, as it is said, demanded and been refused a share of the spoil, the circumstance gave rise to a serious quarrel.

Next day the Turks sallied forth in full force, and first attacked the positions occupied by Suderos and Poloyoryakes, who gallantly sustained the formidable onset, counting on the speedy assistance of the Greek forces stationed at Kastellon. When, however, considerable time elapsed, and the expected reinforcement failed to appear, they were compelled to retreat with the loss of thirty men, and were pursued as far as Kumnia.

Valestras counting on the exact execution of his plan in all its details, rushed from his position, sword in hand, and in advance of his troops urged them on by his exhortations and his example. Unexpectedly, however, a very large Turkish force reached the spot, and assailed the Greeks in the open plain. An obstinate encounter ensued, in which the Greeks, after vainly waiting for assistance, were overpowered. Suderos and Poloyoryakes had been previously compelled to retreat to a considerable distance, and, however desirous, were unable to come to their succour. Protopapadakes remained at Kastellon a passive spectator of the action, engrossed with the wretched contentions that had arisen among the troops there regarding the division of the spoils obtained in the above-mentioned skirmish. Owing to these lamentable circumstances Valestras and his followers were obliged to retire, and were pursued with great loss.

About eighty Greeks are said to have fallen in this retreat; and a considerable number were taken prisoners, including Captain Kokkinos, a native of Khios (Scio), an aide-de-camp of Valestras, as well as that heroic leader himself, having dropped down from bodily exhaustion. A Sphakian, one of the followers of Deliyannakes, attempted to save Valestras, while panting and unable to move, by carrying him on his back, and, after concealing him in a thick bush by the wayside, saved himself by flight. The victorious Turks, however, found Valestras under the bush in their return, cut off his head and carried it in triumph to Rethymne. Kokkinos, also, and all the other prisoners were put to death on their arrival at Rethymne.

Thus perished Valestras, a victim, it is said, of a vile intrigue on the part of Aphentules, who suspected that Valestras was aiming at superseding him in his political position, a thing of which Velestras had never dreamed. From this time forward Aphentules applied himself to form an influential party of his own, treating with neglect and injustice many meritorious patriots, whom he unfoundedly regarded as disaffected to his person and influence.

Had the insurgent leaders cordially and vigorously co-operated in carrying into effect Valestras' plan, the victory would undoubtedly have been on the side of the Greeks. Their army assembled on the occasion, was sufficiently numerous, and the plan of operation, delineated by so able a soldier as Valestras, had been unanimously approved. The want of success may be attributed mainly to Protopapadakes, who, with his followers, left their positions without firing a shot, regardless, it would appear, of the fate of their fellow-countrymen. Whether that leader was guilty of treachery, and acted as the instrument of Apenthules, we leave it to time to determine. One thing, however, is certain, that the failure of Valestras' efforts to establish a regular army in Crete was a fatal loss to the patriot cause. The Cretans, whether Turks or Greeks, possess natural courage and energy; and had the Greeks added to these advantages, common to both parties, that of discipline, their ultimate triumph would have been inevitable.

Meanwhile, the most satisfactory success attended the efforts of the insurgents in other parts of Greece, and distinguished victories were daily achieved both by sea and land.

The Greeks now directed their attention to the political administration of the country, and arrangements were made through the authorities for convening at Argos a National Assembly for the appointment of a Central Government, and the adoption of a National Constitution.

Hitherto every district in Greece had a separate and independent Government, and a distinct form of administration. Poloponnesus, for instance, had established a Senate; Western Continental Greece had also a Senate at Mesolonghion ; Eastern Continental Greece had an administration called Areios Pagos ; the Naval Islands were self-governed, each having a separate form of administration ; and Crete, as we have already mentioned, had established at Lutros, at the commencement of the insurrection, a Cretan or rather a Sphakian Board.

This National Assembly of the Greeks at Argos had commenced its preliminary sittings as early as December 1821, and in these the Cretans had taken part. In the meantime the Peloponnesian deputies, suspecting that Hypsilantes was opposed to the convening of a National Assembly, suddenly left Argos, and repaired to Epidauros (Piada), where the proceedings of the Assembly were brought to a conclusion, and the constitution of Epidauros was drawn up and promulgated. The Cretan deputies were unable to proceed to Epidauros, as some of them were seriously ill, and the rest were occupied with important matters connected with the interest of Crete. They were in particular engaged in enlisting troops, Cretans and others, to be put under the command of Valestras, who was at that moment vigorously preparing his expedition to Crete. The Cretan deputies, however, along with the representatives of all parts of Greece, accepted and signed the constitution of Epidauros. Aphentules alone, who was not a Cretan, endeavoured to oppose its adoption by instigating certain unsuspecting individuals to maintain the inexpediency on the part of the Cretans of subjecting themselves to others by a solemn bond, and insist that the achievements of the Cretans and the importance of their island entitled them to form a separate and independent state of their own. These views were not only put forth in conversation, but distinctly uttered in public documents, though all enlightened and patriotic Cretans rejected them as delusive and preposterous.

After the events connected with the engagement at Rethymne, of which we have already given an account, a large number of Aulopotamite insurgents, including the brothers of the murdered Melidones, the brothers Khamalakæ, Joannes and Stavrules, Kyriakos Sguros, Ant. Kallerges, M. Melitakas, Vasilios Hayiomamites, J. Palmetes, together with Zervudakes, with his followers, and other leaders with theirs, concerted a plan with Theodoros Khurdos, and the auxiliaries under A. Mavrothalassites, besides some others, according to which an insurgent force, about 500 strong, entered the province of Aulopotamos about the end of April. The Turks there being dispersed in the villages, were, on the sudden appearance of the invaders, obliged at first to save themselves by repairing to Heracleion. The Greeks thus got possession of a province which had hitherto escaped devastation, and were thus enabled to convey necessaries to their famished families, who were at that time residing in districts which had been from the commencement of the insurrection exposed to the ravages of war. All the male inhabitants of Aulopotamos able to bear arms, speedily equipped themselves in the best manner they could, and joined the insurgent force to aid in defending themselves and their homes.

How Akhmet Kirimes was informed that the insurgents who had entered Aulopotamos retired from it immediately after seizing whatever they could carry away, we do not exactly know. We can, however, state as matter of fact, that Kirimes and his brothers, putting themselves at the head of 347 chosen Turks from Heracleion and other parts, took by surprise, during the night, a strong tower situated in the village of Episcope, at the foot of Mount Ida, and occupied other convenient positions in order to repel an attack. During their march a few of Kirimes' troops having, without his knowledge, separated from his main body, massacred at the village of Khones about ten unarmed Greeks, whose heads they carried to Episcope, and displayed as trophies of their valour to Kirimes and his brothers. These leaders, however, it is said, indignantly replied, "We have come hither not to drive the Christian population to revolt, but, if possible, to protect the province and our own property from injury."

As soon as the Greeks unexpectedly heard of this inroad, Alexios and Andracos, at the head of their usual followers, accompanied by such armed Aulopotamites as happened to be within reach, and many others, instantly proceeded to Episcope, and vigorously endeavoured to blockade the Turks in the Tower. The latter, on seeing the detachment of Theodoros Khurdos approaching, mistook it for a body of Rethymnian Turks coming to their assistance. Under this impression they issued forth to attack the Greeks, who, either as a stratagem or otherwise, retired to the neighbouring hills at the village of Hayios Mamanta. But, on the arrival of Khurdos, they attacked the Turks with great impetuosity, and put them to flight. The enemy left behind them fifteen dead, and carried off some wounded. The Greeks had only one killed, and he was one of the Aulopotamites who had recently taken up arms.

After this, the Turks were so strictly blockaded in the Tower, as to be without water. Firing was kept up vigorously and unceasingly on both sides day and night, the Greeks being eager to get possession of the place before the apprehended arrival of Turkish reinforcements, either from Gortyna or Heracleion. On the fourth day of the blockade the Turks sought an interview with the Greek leaders. The besiegers, through the influence of Kirimes and his brothers, who were highly respected by the Greeks, proposed to allow the besieged to retire immediately to Heracleion on delivering up all their arms, with the exception of fifty muskets for their protection during their march. The besieged were divided in their opinions. Some of them insisted that they ought to hold out in the hope of speedy assistance, and from an apprehension of being put to death if they gave up their arms, while the rest preferred to attempt an escape with arms in their hands. Kirimes and his brothers, however, opposed the latter opinion, trusting to the friendly feelings of the Christians.*

In the meantime an influential Turk of Heracleion, one of the brothers Ladaoglu, put himself at the head of 300 men, and hastened to the aid of the besieged. Encountering, however, at Sclavocampos a body of Greeks, consisting mostly of Anoyani, he was completely defeated, and his followers were entirely dispersed.

On this occasion the Greeks killed a great number of Turks, and got possession of their arms. The Anoyani, those swift-footed mountaineers of Ida, showed on this as on other occasions, that they were not inferior in valour to the Kydonian Lakkiots. Among those who distinguished themselves most were Vasilios Sbokos, Joannes Palmetes, Stavrules Niotes, Stavros Xetrypes and others. At the commencement of the insurrection the Anoyani joined the movement with no

* The Kirimes were in reality Turks of an excellent disposition and large landed property in Aulopotamos. On all occasions they had given every protection to the oppressed Greeks. On this account the victorious Greeks gratefully treated with special kindness those who survived the blockade. It is a mistake, however, to suppose that the Kirimes were, like the Kurmulidæ of Gortyna, concealed Christians, and Turks only in appearance.

other arms than large clubs, and yet, strange to say, with these they rushed to battle, and, frequently putting the Turks to flight, pursued them and stripped them of their arms, which they afterwards used themselves. A young Anoyan mountaineer, with his club on his shoulder, pursued on one occasion to a great distance an armed Turk, and repeatedly called out to the fugitive what was afterwards repeated as a good joke: "I will pursue you, Aga, till you throw down your arms." The fugitive, in reality, first threw down his pistol, on which the pursuer called out "I must have your musket also." The Turk having thrown down his musket, the Greek called out again with a very loud voice "I must have your sword too." The young mountaineer being now fully equipped, allowed the Turk to escape, and called after him, "Good bye, Aga, and thank you." The Aga safely arrived at Heracleion with only the loss of his arms.

After the defeat of the Turks at Sclavocampos, the Greeks at Episcope received reinforcements, and, urging the blockade with greater vigour, soon compelled the Turks to surrender. The objections of some of the besieged were met on the part of the Greeks by the following remarks:—
"Human beings are not cattle to be slaughtered by you, as you have hitherto been accustomed to do. You have heard, no doubt, the result of the engagement of Sclavocampos. The contest is now to be decided by arms." At first the Turks insisted on being allowed to remain in their villages, and in retaining their arms for the purpose, no doubt, of gaining time, as they always entertained the hope of receiving assistance. The Greeks, however, rejected the proposed terms, as it was impossible at this period for Greeks and Mussulmans to live together, while the murder of relatives and friends was still recent, and the survivors still breathed revenge. The besieged at length consented to give up their arms, but on coming out of the tower hesitated to comply. Many of them, indeed, resolved to defend themselves, and in a conflict that ensued three of the besiegers were killed. On this the Greeks assailed the Turks with vigour and indignation, and killed them all except ten, who, taking advantage of the confusion, escaped to the mountains, and ultimately arrived at Heracleion in safety. On this occasion fell the eldest of the Kirimæ brothers, called Mulus; his three brothers remained unmolested, and were soon after-

wards allowed to escape. The Greeks, on getting possession of the tower, demolished it, lest it might again serve as a place of refuge to the enemy.

The Aulopotamites, now generally furnished with arms, advanced to Knossos, the inhabitants of which were encouraged to join the movement, and the number of insurgents there daily increased, and put themselves under the command of Zervudakes ; and by skirmishes and frequent and successful ambuscades the Greeks confined the enemy to the immediate environs of Heracleion.

Aphentules now rewarded Theodoros Khurdos for his recent success by appointing him Tagmatarkhes (Major) and military commander of the province of Aulopotamos. He at the same time conferred the same rank on Alexios Mavrothalassites, as he, too, had greatly distinguished himself in supporting Khurdos. Many inferior officers also received promotion. It is sad to be obliged to record that Mavrothalassites was soon afterwards assassinated by one of the auxiliaries under his command, and the Cretan cause thus deprived of his important services. His death was greatly and universally lamented by the Cretans.

Alexios was a native of one of the cities on the coast of the Black Sea, and, from this circumstance, was called Mavrothalassites. Having formed an intimacy with various Cretans in Samos, he indentified himself with the cause of Cretan independence. He was of a lofty stature and dignified appearance His countenance was not comely, but his features were softened by the goodness of heart that beamed on his face. Brave, enterprising and energetic, he distinguished himself in every engagement, and obtained an influence corresponding to his merit. All Greeks, not natives of Crete, but engaged in the struggle there, readily put themselves under his orders. He had a constant following of about 150 of these. He governed this auxiliary company with great wisdom, and wherever he went, he treated the Cretans, with whom he had cast in his lot, with cordial and brotherly courtesy. The immediate occasion of his murder was, it is said, that he had severely reprimanded and threatened the murderer and checked his attempts to oppress Christian inhabitants of the province of Amarion. Alexios was succeeded in the command of the auxiliaries by Nicolaos Zervos.

The following circumstance, which occurred soon after this, seems worthy of being recorded here.

While Michael Kurmules was sojourning in the province of Amarion, and making preparations to enter Gortyna and attack the Turks at Tympakion, he received a letter from Seriph Pasha of Heracleion, the tenor of which, as we have often heard from Lazarakes, then Secretary to Kurmules, was as follows:—" I have never yet been able to understand by what means the Infidels succeeded in drawing you over to their cause, and inducing you to bear, along with them, impious arms against our holy religion. The Ottoman Empire is little affected by the movements of a few infatuated rayas, and we shall, with God's assistance, soon inflict on them the just reward of their folly and treason. I am, however, truly sorry that you have been misled, and have dishonoured the name of your family, which was at all times held in estimation among the Faithful.

" If you had any grounds of complaint against those Turks of your province, who, as I understand, were constantly annoying you,* and at length, drove you to defection, you ought to have told us at the time, and we should have punished those by whom you were molested. It is not even yet too late for you to return from your delusion, and I pledge myself to apply to the clemency of our long-suffering Sultan and Lord for your forgiveness. Nay, I feel assured that you will not only be forgiven, but rewarded with high dignities, when I have duly represented your case in the proper quarter, and when our invincible arms have subdued those ungrateful rayas who have dared to rise in rebellion."

Seriph wrote in this manner in order to prevent, if possible, in Gortyna, events similar to those which had occurred in Aulopotamos. Kurmules, however, had from his social position, learnt the import of the Turkish proverb: " The Turk drives at ease in his carriage, and catches hares." Accordingly, he paid no attention to the shallow artifice of the Pasha. Neither did ever Kurmules entertain the slightest idea of resuming the profession of the Moslem

(*) Kurmules had, in fact, been frequently denounced as unsound in the faith, and, as we have previously mentioned, was thus often exposed to danger, from which he escaped either by pecuniary sacrifices judiciously and adroitly made, or by means of his personal influence; but mainly by the efforts of the powerful party of which he was the leader.

faith, to which he had been previously compelled to conform in appearance. He at first declined all correspondence with Seriph or any other Turk, to avoid awakening the suspicions of his fellow-Christians, whose cause he had cordially and steadfastly embraced. When, however, he was subsequently requested by Seriph to send a reply to his letter, he resolved, by the advice of his friend Lazarakes, to transmit the following answer :—

" May it please your Excellency !

" I received your letter, and I thank you for all you have the kindness to say. So far, however, from having been misled in taking up arms against the Ottomans, I beg to assure you that my own conscience was my adviser, and gave me no rest till I publicly acted out my inward convictions. I beheld the fearful sufferings which the Christians, who were, and who are my brethren, unjustly endured, while I could not give them efficient protection. I declare to you, moreover, that I prefer my present position to all the imperial dignities which you kindly promise to procure for me."

This put an end to the correspondence. We now return to the state of matters in Kydonia.

After the successful inroad of the Greeks into Aulopotamos, V. Halles, A. Panayotes, and Siphakas thought the moment favourable for an attack, on their part, on the Turks of Selinon and Kisamos, in order to get rid of neighbours whose presence occupied a considerable portion of the Greek forces. It appeared to them of great importance to avail themselves of the five vessels which happened at this time to be cruising on the Cretan coast, under the command of Theodoros Kantarzos, and which had already succeeded in cutting off all communication by sea between the Turks in the fortress and those who still remained in the above-mentioned provinces. Accordingly, Aphentules, at the request of the military leaders we have mentioned, took the necessary steps for this purpose. About the end of April the whole of the Apocoronites, the Skyphiots under Protopapadakes and Siphakas, the Lampæi under Suderos, and the Kydonians under A. Panayotes and Halles, assembled at Galatas, Platanias, and the adjoining villages of Kydonia. Aphentules himself embarking in one of the ships, proceeded from Armeni to Platanias, a village which, from its strong position, enabled him to superintend, in perfect security, the military preparations more effectively from the village's vicinity to the scene of action.

Halles and Siphakas, acting in concert with Aphentules, induced the other leaders to commence their operations by an attack on the Kydonian Turks, who, convinced that the preparations were intended against them, occupied convenient positions in the suburbs, including the village Macryteikhos, situated at a small distance to the west of the fortress. The Greeks, in like manner, occupied positions opposite the river called Kladissos, and a fire commenced forthwith on both sides. For nearly three days an obstinate engagement was kept up day and night, and the number of killed and wounded on both sides was very considerable.

The guns of the batteries maintained an uninterrupted fire on the Greeks, but without effect; while the Cassian ships replied with equal activity, but with no greater result. The determination evinced by the Greeks so alarmed the Turks in the fortress, that nearly all the females and all the unarmed spectators on the ramparts began to utter lamentations for their relatives and friends, and, overpowered by the most gloomy anticipations, gave themselves up to despair.

During the engagement, which was maintained with equal obstinacy on both sides, an Ottoman of the name of Karajules, renowned for his valour, eluded the observation of the Greeks, and, towards sunset of the third day of the battle, occupied a more advantageous position, from which he was able to damage the Greeks with greater effect; and the daring example of Karajules would have induced the rest of the Turks to have attacked the Greeks with great fury and success, had it not been for the deacon Dorothoos Perakes, who, at the head of a party, rushed forward just at the most critical moment from another advantageous position, and killed the enterprising Ottoman. This prevented the further success of the enemy, who, after the death of their champion, whose dead body they had great difficulty in carrying away, began to retire under cover of the following night, and were next day taunted by the Greeks for their cowardice. In the preceding attack more than 100 Turks were killed or wounded. On the side of the Greeks the killed or wounded amounted to 40.

Next day the Cassians, while firing salutes opposite the small island of Hayios Theodoros, in honour of the victory, sunk a Turkish boat with all on board, which was proceeding from Kisamos to the fortress. On that occasion the following accident occurred. One of the iron guns of Th. Kantarzos' ship burst, and a fragment of it killed that heroic patriot. His unexpected death was deeply lamented, not only by the Cassians, but by the whole Greek population of Crete, who keenly felt the loss of the valuable services of so gallant and cordial a friend as Th. Kantarzes had proved himself to be. His remains were interred at Platanias with all military honours.

Th. Kantarzes was one of the most distinguished naval commanders of the island of Cassos. In fact, he was the most intelligent, the bravest, and the most energetic naval officer that the island of Cassos ever produced. With a heart overflowing with humanity, he not only succoured and soothed the Cretan refugees in Cassos, from the commencement of the revolution, but sent assistance to the distressed in various parts of Crete. He despatched to Aphentules at Lutros, rice and other provisions, as well as clothes, to be distributed among the suffering population of Crete. From the first outbreak of the war, Th. Kantarzes had with his cruisers carried alarm into the ports of Syria, Alexandria, and Asia Minor. Frequently appearing on the coast of Crete at the head of a small squadron, he rendered most effective co-operation to the insurgents there, to the great damage and terror of the enemy. He evinced great judgment as a commander, and earnestly stimulated the shipowners of Cassos to give vigorous support to the Cretan insurgents; and pointed out the advantages that would redound to his native island from the emancipation of Crete. His death led to the immediate withdrawal of the Cassian squadron, which, had it remained on the coast of Crete, would, by blockading the Turkish ports, have rendered the most effective service to the Cretan cause.

The main object of the intended expedition was thus entirely frustrated. In the meantime, Aphentules, having returned to Apocoronos, invited leading individuals from the liberated provinces to repair to Armeni for the purpose of signing a lengthened document drawn up by himself alone, and professing to be a provisional constitution for Crete. Aphentules, however, did not possess the requisite knowledge and capacity for such an undertaking; and his real object in attempting it, was mainly to counteract, by a manœuvre of

his own, Petros S. Homerides Skylizzes, who had already
arrived at Lutros as commissioner from the Central Government of Greece, to organize Crete in accordance with the
new national constitution.

Aphentules' document proposed the following arrangements: All military officers were to be under his control.
He was to appoint aides-de-camp, who, as he stated, were to
be the responsible ministers of the future kingdom of Crete.
He was to form a party by gaining over the most powerful
Cretans to support him in carrying out his schemes; and he
was, lastly, to establish a Cretan treasury in such a manner
as he might think proper, he himself being invested with
its absolute direction and control. This attempt of Aphentules
was inpraticable and absurd. All the public revenues arising
from the sale of oil were under the direction of the Board
which Aphentules had established on his arrival, and which
he had not the power to set aside. The other parts of
Aphentules' proposed constitution were rejected by the
Cretans, and, as we shall see, the constitution recommended
by the Central Government of Greece, through its representative, was unanimously adopted. We return to the
military operations.

After this period it was with hesitation and reserve that
the Turks ventured to advance to a distance from the walls
of their fortresses; and in all their excursions they were
constantly exposed to ambuscades, some of the most important of which we shall mention here.

The Turks of Kydonia, taking it for granted that the
Greeks would engage in the customary rejoicings and religious
usages on Easter-day, issued from the fortress on that
festival, without expecting to encounter any annoyance.
Some of them proceeded at dawn to visit their friends in
garrison at the grange of Kokkinon, while others went to
see the Turks then holding strong positions at Pelecapinna
and Taratsos, and intended, in their turn, to attempt
ambuscados against the Greeks. These, however, were
prepared to receive them. Joannes Halles, with about 80
followers, had laid an ambuscade in convenient positions
near Taratsos and Pelecapinna; while I. Khudales, with 50
followers, secretly occupied positions between the grange of
Kokkinon and the fortress. As the Turks were thus unexpectedly assailed, a large number of them were slain.
None of the Greeks fell in this affair; but Khudales, who

had rushed forward to plunder a Turk that had fallen, was severely wounded.

Siphakas, distressed at the damage done by the Turks in their daily excursions for the purpose of cutting down olive trees in the environs of the fortress, for firewood, concerted the following extensive ambuscade with V. Halles, which they executed on the 25th of April. Siphakas occupied the monastery of Chrysopege and other convenient positions around the grange of Kokkinon, while V. Halles undertook to occupy positions at Paregoria towards Taratsos. Manusos Joseph (called also Manusosiphes)* took up a position with about 50 men towards Kubé, situated under the grange of Barbu, where many Turks continued to remain as in a place of security with numerous flocks. Manusos Joseph was directed to detach as large a portion as possible of these flocks, and to commence driving them towards Siphakas with a view to induce the Turks to leave their positions to recover their property. Gregorios Daminos, with about 200 men, was stationed at Scopia (called Morto Vardia), situated on the promontory of Melekhas, with instructions to attack the Turks in the rear the moment they should issue from the grange of Barbu. It was expected that the enemy, thus placed between two fires by Siphakas and Daminos, would unconsciously be driven towards the positions at Paregoria occupied by Halles.

The movement of Manusosiphes completely succeeded. The Turks issued from Barbu to attack him, when he began to retire towards Siphakas, and at the same moment reinforcements from the fortress hastened to their assistance. Siphakas, making his appearance with about 150 men, stopped the advance of the Turks towards Kubé, and Daminos, suddenly starting from his ambuscade, and attacking in the rear the Turks who had issued from the fortress, opposed their retreat either to the grange of Barbu or to the fortress.

The Turks were thus compelled to defend themselves in the plain, which they did very gallantly. During nearly the whole day frequent and obstinate attacks were made on both sides, in which about 70 Turks were killed, including

* This Cretan patriot was afterwards killed on the Peloponnesian island of Sphacteria, together with about 40 other Cretans, after the capture of Navarino by Ibrahim, in 1825. Manusosiphes, remarkable for his bravery, was the cherished leader of the inhabitants of his native village, Melidoni, and had distinguished himself in many engagements.

Nures Abduramanes, a leader of great valour, who fell at
Xylocamara, as he was advancing at the head of a large
detachment to attack Siphakas in the rear. The whole
ammunition of the Turks having been accidentally destroyed
by fire, they were compelled to retreat to Taratsos.

As they were slowly proceeding to that place, they were
followed by the Greeks, who took it for granted that the
enemy would fall into the ambuscades of Halles, while
Siphakas and Daminos would attack them in the rear. They
were, however, disappointed in these expectations, and the
Turks reached Taratsos in safety, owing to V. Halles's having
neglected to occupy, according to agreement, the specified
positions, from which the Turks might have been assailed
to great advantage. In this affair six Greeks were killed,
and 20 wounded. The Turks in the fortress were greatly
terrified on this occasion, and opened a fire on Daminos as
he marched along within a short distance of the walls with
displayed banners. During the whole day the gate of the
fortress was kept shut for fear Daminos should take it by
surprise, the number of defenders being extremely small,
owing to the large detachments which had proceeded on the
above-mentioned enterprise.

After these and many other similar occurrences, V. Halles
destroyed portions of the aqueducts which supplied the
fortress with water, and thus deprived the garrison and
inhabitants of wholesome water. This greatly distressed
them, as it obliged them to use brackish water from the wells
within the walls. Under the circumstances, the inhabitants
would have procured a supply of fresh water from the river
Kladissos, which runs by the fortress, but even this resource
was cut off, as various Greek leaders, and in particular
Ionnnes Malikhutes, remarkable for his address in executing
ambuscades, incessantly harassed and endangered those who
attempted to obtain water from that stream. Malikhutes
continued to perform similar services in other parts of the
environs at the head of ten or twelve chosen followers, so
that his very name soon became a word of terror within the
fortress.

During the same period exploits still more remarkable
were achieved by Gregorios Daminos, at Acroterion. At
the head of a numerous body of Acroterians, he spread
consternation among those Turks who held out in many
strong positions, anxious to retain Acroterion as an advanced

post. Sakires, S. Loras, and Daminos, had shut up about 60 Turks in the strong tower of the village of Kunupidiana, and about 80 others in a similar tower situated at the village of Sternæ.

On the 1st of May an Ottoman courier, carrying from Constatinople imperial despatches to the Pasha of Kydonia, passed through Acroterion, accompanied by nearly 50 chosen Sudiani, having eluded the vigilance of the Greeks. The moment, however, the followers of Daminos, Tambares, and Sakires observed the courier and his attendants, they pursued them with great vigour, and, overtakng them near Argulidés and Plakura, killed 18 of them, including the courier, without any loss on the part of the Greeks. The rest of the Turks, most of whom threw down their arms and whatever impeded their flight, escaped to the fortress of Kydonia. Had not the Greeks on this occasion, agreeably to the wretched practice we have already mentioned in terms of regret, quitted the pursuit for plunder, they would have destroyed the whole of the party.

On the 12th of May, Leras and Daminos made persevering efforts to set fire to the tower of Knuapidiana, and destroy its defenders. These, however, made a most obstinate resistance, encouraged by the hope of immediate assistance from Kydonia. On the arrival of the expected reinforcements, which took place about noon, the Turks assumed the offensive, and the besiegers were in manifest peril till Siphakas most opportunely arrived to their rescue from Nerocuron with about 300 men.

In the meantime, however, 18 Greeks had been killed and about 20 wounded, including Stephanos Loras, who narrowly escaped falling into the hands of the Turks; but, when the approach of Siphakas was announced by a discharge of musketry, the Turks in a body abandoned the tower, and instantly retreated to the fortress.

The Greeks, vigorously pursuing the fugitives as far as Phrudia, above Khalepa, killed about 20, besides wounding a much greater number. Siphakas, renowned for his stentorian voice, repeatedly invited the retreating Turks to stand and fight; but they declined the challenge, some of them shutting themselves up in great consternation at Khalepa, while the rest entered the fortress with all speed. The Greeks, on returning to Kunnpidiana, demolished the tower; while G. Daminos and J. Sakires, with their followers, proceeded against the Turks still remaining at Sternæ.

In the meantime, the Greeks continued to harass the enemy by incessant skirmishes and ambuscades in Rethymno likewise. The details of all these occurrences would be quite superfluous; we confine ourselves, therefore, to a few particulars.

The Turks of Rethymne, as well as those of Kydonia, made frequent sorties to attack the Greeks, whose presence in the environs put them to great inconvenience, but were almost invariably repulsed with loss. Several Jews, it is said, advised the Turks to anoint their banners with the blood of the Bishop, promising them, if they did so, certain victory. In consequence of this, the Turkish mob tumultuously burst open the door of a prison in which the Bishop of Rethymne then lay, instantly led him to the gallows, and, tearing out his heart, did as the Jews had directed. During the ensuing night, various ambuscades were executed on both sides, and a body of Greeks, happening to advance to a position which had been previously occupied by the Turks, found themselves unawares in the midst of the enemy, and had to retire with the loss of about 40 men. This victory confirmed the Turks in the belief that the Jews, whose advice they had followed, really possess the gift of divination.

About the end of April, Petros S. Homerides, already mentioned, at length arrived at Armeni, where Aphentules was then residing, and presented to him an official document, a copy of which is here inserted, as it indicates the objects for which Homerides had been sent to Crete by the Central Government:—

" Ministry of the Interior.

(No. 829 of the Register.)

PROVISIONAL GOVERNMENT OF GREECE.

THE MINISTER OF THE INTERIOR TO MR. PETROS SKYLIZZES HOMERIDES.

"The island of Crete, which, from its situation, its varied and extensive resources, and the devotion of its inhabitants to the common cause of Greek liberty, constitutes a most important portion of the Panhellenium, has, in self-defence, risen in arms against the tyrant, and fearlessly faced all the difficulties and obstacles naturally to be expected in so arduous and bold an enterprise.

"The government rejoiced exceedingly to hear of the promising attitude which the inhabitants have assumed in opposing the implacable enemy, and especially as the oppressors, giving way before their unwavering resolutions, and filled with dismay at their irresistible valour, have shut themselves up in the fortresses and other strongholds of the island, so that the liberated portion of the Greek inhabitants are now living unmolested. This joyous intelligence has led the government to think that, to consolidate the advantages already achieved, and promote further progress, it is of the highest importance that the island of Crete should obtain an enlightened and liberal constitution, in accordance with the principles adopted by the central authorities of the nation.

"The government, with a view to the removal of all internal dissentions that might possibly arise, has resolved, by its decree of ...... March, to send a commissioner for the aforesaid purpose; and has great pleasure in informing you that you have been appointed to this function. So arduous a task could not be better entrusted than to the patriotism of an individual who, as a member of the central authority of the nation, has signally contributed to the establishment of the provisional government.

"Enclosed is a draft of a provisional constitution, which will serve you as a guide in executing your difficult mission. It remains with your experience, intelligence, and judgment, to adopt the necessary measures for bringing your momentous undertaking to a happy issue. You will invariably adhere to the fundamental principles of the national legislation. You will endeavour to establish among our brethren, the Greek inhabitants of Crete, order and harmony, cherishing among them the love of freedom, and respect for constituted authorities, and rousing them to persevering efforts for the final overthrow of the oppressor. You will take care that the elections of the Cretan representatives for the national legislative body be carried out through the free and undisturbed vote of the electors, in order that the representatives of Crete be the most respectable, worthy, and enlightened individuals in the island. You will frequently and statedly transmit to the government all necessary information regarding the political, military, financial, and moral condition of the island, carefully executing the instructions you receive from the government. Your suggestions will be regularly submitted to the Government and will aid it in its efforts to promote and accomplish the entire emancipation of the island. In conclusion, it is fully expected that you will, on all occasions, prove yourself worthy of the confidence of the government, under the assurance, that your services will be duly acknowledged and rewarded."

* * *

"Minister of the Interior, and *Interim* Minister of War.

"*Corinth, 7th April* (o.a.), 1822."

Homerides lost no time in stating to Aphentules the necessity of convoking an assembly of plenipotentiaries of the Cretan provinces, to proceed in accordance with the views of the Central Government. Aphentules, however, unexpectedly opposed the proposal, and not only refused to issue writs for the election of deputies, but endeavoured to persuade the more credulous and inexperienced to support his favourite plan, to which we have already alluded, which was to induce the Cretans to decline subjection to the Central Government, and attempt to establish an independent Cretan kingdom. In vain did Homerides and the more sagacious of the Cretans endeavour to convince Aphentules of the inexpediency and impracticability of his scheme, and represent that the refusal of Crete to act in concert with the central national authority would be signally injurious to the common cause. Aphentules, however, persisting in his absurd scheme, repaired forthwith to Platanea on board a Cassian vessel, expecting that his absence from Armeni would prevent further proceedings in the matter, and that he would be able to gain over the military chiefs of these parts to his views. To such a length was he driven by a foolish ambition.

Homerides, having finally reminded him that it was the duty of the Eparch-General of Crete (for such was the title given to Aphentules in the draft sent from Poloponnesus) to support every measure of the Central Government in respect to Crete, convoked an assembly of deputies by his own authority. When as many of these as the state of the country permitted, had assembled, he submitted to their

consideration the following document, and explained to them
the nature of the mission he was directed to execute in accordance with the national constitution already promulgated, communicating at the same time the draft inserted
below :—

"Ministry of the Interior.
  (No. 828 of the Register.)

PROVISIONVL GOVERNMENT OF GREECE.

THE MINISTER OF THE INTERIOR TO THE PATRIOTIC LEADERS
OF THE CRETANS.

" The Central Government of Greece, unweariedly watching
over the progress of the national cause with a view to the
prosperity of all portions of the Grecian territories, has
recently issued drafts of a government for each of the
islands of the Ægean respectively, as an indispensable and
effectual means of establishing order and progress, and thus
appointed Mr. Petros Skylizzes Homerides commissioner
for carrying out the decisions of the government in respect
to the island of Crete.   This patriot, actuated by an ardent
desire to make himself useful in that prominent island, will,
there is no doubt, successfully execute the instructions of
the government, and fulfil the expectations of the Cretans
in accordance with the draft intrusted to him, which
embodies the fundamental principles of the general constitution of Greece.
" It will be necessary for the Cretans, conformably to the
draft now transmitted to them, to elect the specified number
of representatives to sit as members of the general legislative
body of Greece ; and it is of great importance that, on being
elected, they should forthwith proceed to head-quarters to
devise, in concert with the other members, the most effective
means of achieving the general and entire emancipation of
our beloved country.
" Brave Cretans! the trumpet of fame proclaims far and
near your heroic achievements in the contest, and Greece,
exulting at what you have already accomplished, confidently
anticipates from your valour and patriotism still more
brilliant achievements, when cordial unanimity shall have
been secured among the leaders, and respect for constituted

authorities established among all classes of the citizens. The government, fully aware of your urgent exigencies, will, on the arrival of your representatives, spare no effort to keep you supplied with warlike stores, and all necessaries for securing your triumph over the forces of the enemy. Heaven aid you in the contest for our faith and our country!

"*Corinth, 17th April* (o.s.), 1822.

* * *

"Minister of the Interior and *Interim* Minister of War."

Deputies from the provinces accordingly assembled, and held frequent meetings with the commissioner of the Central Government in the chair. The preceding documents were duly examined, and the existing condition of Crete fully taken into consideration. The constitution required was drawn up and called "The Provisional Constitution of Crete." The government of the island was thus provisionally established in strict accordance with the fundamental principles adopted in the provisional Greek constitution of Epidauros.

At the same time it is necessary to remark, that, in the Cretan constitution, several mistakes were avoided which had slipped into the original draft through an imperfect acquaintance with the affairs of Crete on the part of those by whom it was framed. That large island, for instance, comprehended twenty-four provinces, or cadilicks, as the Turks call them, that is to say, as many as all Peloponnesus, with the exclusion of Maina. Accordingly, it would have been proper to divide Crete into four provinces, if Peloponnesus had been divided into five, but not otherwise; as the population of Crete was then nearly the same as that of Peloponnesus.

When the assembly at Armeni had terminated its labours, and the constitution had been signed, Homerides, accompanied by some of the deputies and several members of the newly constituted local government, proceeded to Platanea, where, for reasons stated above, Aphentules still sojourned, and acquainted him with the results of their proceedings. They succeeded in undeceiving such military chiefs as had been misled by Aphontules. The new order of things was thus adopted by all, not excepting Aphentules himself, who, notwithstanding his previous opposition, had, in consideration of his former services, been appointed by

the Assembly Eparch-General or Governor of Crete, as it
was hoped that for the future he would act with sincerity
for the common interest of Greece. In this capacity Aphentules promulgated throughout all Crete the new constitution. His proclamation on this occasion will be found
annexed to that document below.

The Central Government was, through its commissioner,
duly informed of all that had occurred in Crete since his
arrival. The same functionary sent, likewise, a report of
the progress of the Cretan arms, and detailed the victories
gained at Aulopotamos and Halykæ, and other brilliant
achievements, to all of which he had been an eye-witness.
All that the Cretans at this time asked of the Central
Government, was in consideration of existing circumstances,
the co-operation of a naval force. The Cretans, at this time,
were by land sufficiently powerful, and had defeated the
enemy in many quarters, as will be stated below in detail,
but naval assistance was at this moment a matter of the
utmost importance and necessity, and this the Central
National Government inexcusably failed to send.

The draft mentioned above was as follows :—

DRAFT OF A PROVISIONAL GOVERNMENT FOR THE ISLAND OF CRETE.

PART I.

I. The island shall be divided into four provinces, but
that number may be diminished or increased as circumstances may require.

> The chief town of the first shall be ——
>   ,,   of the second ,, ——
>   ,,   of the third   ,, ——
>   ,,   of the fourth ,, ——

II. Each province shall be subdivided into three districts;
but that number may be increased or diminished as circumstances may require. The chief town of each province shall
be fixed by the Central Government.

III. Each district shall be subdivided into municipalities.

IV. The administration of the island shall be entrusted to
an Eparch-General, or Governor, appointed by the Central
Government of Greece.

V. The Eparch-General, or Governor, shall be at the head of a General Board of Administration, divided into six sections.

1. That of the Secretary-General.
2. That of the Commissary-General of Finance.
3. That of the Commissary-General of Police.
4. That of the Commissary-General of War.
5. That of the Commissary-General of the Navy.
6. That of the Commissary-General of Justice.

VI. In the chief town of each Eparkhia, or province, there shall reside:

An Eparch.
A Commissary of Police.
A Chief Secretary.
A Commissary of War.
A Commissary of Finance.
A Captain of the Port, if the town be a seaport.

VII. The Eparch shall act as representative of the government within the bounds of the Province, and all the other administrative functionaries of the same province shall be under his orders; and, in matters relating to the public service, he shall correspond with the respective functionaries of the General Board of Administration.

VIII. In the chief town of each district there shall reside
A Sub-Eparch.
A Secretary.
A Sub-Commissary of Finance.
      „ of Police.
      „ of War.
A Sub-Captain of the Port, if the town be a seaport.

IX. In the chief town of each province there shall be established a civil tribunal, the president of which shall correspond with the Commissary-General of Justice.

X. In each community there shall be established a Board of Inspectors, consisting of
A President, who shall be the representative of the General Administration in each community.
An Inspector of Finance.
     „ of Police.
     „ of Military Affairs.
An Harbour-Master, if the village be on the sea-coast.

Part II.

GENERAL ORDER OF CORRESPONDENCE.

XI. The Eparch-General of the island will correspond with the Ministers of the Central Government of Greece, and will communicate to the different sections of the Cretan Board of Administration all affairs of their respective competence.

The Eparch will correspond with the Eparch-General; the Sub-Eparchs, with the Eparch; and the Presidents of the Boards of Inspectors, with the Sub-Eparchs.

XII. The Commissaries of the provinces will correspond with the Commissaries-General; the Sub-Commissaries of the Districts, with the Commissaries of the province; and the Inspectors of the Municipalities, with the Sub-Commissaries of the District.

XIII. The police will have a special power and authority, to be exercised under the exclusive direction of the superior police functionaries.

XIV. The Commissaries and Sub-Commissaries of Finance will have a collector and a treasurer.

XV. The national flag shall be bicolor, that is, blue and white, agreeably to the pattern enjoined by the Central National Government.

XVI. The seal of the Cretan Board of Administration will bear Minerva, with the appropriate symbols, and the inscription "Administration of the Island of Crete."

XVII. The seals of all subordinate functionaries in general will bear the same symbols, and will be distinguished from each other only by their respective inscriptions.

XVIII. The number of Cretan members of the National Legislative Body will be in proportion to the population, one member being elected for every thirty thousand souls.

PROCLAMATION OF THE PLENIPOTENTIARIES OF THE PROVINCES OF CRETE.

IN THE NAME OF THE TRIUNE GODHEAD.

"On the 14th of June, 1821, the inhabitants of the island of Crete, roused by the love of freedom, took up arms against Ottoman oppression. Obedient to the sacred voice of our country, and after achieving so far its emancipation, the lawful Representatives of the different provinces of Crete, have met together by invitation of the Central Government of Greece, and, after mature deliberation, have adopted the following constitution for the island of Crete, in accordance with the spirit and fundamental principles of the general constitution of Greece, and we hereby declare and ordain, that the said Cretan constitution shall be strictly and fully received and maintained throughout the island."

Armeni, 20th May (1st June), 1822,—Second year of Independence.

PROVISIONAL CONSTITUTION OF THE ISLAND OF CRETE.

TITLE I.—SECTION 1.

OF RELIGION.

ART. 1.—The established religion of the island shall be the Orthodox Eastern Church, but every other religion shall enjoy toleration.

SECTION 2.

OF THE GENERAL RIGHTS OF THE INHABITANTS OF THE ISLAND.

2.—All Christian natives of the island are citizens, and shall enjoy all the rights of Greek citizens.

3.—All citizens are equal in the eye of the law, without distinction of rank, class, or function.

4.—All persons, not natives of Crete, as shall settle in the island, shall be in the eye of the law the same as natives.

5.—Strangers, desiring to be naturalized, will be admitted conformably to the law of naturalization, to be promulgated by the central authorities of Greece.

6.—All Greeks shall be equally admissible to all functions and honours, and promotion to these shall be the reward of merit.

7.—The property, honour, and personal security of every citizen shall be protected by the law.

8.—All taxes shall be assessed fairly on all ranks and classes of the inhabitants without distinction, and no tax shall be levied except in virtue of a positive and special law.

9.—Devotion to the interest of our country, and the practice of righteousness and beneficence, shall be regarded as the sacred duty of every citizen.

10.—Every citizen shall be bound to uphold this provisional constitution conscientously and to the utmost of his power, yielding obedience to the laws and respect to constituted authorities.

11.—Every citizen shall, moreover, when required by the laws and duly summoned, take up arms in defence of his country, and, on the other hand, every citizen who abandons or evades military service without a written permission from the competent authority, shall be liable to legal punishment.

SECTION 3.

OF THE TERRITORIAL DIVISIONS OF THE ISLAND.

12.—The territory of the island is divided into twenty-four provinces, comprehending the adjacent islets.

The territory of Heracleia shall be divided into the provinces of Heracleia, Knossos, Temenos, Khersonesos, Petra, Lassion. Gortyna, Arcadia. Sitela, Hierapetros, Pyrgiotissa, Monoprosopon, Kaenurion.

The territory of Rethymne shall be divided into the provinces of Rethymne, Mylopotamos, Amarion, Hayios Vasilios, Sphakia.

The territory of Kydonia shall be divided into the provinces of Apocoronos, Acroterion, Kisamos, Selinon.

The adjacent islets are: Dia, Suda, Hayios Theodoros, Krambusa, Ponticos, Elaphonesia, Gaudos, Gaudopula, Paximadia, Gadaronesos, Prasonesos, Elaphonesion, Psira, Triades, Hayios Nicolaos, Spinalonga, etc.

13.—Each province shall be subdivided into municipalities.

14.—When circumstances permit, a more systematic division of the island into provinces will be carried into effect.

SECTION 4.

OF THE GOVERNMENT OF THE ISLAND.

15.—The object of government should be the national welfare, which is to be attained only through the exercise of impartial and effective justice.

16.—The government of the island shall be entrusted to an Eparch-General, to be appointed by the Central Government of Greece.

17.—The said Eparch-General shall have the aid of a general Board of Administration, divided into six sections: that of the Secretary-general, that of the Commissary-general of Finance, that of the Commissary-general of Police, that of the Commissary-general of War, that of the Commissary-general of the Navy, and that of the Commissary-general of Justice.

18.—In the chief town of each province there shall be appointed an Eparch, a Commissary of Finance, a Commissary of War, and, if the town be a seaport, a Captain of the port.

19.—In every municipality there shall be established a Board of Inspectors, consisting of five members, viz., a Sub-Eparch, representing the government in the municipality, a Sub-commissary of Finance, a Sub-commissary of Police, a Sub-commissary of War, and, if the town or village be a sea-port, a Harbour-master.

20.—In the chief town of each province there shall be established a Civil Tribunal, the President of which shall maintain an exclusive correspondence with the Commissary-general of Justice; and in each municipality one of the five Sub-commissaries shall be appointed to act as Justice of the Peace for the municipality, and shall constitute a small debt court for sums not above 100 piastres, and at the same time shall endeavour to effect an amicable arrangement in all matters of greater importance that may be submitted to him, transmitting to a higher tribunal cases of the latter class, when his efforts to effect an amicable arrangement have proved unsuccessful.

SECTION 5.

ELECTION OF PUBLIC FUNCTIONARIES.

21.—In each municipality, the elders and respectable inhabitants shall conscientiously and impartially elect the Sub-commissaries of the municipality. The number of the inhabitants in each community shall not exceed 500 families, and shall not be less than 300.

22.—The Sub-commissaries of all the municipalities of each province shall meet in the chief town of the said province, and the said chief town shall then, in the same way select from among the most respected of the citizens, electors whose number shall be in proportion to its population. The whole electors of the province shall then meet, and after a solemn oath to choose the most worthy and enlightened of their fellow-citizens, shall elect the five provincial Commissaries, who must be persons of education, practical wisdom, irreproachable morals and acknowledged probity. After the election, the Commissaries shall receive their commission signed by the electors, authorising them to discharge, in accordance with instructions given by the electors, the duties of their office. The Commissaries shall then sign a solemn declaration, to be deposited in the archives of the General Board of Administration, that they will discharge the duties of their office with fidelity, diligence and impartiality. After the election of the Eparch and Commissaries of each province as above, the electors of all the provinces shall meet, and elect with the greatest possible unanimity the most competent of their fellow-citizens to represent their respective Provinces in the Central Board of Administration, and shall give the individuals duly elected their written commissions.

23.—In the same manner also shall be elected the deputies who are to represent Crete in the Panhellenic Legislative Body, and the elections of all the above mentioned functionaries shall be annual.

SECTION 6.

GENERAL DUTIES AND RIGHTS OF ADMINISTRATIVE FUNCTIONARIES.

24.—The Eparch-general shall be superintendent of all the Commissaries and of the local administration of Crete. He shall regularly acquaint the

Central Government of Greece with every thing relating to the general welfare of the Island, and report whatever may be required regarding the proceedings of all functionaries under his superintendence.

25.—The general acts and decisions of the Administration shall be signed by the Secretary-General, and countersigned by the Commissary of that department to which the matter in question refers.

26.—The Eparch-general shall be strictly bound never to accede to any treaty whatever, the object of which may be the abolition of the political independence of the Island ; and, should he be convicted of taking part in any such negotiation, he shall be suspended from the exercise of his functions, till the central Government of Greece adopt such measures as the case may require.

27.—It shall be the duty of said functionary to provide for the widows and orphans of all patriots who have perished, or may perish, in the war of independence, and to specify the sacrifices and services of all patriots respectively in the cause of liberty, for the purpose of enabling the Central Government of Greece to assign in due time a suitable reward to every citizen according to his merit.

28.—None of the Commissary-Generals shall exceed the limits of his own authority so as to interfere with the functions of another. Should any such functionary be accused of fraud or unfaithfulness in the discharge of his duties, he shall be brought to trial, and, if convicted, punished according to the nature of his offence.

29.—Till the promulgation of civil and penal codes of laws, the courts of justice shall follow the provisions of those laws which were promulgated by our ever memorable Emperors.

80.—The Provincial Representatives in the General Board of Administration, as well as the Deputies sent to the Panhellenic Parliament, must be upwards of thirty years of age.

81.—In case of the death of any of the Commissaries-General, the other members shall in concert with the Eparch-General, elect a successor.

SECTION 7.

GENERAL ORDER OF CORRESPONDENCE.

82.—The Eparch General of the Island shall correspond with the Ministers of the Central Government of Greece, and shall transmit to each Section of the Cretan Board of Administration respectively, all affairs that come under its jurisdiction. The Eparchs shall correspond with the Eparch-General ; and the Sub-Eparchs, with the Eparchs.

83.—The Provincial Commissaries shall correspond with the Commissary General ; the Sub-commissaries of the municipalities, with the Provincial Commissaries, and vice versa.

34.—The Police shall exercise a special jurisdiction under the exclusive control of the Commissary of Police.

85.—The Commissary-General and Sub-Commissaries of Finance shall have each a Collector and a Treasurer.

86.—The National Flag shall be bicolor, namely, blue and white, according to the pattern adopted by the Central Government of Greece.

37.—The Seal of the Cretan Board of Administration shall bear the effigy of Minerva, with the distinctive emblems, and the inscription, "Administration of the Island of Crete."

38.—The Seals of all subordinate functionaries shall bear the same symbols, and shall be distinguished from each other merely by the inscription.

39.—The number of Deputies representing Crete in the National Parliament shall be in proportion to the population, one Deputy being elected for every thirty thousand inhabitants.

40.—This constitution shall be promulgated throughout the Island ; and the original shall be preserved in the archives of the Cretan Board of Administration.

Armeni, 20 May (1 June) 1822,—being the second year of independence.

———

ACTS OF THE GENERAL ASSEMBLY.

The General Assembly, in accordance with the decision of the Central Government of Greece, accepts Mr. Michael Kumnenos Aphentules as Eparch-General of the Island.

The Assembly, further, appoints—

Mr. Neophytos Œconomos Secretary-General to the Cretan Board of Administration, Mr. Emmanuel Antoniades sectional first clerk, Messrs Georgios Protopapas, Georgios Papadakos and Kh. Ioannes Polakes, Commissaries of Finance, with equal rank and power, and required to sign all documents in such capacity.

Messrs. Andreas Krisarakes and Georgios Sakorrhaphos Commissaries of Police, with equal rank and authority.

Messrs Anagnostes Psarudakos, Andreas Pappadakes, and Theokhares Kuyumzoglu Commissaries of War, with equal authority, who shall all sign documents issuing from their office, so that every such document shall be null and void unless it be signed by all three.

M. Nicolaos Andrulakes, Commissary of the Navy.

M. Manasses Ex-Abbott, President, and

Messrs. Zaccharias Didaskalos, Styllianos Khlonakes and Em. Butsakes, Commissaries of Justice, with equal rank and authority.

Armeni, 21 May (2 June) 1822, being the second year of independence.

(Signatures of the Plenipotentiaries.)

Petros S. Skylizzes Homerides, Commissioner and Chairman of the Assembly.

Anagnostes Psarudakes, Athanasios Archimandrites, Andreas Krisrakes, Andreas Marku, Andreas Phasules, Georgios Protopapas of Sphakia, Georgios Kuletakes, Georgios Melidonnes, Georgios Sakorrhaphos, Georgios Papadakes, Gregorios Kallonas, Georgios Puinnakes, Gregorios Savinaisos, Demetrios Saridakes, D. Apostolides, D. Chrysaphopulos, Euthymios Psarudakes, Em. Stephanakes, Em. Antoniades, Em. Lutsakes, Zaccharias Tsirigotes (s.) Theokhares Kuyumzoglus (h.) J. Andrulopulakes pilgrim, J Stephanakes, J. Boyasoglus, J. Papadakes, J. Stratudakes, N. K. Kyrtomadianos, N. Verycakes, N. Kaphates, O. D. Critovulides, K.

Gerakakes, Luis Staes, Lazarakes Iordianu, Michael Paduvas, Manasses Prohegumenos, Melkhisedek Hegumenos Prevele, Michael Khionakes, Neophytos Œconomos, Nic. Andreas, Stylianos Khionakes

(a) This gentleman afterwards assumed the surname of Praclikides.
(b) Theokhares, too, assumed in the same manner the surname of Agathakes

---

PROCLAMATION OF THE EPARCH-GENERAL.

Provisional Government of Crete.

The Eparch-General to the Inhabitants of the Island.

The Central Government of Greece has appointed me Governor of Crete with the title of Eparch-General. Though aware that my capabilities are inadequate to the arduous task instructed to me, yet, in obedience to the voice of our country, I shall employ every effort to discharge my duties with diligence and success. The first and main object that will occupy my constant attention, will be the social improvement of the Island, the strict maintenance of the laws which guarantee the honour, the life, and the property of all its inhabitants. By obedience to those laws you will show yourselves worthy of national independence.

The Government will, as in duty bound, eagerly cherish and protect those under its maternal control. Do you on your part, as in duty bound, conform to the laws of the Nation, respect the Government, and obey its constituted authorities.

The Administration has been divided into six departments:—1. That of the Secretary General. 2. That of Finance. 3. That of Police. 4. That of War. 5. That of the Navy. 6. That of Justice. To those departments respectively every individual may apply in writing, and submit any affair requiring to be laid before the Government, and will receive replies to his communications, and through the same departments all orders of the Government will be issued. The Commissaries of the said departments, sixteen in number, promise, along with myself, by the following oath, strict adherence to the legitimate ends of the Government and obedience to the Central Government of Greece.

OATH.

" We swear before God and men to be faithful to our country, submissive to the constitution promulgated by the National Assembly of Epidauros, and obedient to the Central Authorities of Greece. Should we violate any of these solemn obligations and engagements, and succeed in evading the penalties denounced by the laws, may we never escape divine vengeance."

Armeni, 21st May (2nd June) 1822, being the second year of Independence.

Michael Kumnenos Aphentulief, N. Œconomos, Ph. Joannes Andrulidakes (alias l'olakes), Andreas Kriarakes, Georgios Papadakes, Manasses Prohegumenos, Georgios Protopapas of Sphakia, N. Andreas, Melkhisedek Hegumenos (Abbot) of Prevele, Anagnostes Psarudakes, Stylianos Khionakes, Zaccharrias Tsirigotes, Theokhares Kuyumzoglus, Georgios Sakorrhaphos, Em. Vutsakos.

In the meantime, ambuscades, slight engagements and skirmishes were taking place on the part of the Greeks over all Crete with increasing energy and effect. Such encounters were undertaken almost daily in the vicinity of Heracleion by the Anoynni and the patriot forces now in possession of Aulopotamos. Such operations incessantly effected in the vicinities of Rethymne and of Kydonia kept the Turks shut up in those fortresses.

We shall mention with some detail what took place at this time at the village of Sternao in Acroterion.

About 80 Turks, as we have already mentioned, were blockaded in the town of Sternao, having been discomfitted by J. Sakires, G. Daminos, and C. Prinoles, after the engagement at Kunupidiana (see page 90), and were reduced to the greatest extremities. No assistance could reach them from any quarter, as the Turks of Kydonia no longer dared to advance beyond Khalepa, owing to their being kept in check by Nicolaos Tambares and Nicolaos Kalathakes, with their followers, who were preparing to occupy Khalepa itself, and to drive the Turks there into the fortress. The Turks of Suda were also effectively blockaded, and prevented from making a descent on the mainland, but the besiegers were disappointed in their hope of reducing the fortress by famine. On the 25th or 26th of May one of the besieged Turks, whose name was Tusunos Tsunos, sent a message to G. Daminos, warning him that if he did not immediately retire from Acroterion, his retreat would be cut off, as a fleet with numerous land forces on board was daily expected at Suda. The Ottoman who sent this message, having certain information on the subject, made the announcement rather for the purpose of frightening Daminos and his followers than of rendering them a friendly service. Such communications from Turks had been frequently made on former occasions, and were now treated by the Greeks as stratagems or idle bravadoes. The effect, however, of this communication was to rouse the energy of the besiegers, and to prompt them to still more vigorous measures against the enemy. In consequence of this the whole of the Turks in Suda would have been inevitably reduced had not a formidable Turkish fleet announced its approach on the 28th, and appeared steering towards the Amphimallic bay (Suda). Notwithstanding its approach, however, the Greeks, though greatly discouraged, continued the blockade during the whole of that day. But the besieged, animated by the arrival of the fleet, sallied forth and assailed the besiegers. How the large number of Greeks then in Acroterion effected their escape will be narrated in the following chapter. Such was the condition of Crete when the first Egyptian expedition arrived there.

CHAPTER III.

The Turks had, for many days, been frequently threatening the Greeks, saying "Our fleet will soon be here with numerous land forces on board, and what will become of you then?" But the Greeks, having for nearly a whole year been accustomed to hear such threats from the enemy, remained incredulous, till on the 28th of May the threatened danger proved a visible reality.

On the morning of that day Egyptian vessels anchored in the Amphimallic Bay (Suda), and commenced a furious firing on the Greeks, though, from the distance, without effect, their object being merely to strike with dismay those with whom they were soon to come to close quarters. The Egyptian fleet had sailed from Alexandria to Crete, had remained a short time at the island of Cassos, and also had been several days becalmed off Heracleion, without ever having been observed by any Greek vessel during the whole of that long voyage.

On the 28th of May the fleet continued nearly the whole day to enter the bay, and before night 114 vessels had anchored there. Of those about 30 were Egyptian vessels of war, carrying the Turkish flag. The rest were transports, and on these floated the flags of not a few of the States of *Christian Europe*. These European vessels, while displaying on their flags the sign of the Cross, were transporting warlike stores and Egyptian troops, and thus aiding the Turkish oppressor against Greeks fighting and perishing under the symbol of the Cross in defence of the Christian faith.

The troops that arrived from Alexandria amounted to about ten thousand, consisting mainly of veteran Albanian mercenaries, and about five hundred Egyptian cavalry, the whole of these forces being under the command of Hassan Pasha, the well known Albanian, who was formerly sent by the Port along with Mehemetali to settle the affairs of Egypt.

The arrival of such reinforcements naturally revived the courage of the Turks in Crete. The vessels casting anchor immediately commenced respectively the landing of the troops, and fired salutes to congratulate their friends and terrify the Greeks. The garrison, issuing from the fortress, hastened to aid the landing of the troops at Halykæs. This new state of affairs greatly discouraged the Greeks, though their despondency was of short duration. Many of them took up a position in Acroterion of Melekha, and their situation was for some time perilous; but the military chiefs Siphacas and Ioannes Halles, then at Nerocnron, roused the courage of their followers, who gallantly determined to hazard their lives in order to rescue their brethren in Acroterion.

The number of Greeks in Acroterion, comprehending soldiers with arms in their hands, women, and aged men, amounted to more than 300. Many of these had been induced to repair thither in order to procure olives and other provisions, and they had considered themselves sufficiently strong to defend themselves from any probable attack. The Turks now soon entirely occupied the Isthmus which joins Acroterion to the main land of Crete, and thus it became extremely difficult for the Greeks in Acroterion to escape from their perilous position.

Siphacas and Halles, apprised of this state of things, immediately hastened at all hazards to their rescue, and attacked the enemy at the head of scarcely 300 men, being all that could be mustered at the moment there. In the meantime about 1,000 Turks from Kydonia had advanced as far as Vlytea, while the troops from the fleet were quietly landing at Halykæ. The Greeks in Acroterion saw with dismay from the hill-tops the impending danger. Halles and Siphacas now divided their small body of followers, and the former, advancing to Halykæ, alarmed and threw into disorder even in the plain, the enemy's infantry and cavalry as they landed; while Siphacas, hastening to Vlytea, defeated the Kydonian Turks there, and drove them back to the fortress. These opportune and simultaneous achievements enabled the Greeks in Acroterion to effect their escape. The armed and the unarmed among them, seizing the favourable moment, passed over, many of them in fact swimming, and, like the Jews of old, passing through the Red Sea, reached the village of Tsicalaria in safety. What is remarkable, is that, though the fugitives were exposed to a vigorous fire from the enemy, only one of all was killed.

All the armed Greeks on the spot, including Siphacas and his followers, as well as the armed fugitives from Acroterion, now joined Halles at Halykæ. The Greeks now maintained, during the whole of that day, an obstinate engagement, both with the Kydonian Turks, who had again sallied from the fortress, and at the same time with the troops from the fleet, and killed a great number of the enemy. Some of the Egyptian vessels in the bay approached the shore, and furiously fired on the Greeks; but the latter soon treated the fire of the ships with contempt, as it produced little or no effect. A considerable number of Egyptian troops, but very few of the Greeks, fell on this occasion.

When night put an end to the combat, the Greeks abandoned their positions in the plain, as these could no longer be held without imminent peril, and again fortified themselves at Malaxa. Next day, Hassan Pasha landed the remainder of his troops, and encamped near Halykæ. The enemy, however, were kept in constant alarm through ambuscades and sallies on the part of the Greeks. Animated by the success of the daring exploits we have just mentioned, Siphacas and Halles now proceeded along the foot of the mountain, to which many of their comrades had in dismay conveyed their families, and, reviving the courage of the Greek forces, generally inspired them with resolution to face the new enemy, and prepared them for fresh victories.

About the same time, however, another piece of intelligence had spread dismay among the Greeks of Crete. It had been announced that Dramales at the head of immense hordes of barbarians had entered Peloponnesus, carrying destruction and desolation wherever he went. The situation of Peloponnesus was perilous at the moment, and that of Crete appeared no less so. To many it seemed, on comparing the two great and simultaneous movements of the enemy, that Hades was opening its mouth, and threatening the Greeks with universal destruction. The horizon of Greece was overcast, and the friends of humanity were saddened at the apparently impending ruin of the Greek cause! But God gave might to the feeble! The Greeks in Peloponnesus were soon victorious over Dramales, whom they compelled to save himself by an ignominious and ever memorable flight, at the head of a small number of his followers. And the Cretans on their part, though abandoned by all, and unaided, repeatedly and in various parts gained victories over Hassan Pasha, whom

they could have entirely annihilated, if the want of warlike
stores had not prevented them from treating his army as
the Greeks in Peloponnesus had treated that of Dramales.

Hassan Pasha encamped, as we have already mentioned,
near Halykae with his whole army, and began forthwith to
make preparations for an attack on the Greeks, availing
himself of the suggestions of the native Turks.   The
Greeks remaining in their position above Malaxa, watched
the enemy they were about to encounter, and waited to see
the Pasha's movement, having the intention of harassing
his rear.   The day after his landing, Em. Antoniades
happened to be walking in the neighbourhood of the
enemy's camp, with Petros Tsucalarianos, who was minutely acquainted with the locality.   Em. Antoniades, on
questioning his military friend about the nature of the
ground, and the facilities for an attack on the enemy,
received such information as clearly proved that the
Greeks, by an unexpected attack on the Turks, might
inflict on them a very important blow.   After this conversation Siphacas, commander of the troops at Malaxa,
was invited to give his opinion on the subject, and, after
obtaining the necessary information from both, exclaimed
with enthusiasm, that he was prepared to attack the
enemy's tents by night, and had no doubt that the
enterprize would be of the utmost importance to the
cause; he added, however, that he required the approval
and co-operation of the Eparch-General to guarantee
success.

The Eparch-General, on being acquainted with the matter,
was convinced from personal observation as well as information derived from others, that the proposed plan was
practicable and most promising.   Accordingly, he officially
wrote to Anagnostes Panayotes and Hales to be ready on the
following day at Malaxa, with all the troops they could
muster.   When, next day, Hales appeared at the ren-
dezvous, and was informed of the proposed attack, he hailed
the plan with enthusiasm, and his hopes of success were
confirmed and increased by a personal observation of all the
localities in question.   It was forthwith agreed that he
and Siphacas should that very night carry the plan into
effect, it being understood that the Lakkiota would join
them at the moment they commenced the attack.   It was
arranged in the presence of the Eparch-General that Siphacas

with his followers should march direct to the Pasha's tent, while Halee and his followers attacked the centre of the enemy's camp, and Mandas, at the head of a body of troops, should occupy the village of Tsucalaria, where the Turks had an outpost. It was further arranged that the Greeks should start from Malaxa about midnight.

The Greek leaders, repairing to their respective corps, communicated the plan to their followers, and directed them to take a short repose till eleven o'clock p.m., and then prepare to march at twelve. But the pleasant sleep of an evening in June did not allow them to awake at the time appointed, and their march did not commence till two in the morning. In an army without order and discipline, the execution of every plan, however excellent, is precarious; and when the Greeks had reached the foot of the mountain, dawn and day-light had overtaken them. Siphacas and Hales, notwithstanding, undauntedly advanced to the position assigned them. In the meantime Mandas reached the position immediately above the village of Tsucalaria, from which he was to make his attack. To arrive at this place in time, he had been obliged to pass over a dyke built of stones without mortar, and the fall of numerous stones created a noise which awoke the Turkish guard in the village. These, on observing an attack from the Greeks, opened a fire, so that before Siphacas and Hales had reached the positions assigned them, the enemy's troops were awake, and, issuing from their tents, were preparing for battle. Siphacas having approached the tents, and hearing much firing, while he perceived at the same time that the Turks were in motion, halted with his followers, and, after twice firing on the Turks and their tents, retired, repulsing repeated onsets of the enemy till he reached the foot of the mountain on which Malaxa is situated, so as to prevent an attack on his rear. The rest of the Greek detachments soon reached the same place, and an obstinate engagement ensued, during which sometimes the Turks, especially after the arrival of reinforcements from Kydonia, rushed upon the Greeks, and sometimes the Greeks, in their turn, rushed upon their assailants, without any decisive advantage on either side. While matters were in this critical position, and when the prospect of victory was rather on the side of the Turks, Anagnostes Panayotes at the head of the Lakkiots and other followers suddenly reached the spot. These, on perceiving the state of matters, rushed with their usual intrepidity on the Turks without taking a moment's rest. The Greeks already engaged were so animated by the arrival and dashing onset of the Lakkiots that they, too, followed their example, and, rushing on the enemy opposed to them, put them to flight, and pursued them with much slaughter to the very tents, but did not venture to advance further in the plain where they would be exposed to the enemy's cavalry.

Here again we have to deplore the inveterate habit of pillaging, when duty required fighting. Had not a portion of the Greeks engaged begun to strip the slain, instead of pursuing the fugitives, the number of Turks killed on this occasion would undoubtedly have been immense. According to subsequent accounts in this action, the Turks had more than 300 killed, and a still greater number wounded. On the side of the Greeks 15 were killed, and a considerable number wounded. Pressed by the want of provisions and water, the Greeks now determined to go up to Malaxa, where, after a solemn thanksgiving to God for their victory, in the presence of the Eparch-General, they were able to refresh themselves with sleep and repose.

Had the Greeks started at midnight according to the plan, and occupied during the night the positions respectively assigned to them, and had all the arrangements been strictly executed, a large portion of the Egyptian army would have been destroyed. Crete would have been saved from numerous calamities inflicted on her by that Egyptian army, and by other Egyptian forces which subsequently landed on the island. The want of discipline which then prevailed among the Greek forces, marred the most hopeful enterprises; and such will ever be the case in an army without discipline, even if it should be composed of lions.

The preceding victory of the Greeks, however, was of very great importance to the cause, as it inspired them with contempt for their newly arrived foes, whom they continued ever afterwards to harass by incessant ambuscades and skirmishes. In the meantime, the Pasha remained encamped in the same position, greatly perplexed, and unable to determine his further proceedings.

One whole year before Marcos Botsares executed his memorable night attack in Continental Greece, on the Pasha of Scodra, an enterprise of exactly the same nature, and of equal daring was attempted in Crete, against the

Albanian Hassan Pasha by Siphacas and I. Hales, and proved to a much greater extent successful than that of the Souliot leader. In fact, had not Crete been an island, Hassan Pasha would, in all probability, have been compelled, like the Pasha of Scodra, to return with his army from whence he had come. But the two chiefs who planned and executed the Cretan enterprise, were like many other Cretans who achieved on various occasions deeds of pre-eminent heroism, less fortunate than Botsares in having their names immortalized by poesy. The patriots of Crete thought more of doing their duty in the cause of their country than of obtaining historical renown. Yet they bled and gained victories in vain, condemned by the Christian Powers to see their beloved native island again subjected to the Ottoman yoke.

In the meantime, the plain of Kydonia was almost entirely in the hands of the Turks. Daminos, Tambares, and Prinolos, however, with about thirty other Acroterians, repaired unobserved during the night, though with imminent danger, from Malaxa to Acroterion, and burnt various fortified buildings there, including the tower of Sternae, all of which they had found unguarded. It had appeared to them important to prevent the enemy from finding a refuge in that position. They further killed ten or twelve Turks, who were scattered about not suspecting any hostile attack. But now the assailing party found themselves in great danger, from which they escaped, in the manner now to be stated.

The Turks naturally determined to use every effort, by ambuscades in various parts, for several days, to cut off their retreat from Acroterion, so that the rest of the Greek forces began to despair of the return of the gallant party. These, reduced to extremities, boldly resolved to force their way openly, and almost through the midst of the enemy. One morning, in the hope of being taken for Turks, they marched within gun-shot of the garrison, along the road to Hayios Lucas, a route which the enemy's forces in pursuit of them had never suspected they would select, and having passed over the plain with great speed, reached Kerameia, their stratagem proving completely successful.

The Greeks having, with so small a force, gained the advantage we have described over the Egyptian army, comprehending so numerous a body of warlike Albanians, they thought proper to make an attack on the enemy in a more systematic manner, and on a larger scale. Accordingly the Eparch-General sent for A. Protopapadakes with all the Apocoronites and Sphakians under his command, and A. Panayotes and V. Halles with their Kydonians. All these forthwith mustered at Malaxa, where they were joined by Siphacas and his followers, comprehending the Acroteriani. The number of all these troops thus assembled, amounted to about two thousand.

Simultaneously, however, Hassan Pasha, the commander of the Egyptians, was preparing his whole force for a decisive engagement. For this purpose he directed the Kydonian Turks to march out of the fortress, and brought Kaures with a large body of warlike Turks from Selinon and Kisamos. With an army now about 12,000 strong, the Pasha determined to make a general attack on the Greeks, and to persevere in his efforts till he made himself master of Malaxa, deeming the possession of that strong position indispensable for his future operations.

Such being the arrangements of the two armies, the Greeks commenced the expected engagement early in the morning of the 12th or 13th of the month, by opening a fire on the Turks that held several strong positions around Tsucalaria. The Turks thus assailed advanced from their positions to repulse their assailants, and a very obstinate conflict ensued. The Greeks, though greatly inferior in numbers, made a very gallant resistance, aided in part by the advantage of their position. They even repeatedly rushed on the enemy with effect, though the Turkish officers were standing with drawn swords in the rear of the troops, and instantly punishing such as began to give way. At length the Turks, notwithstanding the efforts of their officers, were driven from their positions by the determined gallantry of the Greeks, and retired to the strong positions they previously occupied around Tsucalaria. During this engagement the Egyptian ships of war, lying in the harbour of Suda, had got under weigh, and, approaching the beach, kept up an incessant fire on the Greek assailants.

Such being the state of matters, another reinforcement of about 500 or 600 men arrived about noon from Kydonia, under the command of the warlike Kaures. His appearance revived the courage of the enemy, who now in full force and unfatigued, advanced on the Greeks, exhausted with continued exertions, and drove them back.

The Greeks, after repeatedly making a stand, retired to positions at Lower Malaxa, whence they resumed the combat, and maintained it with great gallantry, though with considerable loss. On this occasion they lost about 40 men, besides Konstantinos Paterakos and Manoles Alivanistos. The former of these commanded the Malaxiani, the latter, the Pemoniani. Both of them were brave, energetic, and warlike. With these the Greeks had also to mourn the loss of Georgios Konstantudakes, the brother of Siphacas. He was a man in the 30th year of his age, of remarkable strength of body like his brother, a brave and practised warrior, and a person of great moral worth. The Turks, as they occupied positions more exposed than those of the Greeks, lost upwards of 200 men.

The Greeks, though inferior in numbers, occupied more advantageous positions, and would not have been obliged to retire to Lower Malaxa, had it not been that at the commencement of the engagement the followers of Protopapadakes withdrew. Such an act of disorder in an army without discipline, usually leads to disaster. Those who continue to fight with full purpose to remain, are confounded by the desertion of their comrades, and, as if instinctively, follow the example of the fugitives. The bravest army may be thus discomfited. The rest of the Greeks, however, though thus deserted, gallantly continued the fight, and killed a large number of the enemy.

Siphacas, having likewise being compelled to retire to Punta, remained there at the head of a considerable force, endeavouring, with great gallantry and perseverance, and frequently with great danger, to prevent the further advance of the enemy. On seeing his beloved brother Georgios fall, he seized stones and threw them at the enemy, and at the same time he urged on his followers by raising his stentorian voice. He then succeeded in carrying off the body of his brother, while his friends carried off the bodies of several others.

Such was the obstinacy with which the conflict continued till it was quite dark, and then the Greeks left their positions and repaired to Malaxa. Here the leaders held a council of war and deliberated on what was to be done. Protopapadakes proposed that they should leave their present position,

I

where, he said, they were in want of provisions and ammunition. Hales and Siphacas, on the other hand, persisted in recommending that they should remain at Malaxa, and pledged themselves to procure from Kerameia such a supply of ammunition as, along with what they had, would enable them to maintain their present position, till they obtained further supplies. Their opinion was supported by Aphentules, but, unfortunately, that of Protopapadakes prevailed, as most of his followers, on hearing from him the alleged want of provisions, withdrew about midnight to the village of Kampi. The Turks kept their positions during the whole night with the determination of renewing the combat, and of persevering in their efforts till, at all hazards and with any sacrifice, they got possession of so important a position as Malaxa When, at daylight, they perceived that the Greeks had evacuated the place, they immediately entered it, and secured it by a powerful garrison under the command of Mustaphas, then only Colonel. Hassan Pasha, after making this arrangement, marched with the rest of his troops to Kladissos and encamped there.

Ten or twelve days after the arrival of the Egyptian fleet, about fifteen Greek (Spetziot) vessels of war appearing off Suda, attacked two Egyptian vessels in the harbour, and greatly damaged one of them. After remaining seven or eight days on the Cretan coast, the Spetsiot vessels disappeared; the reason of this, it was said, being that an expected Hydriot squadron had failed to join them.

Had a Greek squadron of considerable force, such as the resources of Greece could have supplied, been despatched in due time to reconnoitre the Egyptian fleet the moment of its starting from Alexandria, the Greeks might have taken all or most of the transports, got possession of the immense military stores, and destroyed the numerous Egyptian and Albanian troops, on board. They might also, in all probability, have burnt some of the enemy's vessels of war, as the Greek seamen had frequently done in other parts. The result of what might have been achieved, would not only have saved Crete, but secured the whole of Greece from the dangers which, soon afterwards, all but overwhelmed her. Had this first expedition of Mechmet Ales failed, it is very unlikely that he would ever have attempted another. Unfortunately, however, he was permitted twice afterwards to land troops and warlike stores in Crete, without the slightest molestation, and succeeded, by the immense superiority of his resources, in exhausting the Cretan insurgents, and constituting Crete a safe and convenient centre of operations, by which he was able to overrun and desolate Peloponnesus, and threaten the entire destruction of Greece. He would, in fact, have accomplished the reduction of all Greece, had not the Allied Powers stretched out a timely hand to save her.

Leaving for a moment Hassan Pasha at Kladissos, we shall cast a glance at what was going on in the Eastern parts of Crete.

When the Egyptian fleet arrived off Heracleion, Hassan Pasha had an interview with Seriph Pasha, at which, according to report, it was resolved that both should take the field simultaneously on opposite sides of the island, in the hope of thus being able to suppress the insurrection. At the same time Hassan landed about 500 chosen Albanians, to serve under the immediate orders of Seriph.

The plan they concerted was far from having the success they anticipated. Hassan Pasha encountered in the west, where he landed, vigorous resistance; and Seriph Pasha forthwith encamped at Hayios Myron, a village of Knossos, but his appearance had only the effect of raising in arms the whole Christian population of the Cretan provinces.

M. Kurmules deemed the moment opportune for an offensive movement, and his plan was approved by the Government. Accordingly, an attack was planned on the Turkish army encamped near Tympakion, and consisting of about 2,000 men, under the command of Agriolides and Mustaphas Capsales. A Greek force assembled at Platanos, a village of Amarion, and prepared for the enterprise. This force consisted of Sphakians under Vurdumbas, Lampei under Suderos, Rethymnians under G. Deliyaunakes, Amarriots, and all other insurgents from the Eastern provinces, under Kurmules. The attack took place in June. Though the position of Tympakion was less favourable to the Greeks than to the Turks, the latter having a small body of cavalry, the former gallantly and skilfully executed their enterprise, but were at length, after a great deal of hard fighting, obliged, by the nature of the position, to retire to an upland village called Clema, in the same province. In this engagement, there fell more than 30 of the Turks, and about 15 of the Greeks.

Five or six days afterwards, the Greeks made a second attack on the enemy in the same position as before, but without any further success than the capture of two Turks, whom they set at liberty the following day. The enemy now perceiving that the number of the insurgents was constantly and rapidly on the increase, requested through their commanders a few days' truce. To this the Greek leaders, by the advice of Kurmules, acceded, though the object of the enemy was to gain time for the arrival of reinforcements, as well as for quietly removing their families and effects to Heracleion.

Meanwhile, however, Kurmules also taking advantage of the truce, immediately began to take possession of the upland villages on the side of Mount Ida, such as Borrhizia, Zaros, Gregorias and Yeryere, as far as Kuduni, a position opposite Asita, a village of Knossos, and armed all the inhabitants with great despatch He further sent Apostoles Karatares, Demetrios Kutricas, and J. Hulos, and some others, to raise and arm the Capetaniani and the inhabitants of other upland villages near the coast.

The Turks thus suddenly found themselves in the plain, surrounded by hostile forces, and were compelled to retire from their position, gradually and in detachments. The Greeks, advancing in great strength, attacked them as they continued their retreat from Tympakion, and, putting them to flight, pursued them as far as the village of Hayia Varvara, where the fugitives made a stand. In this engagement, in which more than a hundred Turks were slain, Kutricas greatly distinguished himself, having, it is said, killed nine of the enemy with his own hand. On the side of the Greeks, only three were killed, and twenty wounded; but a large quantity of valuable arms, as well as horses and other beasts of burden, and all the enemy's military stores, thrown away during the pursuit, fell into the hands of the victors.

In consequence of this victory, the Greeks remained in possession of the extensive province of Gortyna. It was exposed, moreover, to the whole wrath of the Heracleiot Turks, who, owing to the level surface of the country, were able to overrun it, laying it waste, and destroying great numbers of the inhabitants. Kurmules hastened to protect it from these calamities, by immediately locating select bodies of troops in advantageous positions within the province and on its frontiers Apostoles Karatares was stationed at Kapetaniana, I. Hulos at Pompeia, D. Kutricas at Kuse,

Apostolos Psomadakes at Tympakion, Stylianos Ha'jidakes at Vorrhizia, Ioannes Khelidones at Gregorias, and Georgios Khalkias elsewhere. These and other leaders of military capacity and local influence supported, with great alacrity, all the arrangements of Kurmules, who now conceived the idea of forming a small body of cavalry, which he gradually accomplished, and soon rendered it effective and formidable. By such efforts to protect the province, he daily became more and more a terror to the enemy.

Seriph Pasha himself was now roused to act with the utmost energy to check the Gortynian insurrection. He not only harassed the insurgents by daily incursions, but prepared such measures as he hoped would be sufficient to overpower them; in particular he determined to use every possible means of overwhelming the gallant Anoyani, who, along with the Aulopotamites and Knossians, greatly annoyed the enemy by frequent ambuscades from Knossos.

Accordingly, in the month of July, about 2,000 Turks, marching up the side of Mount Ida, attacked the village of the Anoyani, carried off whatever effects they were able, by their sudden arrival, to seize, and killed about ten unarmed Anoyani, the rest of whom, however, escaped to more inaccessible positions on Mount Ida. After remaining at the village for seven or eight days, during which they continued to urge the Anoyani both by threats and by promises to submission, but without any effect, they came down to Hayia Varvara in Gortyna, whence they frequently had encounters, and sometimes obstinate conflicts with the forces under Rusos, Suderos and Kurmules.

The Greeks, distressed by the heavy pressure of the Turks in those parts, now thought that a diversion from the side of Knossos would be opportune, or rather deemed it of the utmost importance to make a general attack on the Turks, who had descended from Anoya, and thus not merely relieve the warlike Anoyani, but drive the Turks from a position, the possession of which enabled them to harass the insurgents both of Aulopotamos and of Gortyna. A Greek force was, therefore, speedily mustered at Gonia, a village in Aulopotamos, consisting of Sphakians, of Kometiani, and Muriots under Poloyoryakes, a detachment of Rethymnians and Amariots under Strates Deliyannakes, the whole of the Aulopotamite and Knossian insurgents, and the corps of auxiliaries under Nicolaos Zervos. After the departure of the Turks from Anoya, the Greeks proceeded to Krusson, an upland village of Knossos, to attack Seriph Pasha, then at Hayios Myron.

On the 18th of the month a small detachment of Greeks, about eighty, mostly Anoyani, descended at day-break to the plain of Knossos, and, collecting under the very eyes of the Pasha, a large number of cattle, began to drive them with all possible haste towards Krusson. Seriph, immediately on perceiving this, ordered a body of his attendant Albanians to attack the foraging party. On this, 370 men, including 15 Cretans, one of whom was Macryboyazes of Knossos, issued forth and pursued, as far as Krusson, the party that were driving off the cattle, and killed two of them.

This unreflecting temerity of the Albanians led them into an ambuscade. The Greeks, who, unknown to the Turks, held strong positions around Krusson, instantly surrounded the pursuers, and attacked them with great determination. An obstinate conflict ensued, in which the Albanian Turks, perceiving the imminent danger to which they had exposed themselves, and finding themselves completely surrounded, made a desperate defence, and, attempting to cut their way through the assailants, were nearly all killed. The remainder, after frequent narrow escapes, took refuge, after nightfall, in the church of Saint Kharalampes, belonging to the village. From this position they made a last attempt to defend themselves, but were immediately surrounded by the Greeks, many of whom, especially natives of the village, ascended to the roof of the church, and, opening an aperture in it, let down pieces of cloth steeped in oil, as well as other combustible materials, to which they set fire, and reduced the refugees to extremities, so that some of them rushing from the building were shot down by the surrounding Greeks, while the rest perished in the flames within. Only two were saved, one of whom was a Cretan Turk, and the other, the above-mentioned Macryboyazes.[*] These, concealing themselves under dead bodies, saved themselves during the night, and announced the disaster to Seriph, who, on hearing the intelligence, instantly fled to Heracleion. Had the Greeks followed up their advantage by an immediate attack on the enemy at Hayios Myron, they would, to a certainty, have taken Seriph himself. But they let the opportunity slip, yielding to the temptation of plundering the slain. The spoil they obtained was of great value,

---

[*] This person was afterwards murdered by the Turks, whom he had hitherto served with fidelity.

consisting of the gold found in the girdles of the Albanians, and of richly ornamented arms. The Greek loss in the whole affair amounted to about 25 men.

After the destruction of the Turkish Albanian detachment at Krusson, and the Pasha's retreat from Hayios Myron, the Turkish forces occupied in harassing the Gortynian insurgents, retired from the province, dreading an attack from the victors of Krusson. Vurdumbas, Sideros, and Kurmules with their followers, now left their positions to undertake offensive operations. On the west of Ida they now harassed the Turks in the environs of Heracleion by incessant skirmishes and ambuscades, while Th. Khurdos with the Aulopotamites and Zervudakes with the insurgents of Knossos, did the same on the east of that mountain. The aqueducts that supplied the fortress with water, were soon destroyed, a service in which Poloyoryakes and his followers effectively aided.

As all these occurrences greatly encouraged the Greeks, A. Kuscumpes, Nicolaos Zervos, Panayes Suliotes, Vuzomarcos, Manias Valases, and a Maniat called Spyros, immediately after the victory at Krusson, lost no time in advancing at the head of a considerable force into the provinces situated farther to the east, and called the population to arms. The call was responded to mainly through the efforts of influential natives of those parts, who had happened to be in arms from the commencement of the Greek revolution, either repairing, like other Cretans, to other parts of Greece, or remaining at home and co-operating with the insurgents elsewhere. The inhabitants of these provinces, having in the meantime armed themselves as well as they could, eagerly embraced the national cause. The yoke of oppression could no longer be endured, and the opportunity was seized of declaring the resolution they had long cherished of joining their brethren.[*]

The want of arms, however, was greatly felt, and the insurgents in other parts of Crete had neither arms nor military stores to spare. Of the supplies transmitted

---

[*] Manoles Kazanes, a native of the province of Lasithon, a person of remarkable fleetness of foot, as well as daring, frequently went by night, sometimes to Sphakia, and sometimes to the neighbourhood of Rethymne, and after interviews with insurgents in those parts, returned again by night to Lasithon, communicating information and directions to his friends and neighbours. This meritorious patriot performed many distinguished exploits during the war of Independence.

from time to time by Greeks and Philhellenes in Western
Europe to Peloponnesus, no portion reached Crete in the
times of her greatest need. The contest was common to all
Greece, and the interests of all sections of the Panhellenium
were inseparably connected,—considerations which should
have led the Central Authorities to send opportune and
effective aid to the Greek cause in Crete. The Cretans were,
notwithstanding, left to maintain the struggle unaided and
alone. The recent insurgents made every effort to procure,
by the greatest pecuniary sacrifices, arms from those of their
countrymen who had joined the national cause at an earlier period, and who had obtained from the spoils of their vanquished
enemy more arms than they required. Still a large number
of the recent insurgents remained partially or entirely
unarmed. The consequences of this were, as we shall by
and by see, disastrous. The newly revolted provinces
suffered extremely from the frequent and exterminating
inroads of the Turks, eager to prevent the insurrection
taking root in those parts. Besides being in want of arms,
these insurgents had no place of security to which they
could convey their families, and secure military stores.
With due foresight and energy, the Greeks might have
converted the province of Lasition, so rugged and so difficult
of access, on account of the surrounding mountains, into
another Sphakia, where the inhabitants of the neighbouring
parts might, in moments of danger, find a safe retreat.
The inexperience, however, of the inhabitants of these parts
was so great, that they do not appear to have thought of
such measures. It has already been stated that the struggle
in Crete received no aid from other parts. It is but just,
however, to mention here a circumstance which does honour
to the late Varvakes, from whom alone Crete, during her
arduous contendings, received assistance.

Fame had long before made known that this worthy
patriot, a Greek merchant of immense wealth, in Russia,
had aided, not merely his native island of Psara, but Greece
generally, by promoting laudable undertakings and establishing useful institutions. His reputation for patriotic
beneficence induced the leading inhabitants of Kydonia in
Crete to apply to him for assistance in their efforts to
support the Hellenic or Grammar School, which had been
established there by Hadji Nicolos, as has already been
mentioned at the commencement of this work, but which was

now in danger of being abandoned for want of funds, in consequence of the impoverishing burdens imposed on the inhabitants by Turkish tyranny. A memorial was accordingly addressed to him about the end of the year 1820, and signed by Callinicos, the bishop of Kydonia, Nicolaos Kydones, Nicolaos Renieres, Constantinos Yeracakes, Stavrakes Samaripas, Georgios Papadakes, Manoles Heliakes, Stephanos Vasilopulos and others, requesting his aid towards maintaining the school. Vasilopulos undertook to deliver the memorial to Varvakes, who then resided at Taganroc.

Vasilopulos, after various wanderings, at length reached Taganroc, but not till the Greek insurrection had broken out in Dakia (Moldo-Valachia) and spread over all parts of Greece. On delivering the memorial, he explained to Varvakes, by word of mouth, that his mission related in reality not to the school, but to the insurrection. This explanation made Varvakes hesitate to comply with the request of the memorialists : " You have," said he, "a rich fellow countryman, a native of your own island, established at St. Petersburgh, I mean Kallerges. It is his part to come forward and aid the cause of his native island." After various objections, Varvakes handed over to Vasilopulos 25,000 Russian roubles, and the latter with this sum repaired without loss of time to Marseilles, and purchased 900 muskets there, with which he arrived in Crete in the month of July of the same year, that is, at a moment when they proved of great service to the cause in various parts of Crete.

After the preceding brief and necessary digression, we resume our narrative of Cretan affairs, giving in the first place an account of the proceedings of the recent insurgents. Inexperienced in war, they naturally put themselves under the conduct of military leaders of skill and capacity. The Khersonesite or Pediadite appointed as their commanders Georgios Kampasacalca and Zakharias Apostolakes; the Mirabeliote, * Manoles Lutsakes, Mikhales Magulakes,

* This delightful province, which, in the ecclesiastical division of the island comprehends the district of Lasithion, is the only one of all the provinces of Crete that has not retained the ancient names of the ancient cities within its bounds. The province in question, which bears the foreign name of Mirabelo, contained the ancient Miletos, on the site of which is at the present day the small village of Milatos (the Doric and original form of the name). The ancient Naxos is also to be traced in the poor village which now bears the name of Axos. This last place is still, as it was in ancient

and Konstantinos Stacakes; the Lasitiotæ, Manoles Kazanes, and Vasilios (father of Vasiloyoryes, afterwards appointed); the Arcaditæ, Anagnostes Symianos, and the Hierapytnians, Ph. Tsantirakes. The two Sitians, Ioannes Kontos, and Ioannes Macres, as well as Siphes Temirtaakes and Theodoros Spanos put themselves at the head of the Sitians as they continued to rise in arms, the province of Sitein having, owing to its remote situation, not yet openly espoused the national cause. All these corps, together with a considerable force under the command of Kuscumbes, Zervos, Suliot, and Vuzomarcos, immediately blockaded the numerous Turkish garrisons of the fortress of Lato or Spinalonga, as well as the garrison of the fortress of Hierapytnos, and continued to alarm and harass them by incessant skirmishes and ambuscades on the east, while on the west the Gortynians, Cnossians and Aulopotamites were assailing the Turkish forces in the vicinity of Heracleion.

Such was the situation of affairs in the Eastern provinces, when the Egyptian commander marched in that direction with his formidable hordes from the west of Crete.

It is necessary, in the meantime, to cast a glance at the political affairs of Greece at this period. The alarm, produced by Hassan Pasha's arrival in Crete at the head of a numerous Egyptian army on the one hand, and on the other by Dramales' simultaneous invasion of Continental Greece, and then of Peloponnesus, at the head of an overwhelming barbarian host from Constantinople, had thrown the whole Greek nation into the utmost perplexity. Quitting every pacific occupation, the Greeks, with one heart and soul, and with the greatest energy, directed their attention to warlike affairs, to save the nation from her impending danger. In consequence of this state of things, the Cretan Administration was utterly unable to observe the ordinary forms of proceeding, while in Peloponnesus all that remained of the National Parliament and the National Government consisted of a few individuals, who retiring to Hermione, with Athanasios Kanacares as Vice-president of

times, famed for its excellent supply of hones or whetstones. The ancient Olous is to be found in the village now called Elunta. Near the port of Saint Nicholas are the ruins of another ancient city, probably Minoa. We are not aware if there existed an ancient city called Petra, the present name of a Bishop's see. Out of veneration to the memory of Minos we designate the province of Mirabelo, by the name of Minoa, from the ancient city it contained according to Strabo and other ancient geographers.

the executive power, endeavoured to maintain there the shadow, at least, of a Central Authority.

The Cretans, as we have already mentioned, had been invited to send representatives to the National Parliament; and, had not their attention been engrossed by the impending dangers, they would, like the Peloponnesians, have sent one or two representatives from each Province (or Kadiliki) conformably to the new Cretan Constitution. The Cretan Administration took such measures as circumstances permitted, and, as appears from the documents below, sent three, one of whom alone, Homerides, took his seat in the National Parliament, after the restoration of tranquillity by the overthrow of Dramales.

As Homerides had been an eye-witness to the landing of the Egyptian troops in Crete, and was about to proceed to Peloponnesus, he was especially directed by the Cretan Administration to acquaint the Central Government with the critical situation of affairs in Crete, and to urge the necessity of immediate assistance. He, accordingly, made known the results of his mission to Crete, reporting in becoming terms the progress of the Cretan arms, and the firm determination of the Cretans to persevere in the vigorous prosecution of the War of Independence. He pointed out, at the same time, the absolute necessity of instantly despatching to the patriots of Crete a naval force with five or six thousand stand of arms, of which there was extreme scarcity in Crete, while the Central Government now possessed a considerable supply. This urgent application, however, led to no result.

No. 9.
THE PROVISIONAL GOVERNMENT OF CRETE
To His Excellency JOANNES KOLETTES, Minister of the Interior and Interim Minister of War.

Sir,

A general Convention of Cretans has appointed as their Representatives in the Panhellenic Parliament, Ioannes Mikeles, Petros S. Homerides and Athanasios Archimandrites, for whom we now solicit Your Excellency's good offices, requesting you to present them as such in the proper quarter, that they may be duly admitted as members of the National Parliament, and take part in its deliberations on the general interest of Greece, and especially in all affairs relating more immediately to the island of Crete.

We have the honour to be, with profound respect, etc.

MICHAEL KOMNENOS APHENTULES, *Eparch-General*

(Then follow the other signatures, the same as in the preceding documents.)

No. 10.

THE PROVISIONAL GOVERNMENT OF CRETE

To M. Petros Skylizzes Homerides.

Sir,

The inhabitants of Crete, convinced of your experience and capacity in the direction of public affairs, and grateful for the services you have rendered their island during the struggle for independence, have appointed you through the Eparch-general and the Commissaries-general to sit as lawful Representative of Crete in the Panhellenic Parliament, and they hereby give you power and authority as such, and direct you to use all diligence, in concert with the other members of the National Parliament, to promote the general interest of Greece, and to devote special attention to whatever concerns the affairs of Crete.

Prosneron, 14th (o.s.) July, 1822.

(Here follow the signature of the Eparch-General and others, as in the preceding documents.)

The Cretan Administration now determined, in compliance with the demands of the military leaders, to reward such patriots as had distinguished themselves in the victories obtained since the arrival of the Egyptian expedition, and to prompt the patriot forces to further achievements, by military promotions.

The Cretan insurgents had till now been obliged to serve without pay, and even to provide arms and all other necessaries, each from his own private resources. Military rank was the only recompense bestowed, and this, which was regarded as an acknowledgment of pre-eminent valour in the field, was highly appreciated, and effectively stimulated to further achievements. Accordingly the Eparch-General issued the following proclamation:—

No. 7.

PROVISIONAL GOVERNMENT OF CRETE.

PROCLAMATION.

Prosneron, 27 (o.s.) July, 1822.

It is hereby made known to all whom it may concern, that all military officers shall, on entering the civil or financial service, immediately lose their military rank. In such case their military commissions shall merely be regarded as a certificate of their military services in the national cause, and all such individuals shall, in signing documents in their civil or financial capacity, abstain from adding to their names the military rank they previously possessed.

Moreover, military officers are by law prohibited from accepting civil or financial functions till the struggle for the defence of our faith and country be terminated. When the national independence shall have been achieved, any military officer shall be at liberty to retire from the service, and to accept any other public function to which he may be appointed. Such are the provisions of the national laws, and due notice of this is hereby given to all.

MICHAEL KOMNENOS APHENTULES, Eparch-General.

We now return to the state of matters in the province of Kydonia.

The Albanian Hassan Pasha, after having placed a garrison in Malaxa, and thus secured his army against an attack from that quarter, remained for some time on the banks of the Kladissos, without attempting anything further. His inaction arose either from the discouragement caused him by the events at Halykae and Tsucalaria, and subsequently by those in Gortyna, as well as by the simultaneous destruction of so many Albanians at Krusson, by all which the plan he had previously formed with Seriph Pasha of Heracleion, had been completely baffled; or to the perplexity into which he was thrown, by intelligence daily received from Peloponnesus, announcing the overthrow and almost total destruction of the formidable army under Dramales, events which naturally alarmed him about his own position, shut up in the island of Crete, and suggested the danger of an attack that might be directed against him by the Greek troops now triumphant in Peloponnesus. It now occurred to him to try by policy and deception to avert the impending danger; accordingly, he immediately set at liberty all surviving Christian prisoners in the dungeons of the fortress, including the Bishop of Kydonia, who had been nearly a whole year groaning there amid filth and consequent disease. The Pasha invited the Bishop to his tent, and treated him with apparent kindness and respect.

The Turkish troops had, at the same time, been directed not to undertake any hostile movement, either from Malaxa or from the Kladissos, although, meanwhile, the Greeks, and especially the mountaineers of Kydonia, continued, in spite of the Pasha's pretended change of policy, to harass the Turkish forces by daily ambuscades.

The Pasha, after these demonstrations, for the purpose of deceiving the Greeks, determined to employ for the furtherance of his purpose, the instrumentality of the Bishop, whom he directed to address the following pastoral to the insurgents:

"Christians, my children in the Lord! Be it known unto you, that the illustrious Commander-in-chief Hassan Pasha, moved by feelings of philanthropy, has liberated from prison many other Christian brethren, as well as myself. Now enjoying his kind protection, as my Deacon

will inform you, I am compelled by a sense of gratitude
to bear public testimony to the Pasha's beneficent and
righteous intentions.

"Let me entreat you, my dear children, to reflect seriously
on what you are about, and consider what a formidable
adversary you have in the Viceroy of Egypt. My paternal
advice to you is to lay down your arms, and to offer your
submission to so humane a dignitary as the Commander-in-
chief, whom the illustrious Mechmet Ales selected for his
conciliatory character, and sent to restore tranquillity in
this island, with instructions to punish henceforth, with the
strictest severity, all disorderly persons, whether Turks or
Christians, but to protect all well disposed persons without
distinction. The Pasha promises to forgive all that you
have hitherto done, as he believes that you are driven to
desperation by the oppressions you previously endured from
the disorderly Turks of Crete. Follow then my counsel,
children in the Lord, preferring a quiet and peaceful life to
your present condition, in which yourselves, your families,
and your effects are exposed to incessant calamities."

The Bishop addressed the insurgents in this manner, not
from choice but the pressure of circumstances. It could not
be expected he would disregard the commands of the Pasha,
and he was still suffering both in body and mind from the
effects of his long and cruel imprisonment. The Pasha was
pleased with the contents of the pastoral, which he immediately put into the hands of the Deacon, with instructions
to repair to various parts, and read it to the insurgents.
Ioannes Hales, then at Kerameia, on ascertaining these
particulars, arrested the bearer of the letter and instantly
consulted his brother Vasilios on the subject. The two
brothers repaired forthwith to Prosneron, then the seat of
the Cretan Administration, and obtained from it to publish
a suitable reply to the pastoral to obviate its possible effect.
The bearer had further informed them, that the Pasha
intended to employ many similar manoeuvres, and that the
Bishop was in great distress of soul on account of having
issued, though by compulsion, the pastoral in question. The
reply was in the following terms:

"Venerable Bishop.—We had not entertained the hope
of your being still alive, after the slaughter of so many
thousands of our brethren, and the cruel martyrdom of so

many of our clergy of all ranks. We rejoice that the philanthropy of Hassan Pasha has released you from the sufferings of imprisonment, and we are disposed to infer that the Pasha must be a man of prudence and justice. We were surprised, however, at your advising us to submit again to the yoke. In giving us this advice you seem as if urging us to tie our own hands, and prepare ourselves again to be slaughtered at the caprice of our oppressors. Owing to the cruelty of the Turks in Crete not one of us would have been this day alive, had we not, in due time, taken up arms in self-defence. Our unalterable resolution is to protect ourselves from the most fearful oppression, or die with arms in our hands. We, therefore, request you not to write to us any more on this subject. On this point, neither your prayers nor your threatenings could shake our determination. We sincerely pray and trust that Hassan Pasha may not, at any time, abandon you to the ferocity of the Cretan Turks. Our own Commander-in-chief has Turkish prisoners, Musuragas of Rethymno and others, and he treats them with the greatest humanity, though they were taken in battle."

Nearly at the same time an Albanian of distinction repaired from Malaxa, with two followers to the village of Kampi, where he had an interview with Siphacas, in which he addressed him as follows: "Trusting my life to your military honour, I have come to see you and your brave followers, with whom we have been fighting. We have come with the permission of our Bimbashi (Colonel), though he tried to dissuade us from coming, assuring us you would kill us the moment we put ourselves into your power. Hassan Pasha told us before we left Egypt, that we were going to the Morea, but that in our way we should touch at Crete, and seize a few rebels there, and thus restore order. Instead of finding a few disorderly persons, we have found a hostile army, numerous and warlike." "What sort of order," asked Siphacas, "does the Pasha intend to establish? Is he aware of the cruel oppression the Christians so long endured in this island?"—"He received instructions before he left Egypt," rejoined the Albanian "to seize some of the insurgents here, and punish them, compelling others to follow him as soldiers to the Morea In regard to the rest of the Christian inhabitants, the most intelligent of them are to be sent to Egypt, and Egyptians are to be brought to

Creto, to cultivate the lands along with the rest. He has instructions however, to inflict punishment on many of the Cretan Turks also. Of all these I can give you perfect assurance, and moreover I know, that Mechmet Ales and the Sultan have promised to leave Hassan Pasha at Creto as long as he lives* after he puts down the insurrection here and assists in suppressing the Morcot insurgents."

After these and similar communications the parties took leave of each other before sunset with mutual satisfaction, having, after eating and drinking together, cordially shaken hands. Siphacas communicated to his friends and followers all that had been said at the interview. He even invited the Albanian to pay him another visit, hoping to obtain further information from him, and conjecturing that the Albanian was in reality a Christian, serving in the Turkish army, a thing very usual among the Christian Albanians.

The Albanian, on returning to Malaxa, was questioned by Mustaphas the Colonel as to the result of his mission, upon which he spoke as follows: " I saw troops healthy and vigorous, well armed, full of spirit and not, as we have been told famished and disheartened. They treated us with great hospitality and courtesy, and they invited us to return whenever we pleased without dread or fear," and he added other particulars to the same effect. The Albanian paid another visit to Siphacas and I. Halcs at Keramcin, and affirmed all that he had stated on previous occasions

The Egyptian Commander, having ascertained from the reply to the Bishop's pastoral, as well as from the report of the Albanian's interview with the insurgent leaders, that the Greeks were desperately exasperated against the Turks of Creto, resolved to turn this feeling to account. He, accordingly,

* Nearly the same statements as those of the Albanian were contained in an anonymous letter sent from Alexandria to Crete, on the arrival of Khusein Bey, successor to Hassan Pasha. That letter warned the Cretan insurgents to beware of the schemes of Khusein Bey, and informed them that Khusein was a man of great enterprise, energy, and cunning, and that he would spare no amount of money in order to accomplish his intentions. As to Mechmet Ales' schemes in reference to insurgent Greece, there remains not a shadow of doubt. In fact, Lord Palmerston in his speech, delivered in the British House of Commons, in 1850, on the affairs of Greece in connection with the blockade of Pireus, he distinctly stated, that the intention of the Pasha of Egypt was, if he had been allowed to suppress the Greek insurrection, to fill it with Arab inhabitants, and to transport into Arabia, the whole surviving Greek population. Lord Palmerston added, that the object of British intervention was to save the Levant from such a catastrophe.

thought proper to issue a lengthened proclamation, in which he expatiated on the enlightened policy of Mehmet Ales, the Viceroy of Egypt, gave an historical account of his achievements, dwelt on the mildness of his government, and on the prosperity and contentment of his subjects, adding that every enterprise of the Viceroy had been crowned with entire success; and denounced with great bitterness and indignation the brutality and hardened wickedness of the Cretan Turks'; and slighly hinted his intentions in reference to them, and the beneficent measures about to be adopted for the improvement of Crete. In conclusion, he earnestly exhorted the Greeks to lay down their arms, and become definitively subjects of the humane Mehmet Ales, and solemnly promised all them perfect security of life, honour and prosperity, and this he proclaimed, with perfect confidence, as if the Cretans had not been aware of the wretched condition of Mechmet Ales' subjects in Egypt, who are not merely serfs, but abject slaves, and as if it was not at all known that the intention of the Viceroy was, after the reduction of Crete, Peleponnessus and continental Greece, to transport the inhabitants, some to Arabia, and some elsewhere.

Hassan Pasha immediately published this proclamation throughout the provinces of Kydonia and Apocoronos, and sent copies of it to the Pashas of Heracleion and of Rethymne, directing them to make it known in all other parts of Crete. These Pashas, however, declined publishing the proclamation, on the grounds, it is said, that Hassan Pasha invited, by it, the inhabitants of Crete to become definitely subjects of Mechmet Ales, instead of calling upon them to submit to the Sultan, to whose government the island was still directly subject.

The military leaders A. Panayotes, V. Halles, and Siphacas, on being apprised of all this, returned to Prosneron to consult with the Administration on what was proper to be done under the circumstances. Hassan Pasha hoped to induce the Christian population to submit, as they were worn out and prostrated, he thought, by the sufferings to which they had been exposed, and he flattered himself that by some means or other he would gain over some of the military leaders. A difference of opinion prevailed in the meeting at Prosneron on the subject of a reply to Hassan's proclamation. Aphentules, the Eparch-General, thought

K

that no public notice whatever should be taken of the matter, but Œconomos, the Secretary-General, insisted on the contrary, and, as the military leaders agreed with the latter, his opinion prevailed.

Accordingly, they drew up and published an historical review of the manifold and cruel sufferings which the Christian population of Crete had for many ages endured under Mussulman oppression. They expatiated on their more recent sufferings, on the wretched and precarious position of the Christian among Turks, recorded some of the outrages frequently perpetrated on Christian families, in consequence of which no Christian, on leaving his abode for the labors of the day, could tell if he should ever see his wife and children again, except either dead or dishonoured. They referred to the massacre at Heracleion, Sitcia, and in other parts, and mentioned the well-known determination of the Turks to exterminate the entire Christian population, while, in the meantime, they treated with more wanton cruelty than they did the very brute beasts. After declaring that such a state of oppression could no longer be endured, that the Greeks to a man had sworn by the faith and the dust of their fathers that they would rather die with arms in their hands than again submit to any yoke of bondage whatever, as they were well aware of the condition of the life which the subject population led under every form whatever of Moslem rule. Other remarks were added with special reference to the existing difference between the Sultan and the Viceroy of Egypt.

This document was signed by several military leaders in spite of the opposition both of the Eparch-General and of various Cretans, who disapproved the expressions employed in several passages; and was given to the deacon, as Hassan Pasha's messenger, to be delivered to that functionary. The deacon soon afterwards returned with a communication from the Pasha, in which he threatened to take the field forthwith against the insurgents, and declared that the leaders who had signed the document would be responsible for the sufferings to which the Christian population would be exposed. The deacon did not again return to the Turkish camp, as Callinicos Sarpakes, the amiable and excellent bishop of Kydonia, was now dead, having expired in a tent adjoining that of the Pasha. The venerable man's death arose partly from the hardships and horrors of a long imprisonment; and finally from his mental anguish on being compelled to issue pastorals so little in accordance with his own sentiments. The deacon, who had submitted to indescribable sufferings from attachment to the bishop during his imprisonment, was still in the Turkish camp, when the bishop died, and was permitted to superintend his burial.

The possession of Malaxa by the Turks caused Siphakas and Hallos great uneasiness and annoyance, as it prevented them from making themselves entire masters either of Apocoronos, Kerameia, or the greater part of Kydonia. They accordingly took occasion from the Pasha's recent document to commence preparations in concert with the Eparch-General for retaking that important military position.

On the 20th of July A. Protopapadakes, V. Halos, A. Panayotes and Siphacas held a council of war, and arranged the following plan of attack. Protopapadakes was, by night, and while the enemy were asleep, to occupy the summit of the height, called Pupa, to the east of the fortress of Malaxa, while Siphacas was to occupy the southern part of the same height, that is, the olive-grove. Both these leaders were, at a given hour, to commence a simultaneous attack on the garrison, which was about 800 strong. Hales and A. Panayotes, at the head of the Lakkiots and other mountaineers, were, after occupying positions at Digenes to the west of the fortress, to be prepared to fall upon the Turks in the flank, when these should be compelled to commence a retreat down the hill, the Greek leaders being fully assured that the Turks could not long retain their positions, if the arranged plan were punctually executed.

After these arrangments Protopapadakes rushed with impetuosity from his position, firmly resolved to have the honour of alone driving Mustaphas from Malaxa as he had done before, and was eager to atone for his having, through the desertion of his followers, been obliged to retire and allow the Pasha to get possesion of it. But his conduct in begining the attack before the appointed moment, and that of Siphacas in not immediately hastening to his assistance, rendered the plan a failure. The Turks, roused from their sleep by their sudden assault instantly flew to arms and made a determined resistance, and, as they were attacked only at one point, they were able to strengthen their positions all around the fortress, so that when Siphacas advanced, he found the enemy too well prepared to receive him.

An obstinate conflict now ensued between the Greeks under Siphacas and Protopapadakes and the enemy, who perceiving the danger of their situation increasing, resolved to effect their escape to the plain. On commencing their retreat in small parties down the hill, they suddenly found themselves in the presence of Hales, who, having inconsiderately occupied a position different from the one assigned him, opened a fire on them before the proper time. The retreating Turks, alarmed at this unexpected attack, instantly returned to their previous positions, from which they maintained a gallant resistance till about mid-day.

In this conflict a very considerable number were killed or wounded. Mustaphas himself was, it is said, wounded in the heel. On the side of the Greeks Propapadakes, with about 30 of his followers, mostly Sphakians, and 7 of the followers of Siphacas were killed. The wounded in both corps amounted to 20. Owing to the death of Protopapadakes and the mistakes of Siphacas and Hales, which we have mentioned, the strong and important position of Malaxa remained in possession of the Turks, who, after fortifying it more strongly than ever, spontaneously evacuated it not very long after. Had not the want of strict military discipline among the Greeks marred the execution of a plan admirably devised, the Greek arms would have been crowned with a brilliant success. Had the enemy, as was anticipated, continued their retreat from Malaxa, the Lakkiots and other mountaineers would, as arranged, have fallen upon them in their descent, and, while these were exhibiting their usual impetuous daring, inflicting fearful loss on the fugitives, the rest of the Greeks would have poured down from Malaxa upon the enemy, and the general result would have signally discredited and humbled the prestige of Hassan Pasha. But the want of discipline now, as on so many occasions, proved disastrous to the Cretan cause.

Anagnostes Protopapadakes, one of the most prominent of the insurgent leaders in Crete, was a native of the mountainous village of Askyphi, in Sphakia. Gifted with great practical sagacity, he was of all the Cretan leaders the most ingenious in devising, and the most dexterous and energetic in executing, military operations. He was of small stature, but of great vigour and courage. As a military leader his great endowments were tarnished with numerous and varied infirmities, derived from the disadvantages of his previous

training. These frequently rendered all his great qualities
useless or hurtful to the public cause. Had his life been
spared, the imperfections of his character might, through
favorable influence, have gradually disappeared; and as his
patriotism was sincere and earnest, he might ultimately
have rendered to his country the most important services.
His excess of daring was the cause of his death, which,
from his merits as a soldier and a leader, was deeply regretted by the inhabitants, as well as the authorities, of
Crete. In acknowledgment of his services his son, Manoles
Protopapadakes, then scarcely 25 years of age, obtained the
rank and position held by the deceased. Owing to the comparative inexperience of Manoles Protopapadakes, this young
leader was directed to act under the guidance of his paternal
uncle, Polios, a person not inferior in valour and energy to
his late brother Anagnostes Protopapadakes, who, at his
death, was about 50 years of age.

Towards the end of July, that is on the 29th or 30th, the
Turks unexpectedly evacuated Malaxa, and proceeded to
Kladissos. Malaxa was immediately occupied by Siphacas.

Hassan Pasha was now preparing to commence his great
movement against the Greeks. This, of course, made them
prepare for resistance. The now leader, Manoles Protopa-
dakes, with those under his command, Sudoros, with a portion of the Rethymnians and Amariots, and nearly all the
Sphakians, acting along with Kydonians and Apocoronites,
were now mustered, and altogether formed an army of about
4,000 strong, ready to meet the enemy wherever he might
advance.

On the first of August, about sunrise, the Turkish army
marched from the river Platanias, where it had encamped
and proceeded in full force, consisting of infantry, cavalry,
and artillery, against the Lakkiots, Therisiani, and other
mountaineers. This was done agreeably to the invariable
usage of the Turks on undertaking a general movement, as
they always regarded it as a preliminary necessity to reduce
the mountaineers before carrying into effect general measures
against the rest of the insurgents. The Greeks, on their
part, occupied every advantageous position, from which they
could make head against the enemy, now so superior in
numbers and resources. The brilliant victories they had
achieved the preceding year in this very district, which was
to be the scene of war, roused them to the most determined

resistance, and made them dispute every foot of their own glorious mountain homes.

In the nature of things, however, the Greeks, often in want of the very necessaries of life, and having to contend with an enemy so superior in numbers and so amply supplied with all kinds of stores, were often compelled to retire. Accordingly, Hassan Pasha continued to advance up the side of the mountains, fighting his way day and night with great loss; and, after meeting with great resistance, he succeeded on the third or fourth day in sacking with every indication of fury the villages of Lakki, Therison, and their environs. The Greeks, retiring to still more rugged and inaccessible positions, continued to harrass the invaders by incessant attacks. But Hassan Pasha, with equal obstinacy, persisted in his upward march, determined, as it appeared, to accomplish his object, though at the loss of ever so large a number of his forces.

The conflict was kept up with unabating determination on both sides, day and night, from the 1st to the 6th of August, the Pasha being resolved to overwhelm, by persevering efforts, the Greek patriots, who, in spite of hunger and hardships of every kind, continued to resist with undiminished heroism. The ceaseless sound of firearms, echoed day and night among the lofty mountains, spreading awe and alarm afar. Still the Greeks fought on, and by constantly seizing advantageous positions, inflicted great loss on the enemy, whose cavalry and artillery were of no avail in such a country. The enemy, during the night, carefully transported to the fortress their wounded and dead, lest their corpses should be exposed to the eyes of their adversaries, in those very parts, where still lay the bones of so many Moslems, who had previously fallen there.

The enemy, taking advantage of some inadvertency on the part of Siphakas, attacked his detachment with great fury, and dispersed it. At length, Hassan Pasha resolved to quit the rugged mountain district where he now was, and, on the night of the 6th-7th of the month, he marched for the plain of Kydonia, to encamp near the villages of Perivolia and Murnies. He was afraid of retreating by day, lest his troops should be attacked in various passes by the Greeks. He is said to have lost during the whole time he remained among the mountains, about 500 men. The Greeks, during the same time had more than 60 killed, besides a considerable number wounded.

The formidable expedition of Hassan Pasha thus entirely failed, and proved more damaging to himself than to the Greeks in the provinces adjacent to Kydonia. All that he accomplished was the destruction of the small and rude huts, which the mountaineers had, after the previous desolation of their villages, erected to shelter their families. His cavalry was of no use to him among the mountains, and the adversaries he encountered he was unable to reduce by force, stratagem, or policy. He therefore thought proper to try what he could accomplish in some other and more promising part of the island.

Without allowing the fatigued and exhausted Greek troops time to occupy the defiles and advantageous positions near Malaxa, and thus render it difficult and dangerous for his army to advance by that route, he again took the field on the 11th or 12th of August, and despatched part of his infantry and the whole of his cavalry, to Keramcia, whilst he himself, with the remainder of his infantry, passed through the defiles called Gyrismata, between Apocoronos and Kydonia, and entered Apocoronos without opposition, as the small number of Greeks then in Malaxa had found it expedient to evacuate it. During his stay of five or six days in the province of Apocoronos, he displayed the same fury in the work of desolation, as he had done at Lakki and Therison. None of the inhabitants, however, fell into his hands, as they had previously repaired to Vothonakia* and other strong positions in Sphakia†. He now encamped outside the fortress of Rethymne, but he did not reach that place without sustaining considerable loss in passing the narrow stream of Halmyros, as a body of Kephalliani, Prosneritæ and Halicampitæ, along with Manusios Protopapadakes, remarkable for his dexterity in conducting ambuscades, and on this occasion accompanied by other Skyphiots, suddenly fell upon the Pasha's rear, and killed about 20 of the enemy. The assailants would have

---

* Vothonakia, situated at the foot of the White Mountains, but above Zkriphe, Phre and Melidonion, villages of Apocoronos, is capable of affording in moments of danger a safe retreat to a large portion of the families of the Apocoronitæ, provided timely means were employed to secure the entrance by adequate fortifications. A stream of very delightful water flows from the mountains into what is called Middle Vothonakia.

† In such circumstances, the Askyphiots and Imbriots gave the refugees from other Provinces free admission into their vineyards. The family of the Manusoyannakæ from Imbros, besides this, distributed among the destitute, large supplies of bread and meat.

inflicted a much greater loss on the Turkish army, if a detachment of cavalry had not returned to the rear, and dispersed the assailants.

From Rethymne Hassan Pasha proceeded to the monastery of Aulopotamos, called the monastery of Khalepa, and encamped there on the 30th of August. Here he found adversaries still more vigilant and on the alert. The Anoyani under Th. Khurdos, along with some mountaineers of the Province of Aulopotamos, attacked the Egyptians at their tents the morning after their arrival. The Egyptians defended themselves in various ways, planting guns on the hill called Phlamura; the guns, however, did them more harm than good. The Greek troops at a distance, hearing the cannonading, hastened from all points to the assistance of those who were making head against the Egyptians. In the afternoon, various Greek detachments, unexpectedly assailing the enemy from different quarters, killed about 25 men. One of the Greeks was slightly wounded, and this was all the damage they sustained in the affair.

Next day at an early hour he removed to Sclavocampos, a more rugged position, where he encountered more formidable opposition. There, not only the Greek troops just mentioned, but, along with them, the Knossians under Zervudakes, and the Anoyani under B. Sbocos, brought on a conflict, which was kept up with great obstinacy between Kamarakion and Gonia, almost till it was night, the Turks striving to force a passage to Heracloion, while the Greeks fought with great determination for the purpose of keeping the enemy in the same position, as it appeared to them that they could assail the Turks more effectively there on the arrival of the expected reinforcements under Siphakas, who, according to intelligence, was pressing on in the rear of the enemy with a large veteran force. The intelligence proved correct; for on the Pasha's departure from Apocoronos, Siphakas and J. Halles instantly collected a body of Kydonians and Apocoronites, amounting to upwards of 300 chosen men, and, having been joined on their march by Rethymnians and Greeks from other parts, advanced on the enemy's rear. Night coming on put an end to the conflict at Sclavocampos, in which about 60 Turks, besides from 10 to 12 of the best of their cavalry, were killed. On the side of the Greeks nine were killed, and a few wounded.

Hassan Pasha, aware of the difficulty of his position at

Sclavocampos, where his cavalry was of no use to him, hastened to leave it on hearing the same day, it is said, from a small vessel from Rethymne, which anchored at Balo, that Siphakas was approaching. Leaving a large part of his baggage, he proceeded by a rapid night march to the more level province of Knossos, where his cavalry could freely operate.

The Cretan Greeks always avoided a conflict with cavalry in the open plain. However much confidence they might have in their own swiftness of foot, the sight of enemy's cavalry in the plain was always an object of dread to them. This was very natural to troops, who, whatever might be their bravery, had neither discipline nor bayonets. It frequently happened that the enemy's cavalry inconsiderately penetrated into rugged localities and narrow passes, which abound in Crete. In such circumstances, discipline and military experience might have enabled the Greeks to achieve brilliant results. But, unfortunately, these were wanting among the patriot troops of Crete; and their leaders, though men of great bravery and enterprise, did not possess sufficient influence over their followers, or sufficient skill in directing the movements of a considerable body of troops On the present occasion, the success which had been achieved was prevented, partly also by remisness on the part of the above-mentioned leaders, who did not make all possible exertions to reach Sclavocampos in time.

Having thus failed to effect a combined attack on the enemy, the Greeks, more than 1000 strong, left Strumbula, a table-land which separates Knossos from Aulopotamos, on the 8th or 9th of September, with the intention of bringing the enemy to a conflict below the village of Hayios Myron. Hassan Pasha was now encamped near the fortress, and resting his troops. The native Turks, however, with a detachment of Egyptian cavalry, forming both together a body of nearly 2,000 men, advanced on the Greeks, and commenced a resolute combat, which was kept up with great obstinacy on both sides till nearly mid-day. In this action, about 13 of the enemy were killed, and a great number wounded. Of the Greeks only four were wounded, and none killed. Siphakas and J. Halles immediately after this affair, proceeded to Gortyna, to concert measures with Kurmules.

Hassan Pasha, discouraged by the difficulties he encountered in western Crete, now resolved to march to the eastern provinces, for the purpose of checking, if possible, the insurrection which had begun to spread there. He instantly commenced, as we shall see, inroads fitted to strike the insurgents with dismay. Before, however, giving an account of these, we shall first narrate what took place at the same period in Apocorono, off which the Constantinople fleet had just arrived in the Amphimallic bay (Suda) on its way from the coast of Messenia in Peloponnesus, from which it had sailed without molestation, after having provisioned the fortresses of Modon, Coron and Patras, still in the hands of the Turks.

On the 23rd or 24th of September, seven vessels of war belonging to this fleet anchored near the land, and, next day nearly all their crews, accompanied by many Turks of Suda, went on shore to water either at the river Kœliares, opposite the village of Kalyvæ to the west, or at the stream which runs by Kalami below the ruins of an ancient fortress now called Œconomika or Palæokastron. The party that went on shore, amounting in all to about 800, instead of confining themselves to obtaining a supply of water, resolved to enter the neighbouring villages and assail the inhabitants.

Andreas Phasules and also George Mavrakes commander of the Armeniani, happening at this moment to be in the village of Kalyvæ with about 30 or 40 Kalyviani, Armeniani and Tsivariani, gallantly resisted the assailants for a long time, and used every effort to prevent the Turks from advancing further, and, at the same time, sent word to the rest of the Apocoronites to hasten to their assistance.

While the Turks were on the point of entering the villages mentioned, the inhabitants of which had saved themselves by flight, George Papadakes arrived at the head of about 80 Ziziphiani, Nipiani, Phrediani and Vaphiani, and was immediately reinforced by other bodies of Greeks from the villages of Kephaladæ, Vamos and Gavalokhorion. All these instantly fell upon the Turks, who were advancing towards the interior, and, at once, putting them to flight, overtook them below Palæokastron, while the fugitives were rushing to their boats on the beach. The vessels, already mentioned, immediately got under weigh, and coming as near the land as possible, endeavoured to protect the fugitives by opening a furious fire of grape-shot on the pursuers. The wretched fugitives were now between two fires, being shot down by the Greeks who were firing on them under protection from Palæokastron, and at the same time exposed to the grape-shot from the ships. Many of the boats were sunk with all on board. The loss on the side of the Turks amounted to upwards of 150 men. Only one Greek was killed in this affair, Alexandros Mityleneos. He received a grape-shot wound on the brow as he recklessly exposed himself for the purpose of seizing the arms of a Turk who was in the act of entering one of the boats.

This Alexandros was a native of the island of Lesbos (Mitylene), whence his surname of Mityleneos. He came to Crete at the commencement of the insurrection to take part in the war of independence, then only in the 25th year of his age, and, having received an excellent education for the time, he exhibited an enthusiastic zeal for the freedom of Greece. His death was generally and deeply lamented by the Cretans.

G. Papadakes, overjoyed at this victory, ran about the country day and night, collecting the most warlike combatants in Apocoronos. He then began to harass the enemy, sometimes by ambuscades in the vicinity of the Kœliares and of Kalami, and sometimes by raids as far as Halykæ, accompanied by Petros Tsacalarianos and Ioannes Pitropakes, persons renowned for their address and activity in *guerilla* warfare. His immediate object was to prevent the enemy from obtaining supplies of water without great risk. Seven of a Turkish party, while drawing water from the stream flowing from Hayia Paraskevo, were killed, and one of their boats was burnt. Papadakes, however, not confining himself to such minute exploits, lost no time in calling to his assistance Siphakas, then in Gortyna, apprehending that the Turks would take advantage of Siphakas' absence, and undertake some movement of a more formidable nature in Apocoronos.

On the 30th of the same month the whole remaining part of the fleet, consisting of 48 large vessels of war, a large proportion of which were ships of the line, entered the harbour for the purpose of avenging the recent outrage on the part of the Greeks. A body of about 3,000 men, consisting partly of troops and sailors from the fleet, and partly of Turks of Kydonia and Suda, proceeded during the night of passed unobserved the Greeks stationed at Malaxa and Tsucalaria, they succeeded in advancing through the defile of Gyrismata before daylight. A detachment of them proceeded to Palæocastron, and slew about twelve Greeks stationed there. The main body descended about dawn to make a sudden inroad into Apocoronos.

In the meantime the inhabitants of the neighbouring villages had been alarmed by the firing at Palæocastron and Gyrismata. While some of them conveyed their families to places of safety, Georgios Papadakes, Nicolaos Konstantudakes, brother of Siphacas, and Alevizos Sphakianos, who were then at Neokhorion with about 90 men, collected a few more from the village of Makhœru, and attempted, by keeping up an incessant fire, to make head as far as possible against the Turks till the Christian population should be apprized of the Turkish inroad. As however, the Greeks, were unable to stop the advance of the Turks for any considerable time, the enemy, after being impeded for two or three hours, ascended to the above-mentioned villages, and, while they advanced without opposition, shouted aloud that they intended to sleep the following night in Sphakia. The enemy's wing that proceeded eastward, was soon on the point of entering the village of Nipos, and their wing that was advancing to the west, had already entered Melidonion, which is at a considerable distance from Nipos, as the inhabitants had abandoned it, and were conveying their families to places of security.

Siphacas had reached Melidonion, his native village, the previous day, having returned in great haste from Gortyna. Unfortunately, however, he was suffering from dislocation of one of his feet, and entirely unable to walk. While sitting on horseback surrounded by 30 of his townsmen, he saw from a distance the Turks entering Melidonion with torches in their hands to set fire to his own house, the only one that had remained undemolished. He shouted with a voice of thunder: "Why allow them to advance, brave comrades! fall upon them fearlessly! hold on a little; 500 Sphakians are hastening to our assistance, and are already at hand. The Lakkiots also will be with us in a few minutes." Scarcely had he finished his stirring appeal, when about 80 musket shots were heard announcing the approach of Mutsoyannes and Panayotes Myiyas with a body of Kampiani and others. The Turks were alarmed at this incident, and immediately began to retire, on which the Greeks fell upon them with great fury, and, pursuing them as far as the heights to the west of the village of Makhœræ, killed a number of them.

At the very time these events occurred at Melidonion, about 100 Prosneritæ, Halicampitæ and Vaphiani, under the command of Georgios Velestines, Mertiminnos Perakes, Ioannes Yannares and Antonios Peneses, were approaching the village of Nipos. On seeing from a distance the flight of the Turks from Melidonion, they instantly fell on the enemy at Nipos, and, though scarcely amounting to 300 men including reinforcements from the villages Phre, Ziziphé and Pemonia, they put to flight the immense Turkish force, consisting chiefly of Asiatics, that had landed from the fleet to avenge the disgrace they had a few days before suffered from the Greeks, and, as they gave out, to carry off Cretan female captives. Upwards of 250 of the enemy were, it is said, killed during their retreat; and, what is remarkable, during the whole affair not one of the Greeks received the slightest injury. The whole of the enemy's loss was confined to Turks from other parts, as the Cretan Turks, acquainted with the localities, had occupied strong positions, while the former, unexpectedly encountering the Greeks stationed between Armeni and Neokhorion, were exposed to a deadly fire without attempting resistance. Many of them even threw away their arms in despair. Had the whole Greek force in those parts vigorously joined in the pursuit, those unfortunate strangers would have been cut off to a man, and the fleet would have been without sufficient hands to take it back to Constantinople. But the Greeks, unrestrained by discipline, began to spoil the slain. Siphakas was prevented by the accident we have mentioned from being present in the pursuit, a circumstance much to be regretted, as his great influence over the troops would have enabled him to maintain greater discipline, and to inflict more signal loss on the enemy. The pursuit, it is true, was led by N. Konstantudakea, the brother of Siphakas, a person of equal courage and enterprise, but, owing to various defects in his character, and especially to his grasping disposition, he possessed far less influence in the army than his brother. Siphakas himself was so far from wishing to appropriate an undue share of the spoil, that on every such occasion he was the foremost of all in pursuing the enemy. He had thus so gained the respect and regard of the army, that the alacrity of his followers made him victorious in almost every enterprise.

After these occurrences a line of Greek troops was formed, extending from Gyrismata to Halmyros, and composed almost entirely of Apocoronites and Keramciani, as the danger more immediately threatened them. Siphakas and J. Halles moved about day and night to watch the movements of the fleet, as they suspected a fresh landing might be made to avenge the previous disasters. The Greeks, in the meantime, suffering grievously from want of provisions, owing to the frequent desolation of the country, were frequently reduced to the necessity of living on wild herbs without bread, and sometimes without salt. At times their sole food consisted of acorns and dry keratia (carob-pods). Privations and the want of proper nourishment, produced disease and in many cases death. For seventeen days, during which the Greeks were on the alert along the coast in apprehension that troops would be landed from the fleet, they lived on shell-snails and wild herbs, which they boiled in fragments of pitchers, and ate without salt, using oranges and lemons instead of bread. The recent Turkish inroads and Hassan Pasha's late invasion had completely destroyed the crops, the oil, and every ordinary sort of nourishment throughout Apocoronos and the neighbouring provinces. On the 13th day Siphakas brought to the troops seven loaves, and these, though black and of barley, mixed with various coarse materials, was so highly appreciated, that they were distributed as sacramental portions and thought sweeter than honeycomb. Such were the indescribable sufferings that the Greeks of Crete had to endure in struggling to shake off a cruel and brutal yoke, to which the tortuous policy of European powers has again subjected them.

The fleet, on the 18th day from its arrival, appeared to be preparing some movement. It had on previous occasions sent a large number of boats sometimes to Halykæ, and sometimes to the river Koeliaros, either as a feint, or to water in reality. As often as this occurred, detachments of Greeks instantly repaired to those spots to repel the enemy. At length, after many such movements, the fleet sailed out of the harbour one afternoon with a great parade of Moslem prayers and supplications, and steered for Constantinople, after having lost 400 sailors in Crete; and the only captives it carried away in triumph from Crete consisted of one woman of 60 years of age, taken at the village of Provarma, and two children taken at Armeni.

In addition to the other calamities which the war of independence brought on Crete, the plague was imported by the Egyptian troops recently arrived. The Turks suffered more than the Christians from this scourge, as the former use no precaution against the spread of contagious or infectious epidemics, and consider as a matter of faith that death from such causes is ordained and inevitable. They were moreover in more immediate connection with the Egyptians. The malady spread to a great extent, owing to the crowding of large multitudes within the walls of fortresses, the air itself thus becoming pestiferous. The number who perished under such circumstances were proportionably greater than otherwise might have been.

The pestilence made fearful ravage among the Turks confined in the town of Rethymno, who, besides the sufferings thus inflicted, were incessantly harassed by the hostile operations of Greeks in the environs. These sometimes presented themselves almost under the walls and challenged the Turks to battle, and at other times kept them in alarm by frequent ambuscades. The Turks, roused by these proceedings, frequently made sallies, but always returned with loss. They soon began, however, to imitate the operations of the Greeks, and attempted ambuscades in their turn. On one occasion, about 80 Turks from Rethymno proceeded as far as the village of Kastelon, but were driven back by nearly an equal number of Greeks, suddenly collected from the neighbouring villages. Seventeen of the Turks were killed in this affair, and the rest pursued nearly to the walls of the fortress. In the villages above mentioned and the vicinity, the Greeks more frequently assumed the offensive, so that skirmishes and mutual ambuscades were of daily occurrence. In one of these encounters, during the month of October, a party of Greeks fell into a Turkish ambuscade near the village of Armeni, and lost about 20 of their number, including Deliyannakes. Many similar encounters took place also in the vicinity of Rethymno.

The military chief Georgios Deliyannakes was a native of the mountainous province of Sphakia and of the village of Asphendi. Soon after the commencement of the war of independence he was, on account of his capacity, valour, and military experience promoted to the rank of pentacosiarkhos, then conferred by the Cretan Board as the reward of distinguished services. He was a man of great self-respect, with high feelings of honour, courteous bearing, always conciliatory in his intercourse with persons of all ranks, and at pains to gain the respect and attachment of the soldiers, with whom he thereby often achieved brilliant exploits. At the time of his death G. Deliyannakes was about 30 years of age.

The successive loss of her most able military leaders was a great misfortune to Crete, as they were always the first to meet danger and take the lead in circumstances which required skilful direction and united command for the success of military operations. The common soldiers were always ready to follow with alacrity favourite leaders, though they had nothing to recommend them but superior valour and enterprise. None of the leaders could give pay to his followers, as the local government was destitute of funds, so that popularity with the army was the only means by which a leader could collect and control his troops, and lead them to victory. While the successive loss of the ablest military leaders was very distinctly felt, their followers were not as yet impressed with the conviction that their own safety, success and glory ever depend on the safety of an able leader, whom it is their interest to watch over with constant solicitude, and preserve from danger. In this, however, they resembled the Cretan Turks, for among them, too, the most able leaders were constantly exposing themselves to the greatest danger, and successively dropping off.

This appears to be the appropriate place for mentioning the recent proceedings of Aphentules, Eparch-General of Crete. We shall prefix a few words relating to his previous history.

Michael Aphentules was the son of an Asiatic Greek, and born at Nisna, a town in Russia. On growing up he had for many years, it is said, served as steward in the house of Tatikhef, the Russian ambassador in Spain; and afterwards accompanied him to Vienna in the same capacity. During the Congress of Vienna Aphentules was sent to St. Petersburgh, as bearer of despatches to the Emperor of Russia. This commission was the only public service he ever held under the Russian Government. At the commencement of the Greek war of independence in 1821, he accompanied Alexander Kantacuzenos to Greece. Happening

to be in his suite at the capitulation of the fortress of Monemvasia, he was apprised of the invitation Kantacuzenos
received from the Cretans to accept the Government of their
island.   On Kantacuzenos' declining the honour, Aphentules
contrived, in the manner already mentioned, to procure the
appointment for himself, and, proceeding soon afterwards to
Lutros in Sphakia, was accepted by the Cretans.   Though
in reality self-elected, he appeared in Crete as military
Commander-in-chief and Civil Governor-General.

Aphentules, on his arrival, found the Cretan insurgents
animated with the utmost ardour, and fully determined to
shake off the yoke of oppression.   They had already gained
numerous victories, and they were now in a condition to
achieve others still more important, had Aphentules, whom
they now put at the head of affairs, possessed honesty and
capacity for his position; but, as we have already seen, he,
from the very outset, committed both blunders and atrocities,
such as his assassination of Semertsakes, his treachery to
Valestras, and other delinquencies, to which he was prompted
by a suspicion that the individuals whom he cut off wished
to deprive him of his office

He was, moreover, dissatisfied with the new order of things
introduced by the Assembly at Armeni, in accordance with
the national constitution; as the new arrangement gave
others a share of the authority, which he desired to retain
for himself alone.   His dissatisfaction produced at Prosneron
dissensions between him and the Secretary-General, whom
he pretended to treat as a mere subaltern, bound to obey
without having the right of judging and deciding for himself
on affairs relating to his own department; whereas, the new
constitution gave the latter authority to decide and act in
co-operation with the Eparch-General, instead of merely executing that functionary's decisions.   Aphentules, agreeably
to his pretensions, published the following proclamation on
the 8th of July, a most critical moment for Crete, from the
impending danger caused by the arrival of Egyptian troops.
He was about to visit Peloponnesus, and the object of his
proclamation was to excite public indignation against certain
individuals, in connexion with the cause of his departure.
Ho admitted that Peloponnesus had been reduced to the
greatest extremities by the invasion of Dramalis; and such
being the case, he could not expect to find there the public
functionaries at leisure to consult with them, or able to give

L

him the supplies and assistance which he assured the Cretans he was going to bring. The proclamation was as follows :—

TO THE VENERABLE CLERGY, THE NOBLE PENTACOSIARKHI, GALLANT COMMANDERS, WITH ALL OTHER OFFICERS AND SOLDIERS OF THE PATRIOT ARMY, AND TO THE HONORABLE COMMISSARIES, WITH ALL OTHER CHRISTIAN BRETHREN IN CRETE, GREETING—

The existing state of public affairs peremptorily requires me to leave my post for a brief space, and to hasten for a few days to Peloponnesus. This short voyage, though arduous and irksome to me, is absolutely required for our interests.

Both your welfare and the satisfaction of my own conscience require me to repair to Nauplia (a,) to consult with the Central Authorities and the members of the National Parliament, and to see that due measures be adopted on various matters relating to Crete, and I have no doubt that the result of my exertions will be satisfactory to the Patriots of Crete, great and small.

Do not imagine that I am quitting Crete from personal fear (to such a feeling, thank God, I am a stranger). I came among you, not to abandon you in the hour of difficulty or of danger, as the hireling leaves his flock, when the wolves are coming to devour or disperse it. No, brethren, there is at present nothing to fear.

As, however, I cannot procure you the supplies and aid you require, and as I am sure of obtaining these at once at head quarters, I feel it my duty to absent myself from you for a few days, in order to make your situation known, and to return forthwith to my post. Entertain no apprehension that I have the slightest intention of not returning to Crete.

I require and implore you all in the name of the Most High to be up and doing, and I trust that during my absence each of you will discharge his duty to his country with even greater zeal and diligence than if I were present, thus evincing, to my great delight, the sincerity and fervour of your attachment to your country

In due time I shall take care to represent the services of all deserving patriots to the Central Authorities and the National Parliament of Greece, who will, without doubt, express their sense of them in due terms. (b.) Prosneron, 9th July (o.s.) 1822.

MICHAEL KOMNENOS APHENTULIEY, Eparch-General.

(a) Nauplia was taken by the Greeks on the 30th November (St. Andrews day), 1822 (o.s.) At the date of this proclamation it was still in the hands of the Turks, but the Greek Government was in the vicinity.

(b) See "Regeneration of Greece," Vol. I. No. 181.

Soon after this Hassan Pasha took the field with the whole of his forces, threatening general destruction and desolation. This obliged the . Cretan Administration to remove from Prosneron to Sphakia. Aphentulea, however, took refuge on board the vessel of Scalisteres of Khios (Chios), which he always had at hand and in his service. The other members of the Administration remained at Prosyalos, which is called the chief town (Khora) of Sphakia, and preserved the shadow at least of a Government in Crete during the crisis in question.

When, as we have already mentioned, the Pasha marched in force to the Eastern parts of Crete, the Administration proceeded on board the vessel of Valsamakes to Kaloi Limenes of Gortyna, for the purpose of establishing order and encouraging the insurgents there. But on that occasion, too, Aphentules, the Eparch-General, after remaining a few days at Pompeia, returned on board, while the other members of the Administration advanced into the interior, and remained for many days at the village of Gregorias, where they continued to exert themselves to promote the national cause, and corresponded with the Eparch-General, who remained in security on board of ship at Kaloi Limenes.

But even while he remained at that place he continued to display the same restless ambition and tortuous policy which had marked the whole of his career in Crete, and which had led him incessantly into blunders and delinquencies. Sometimes he had acted with great duplicity towards the Cretan authorities in general, and undermined certain members of the Administration in particular. Sometimes he sowed dissension between the Anopolitae and the rest of the Sphakians to such an extent as to be on the point of producing a disastrous conflict, and such a calamity would have actually taken place, had not the two parties discovered in time the craft of Aphentules, and come to a reconciliation.

This policy of Aphentules may be attributed to that sort of cunning which usually implies a want of capacity and discretion, and, at the same time, to unprincipled ambition. We record these details, as we think them highly instructive to those who are in danger of entrusting their highest interests and their very existence to untried men, or, we should rather say, we consider the facts in question as a warning to those who are not at pains to place at the head of affairs natives already known and tried, men having an interest at stake, and from genuine patriotism devoted to their country's welfare,—men determined to live and die on their native soil, and thus in every respect infinitely better fitted to consult its public interests and direct its public affairs than strangers. We regret to add that, as will be seen in the sequel, the Cretans did not take a warning from their experience in connexion with Aphentules.

Such then was the state of affairs when the Cretan Administration returned to Sphakia about the middle of October. Hassan Pasha had made exterminating inroads into the Eastern Provinces of Crete, and especially into Gortyna, for the purpose of crushing the armed force under Kurmulca, which in those parts maintained the most formidable resistance. Aphentules landed at Lutros, and from that place addressed to Kurmules and to other military leaders such communications as were fitted to excite among them mutual jealousy, and set them at variance. Meanwhile the other members of the Administration continued their stay at Prosyalos, and under existing circumstances they considered it their duty to send to the Central Government an account of the state of affairs in Crete. They accordingly sent a deputation to present a memorial, a copy of which is subjoined, to complain of the conduct of the Eparch General, and to implore aid from the Central authorities towards averting the impending danger apprehended from the movements of the enemy.

PROVISIONAL GOVERNMENT OF CRETE.

To His Excellency Joannes Koletter,

Minister of the Interior, and *Interim* Minister of War.

After the communications we submitted to your Excellency, dated the 4th and 14th of July, and the 15th of August respectively, containing detailed accounts of the exigencies of this island, and suggesting the means, that would enable us to avert impending dangers, it would be superfluous to repeat the same statements in our present memorial. We, therefore, refer you to our previous communications, and briefly add, that as the Eparch-General insists on resigning his post, we send a special deputation consisting of Anagnostes Panayotu, Georgios Papadakes, Nicolaos Andreu, Emmanuel Antoniades, and Anagnostes Ieronymakes, as representatives of this island, and we direct them to request that another Eparch-General of Crete be immediately appointed, and to represent the urgent necessity of assistance to enable the inhabitants of Crete to meet the great impending dangers.

We consider it superfluous to enter into details, as our representatives now sent, will furnish you by word of mouth with any information required; and as the Cretans entrust them with full power to act and decide in their behalf at the present crisis, and as from personal experience and observation they are accurately acquainted with our affairs, and fully understood our interests, we entreat your Excellency to recognize them as duly authorized, and entirely competent representatives of Crete, and to present them as such to all the other members of the Central Government, and to comply with their reasonable suggestions and requests: and lastly, when you receive from them full and accurate information of the state of our affairs, to adopt the necessary measures in behalf of Crete, thus showing, that you are really interested in her preservation, and that you desire to have her co-operation in the common struggle for the National Independence of Greece.

In submitting these statements and requests to your Excellency, we sign our memorial with the most profound respect.

Sphakia, 29th October (o.s.) 1822.

N. Œconomos, Secretary-General.
Emm. Antoniades, First Clerk.

Georgios Protopapas of Sphakia, Georgios Papadakes. Kh. Ioannes, Androuledakes, Kh. Strates Burdumbakes, Sephes Kukutsakes, Pappa Andreas Scordiles, Kh. Strates Delevanakes, Anagnostes Panayotes, Manases Ex-Abbot, Anagnostes Ieronymakes, Georgios Sacorrhaphos, Andreas Kriarakets, Nicolaos Andreas, Commissary-General.

The deputation took their departure forthwith, but were driven back by contrary winds to Lutros, where they found Georgios Kalamaras* a native of Crete, who had just arrived with several other persons from Hydra.

* Georgios Kalamaras was born in the town of Haylos Thomas in the Province of Gortyna. Fond of learning from his infancy, he went at an early age to Smyrna, where he studied the elements of Greek literature as then taught. He subsequently availed himself of an opportunity of going to Russia, and, through his talents and acquirements, was admitted into the University of St. Petersburg, and there studied the mathematical and physical sciences, devoting special attention to navigation. He was acquainted with Russian and French, as well as Italian, which he spoke and wrote with great ease and accuracy. Owing to his acquaintance with nautical science he afterwards obtained a commission in the Russian Navy, and having attracted notice by his attainments and conduct, and distinguished himself in several naval engagements, he received the order of St. George. He was promoted to the rank of Captain of a frigate, with the right of commanding a vessel of that size in the fleet.

We shall submit to the reader a few interesting details from the biography of this officer. When a Russian squadron, in which Kalamaras served under the command of Leles, was in 1805 or 1806, during the war between Russia and Turkey, despatched to the Ionian islands, it captured an enemy's vessel, on board of which was found, among other articles of merchandise, a quantity of Indian shawls, which were proved to belong to a Greek merchant in Constantinople. In passing judgment on this prize Kalamaras persisted in maintaining that the shawls ought not to be confiscated, though he was directed by the Commander to declare them a lawful prize. At length he was obliged to give in.

On the return of the squadron to St. Petersburgh, Leles brought Kalamaras before a Court-Martial on a charge of insubordination. On appearing in the Court he was not desired by the judges to sit down, an honour to which his knighthood entitled him, but was examined standing. When asked why he had not obeyed the orders of his Commander, "Because," he replied with firmness and emphasis—"When one acts as a judge he is to consult none but God and his conscience." At the same time he deviated from the Russian custom of mentioning the name of the Emperor. He then complained to the judges of not having been allowed to sit down agreeably to the right his rank conferred; and being a person of great excitability and impulse he, very improperly, struck the table with his fist.

In consequence of all this he was condemned to death. His sword was instantly broken over his head, and he was on the point of being sent to Siberia, when the Minister of the Navy, who had a great regard for Kalamaras on account of his distinguished merit, postponed the execution of the

Acquainted with the previous history of Aphontulos, and
having ascertained how he had conducted himself in Crete,

latter part of the sentence, and afterwards, during Napoleon's memorable
expedition to Moscow, employed every means to obtain for him a complete
pardon. Kalamaras thus remained at St. Petersburgh. When, after a suc-
cession of victories, the Emperor repaired to Vienna, and afterwards to
Paris, Kalamaras accompanied him, and thus had an opportunity of perceiving and studying the great events of that remarkable period, and of
greatly improving himself in knowledge of the world, and of adding to
his attainments. At Paris, through the intercession of friends, he obtained
a complete pardon, but was never restored to his rank, or admitted to any
Russian service. Without fortune, and having a wife and family to
support, he then removed to Jassy to find a livelihood, and announced,
through the "Loyios Hermes," his intention of giving instruction in
navigation. The Greek insurrection, however, having broken out shortly
afterwards, he immediately joined Hypsilantes, who appointed him one of
his principal counsellors, in consideration of his great acquirements and
experience. He now addressed a letter to his wife, Anna, a native of Corfu,
and, on account of his present rank, gave her, as he used to do formerly,
the title of *Excellency*. To this letter his wife, who was at that time in
extreme destitution, wittily replied, "I read thy letter, and understood from
it that I am restored to the dignity of Excellency, though I am in want of
daily bread." After the termination of the insurrection in the Principalities, Kalamaras proceeded to Greece, and arrived at Corinth after the
establishment of the National Government there. He received great
attention from Alexandros Mavrocordatos, who duly appreciated his great
attainments and sagacity. Here he was for some time employed in the
department of police, and showed great ability in discharging the duties of
the Minister of Police, Andreas Metaxas, then absent. From Corinth he
wrote a second time to his wife, giving her again the title of Excellency, on
account of the position he held. His wife again wittily replied, "I perceive from your letter that I am still *my Excellency, and still without bread.*"

Kalamaras afterwards, as we have already stated, proceeded to Crete.
Acquainted with the previous history of Aphontulos, as well as with his
conduct in Crete, he contributed to Aphontules' removal, and was sent as
one of the deputation to the Central Government to urge measures in
behalf of Crete. Returning to Kisamos, he guided Tombazes in taking
the fortress of Kisamos, as we shall by and by see, and Tombazes would
have rendered much more important services to Crete, had he duly availed
himself of Kalamaras's knowledge and experience.

When in 1823 it was proposed to invite some prince to become King of
Greece, and the Central Government required the consent of Crete as an
integral portion of the Panhellenium, Kalamaras was employed on the
part of the Cretans to draw up the official reply on the subject, which
contained judicious and important observations under existing circumstances, and was duly appreciated by the Greek public, and produced a
very considerable impression. "Which of the Kings of Europe (said the
Cretans in their reply) are acquainted with this proposal, and are agreed
to carry it into effect? Is it approved by the Western Powers, and in
particular by England? If it is not, then, the inhabitants of Crete beg leave
to state to the Central Government, that they cannot give their consent
to a proposal not approved and supported by England and France, and
that they prefer to act independently, trusting the destinies of Crete to the
protection of Heaven."

Such was Georgios Kalamaras, an excellent mathematician, a distinguished
navigator, a man of great bravery, and an ardent lover of liberty. As
counsellor he was fitted to render inestimable services to his country, but

he, too, recommended as the most expedient course under
the circumstances that the Cretans should set him aside, and
immediately inform the government on the subject. He
was, accordingly, deposed through the following document.
The deputation set off for Peloponnesus, accompanied by
Kalamaras, who had been invested with the same power as
the other representatives of Crete. Such, at length, was
the end of Aphentules' career in Crete, an end caused by his
own indiscretion and misconduct, the details of which we
have already recorded. The document was as follows :—

PROVISIONAL GOVERNMENT OF CRETE.

The sound of Grecian liberty echoed delightfully in our ears, our resolution to be free will remain unshaken, and the love of our country glows in our hearts. The cruel oppression we endure, has made us rush to arms with boundless enthusiasm, determined to prefer honourable death to bondage.

Engaging in this arduous struggle, we felt from the commencement the necessity of having an able and experienced leader. We, accordingly, with perfect sincerity, sent a deputation to Peloponnesus, where as we have been informed, many accomplished and distinguished Greeks had arrived from Western Europe. Deceived, however, by impostors, we had the misfortune to give our confidence to absurd pretensions and false insignia, and placed at the head of the affairs of our beloved island Michael Aphentulief, an individual whom chance threw in our way, and who had assumed, without any right, the borrowed name of Kommenos.

To him we intrusted with perfect sincerity the task of guiding us in our efforts to achieve our emancipation. On trial, however, he soon proved his utter incapacity for the high and responsible position assigned him, but manifested an utter want of attachment to the national cause, a spirit of intrigue and turbulence, and a character utterly incompatible with honour and order, and fitted only to mar our glorious struggle. All this will appear in the sequel.

We will not detail the lawless, selfish, and base manœuvres he employed, and the atrocious means to which he had recourse for the purpose of detaching Crete from the rest of the Greek nation; neither will we enumerate all his unprincipled attempts, after he had been compelled to submit to national unity according to the decision of the Panhellenic Parliament, to excite dissensions and conflicts among the other members of the Cretan

---

as he was unfortunately very excitable and impulsive, he could not be safely trusted with the uncontrolled direction of affairs. Kanellos Vyzantios and Panayotes Nicolaides of Smyrna, well-known men of letters, used to say of Kalamaras "He is an inestimable treasure and a man of great and varied attainments, yet, owing to his reckless impulsiveness he ought to be shut up in a room with all necessaries for his subsistence, and should be used for dispensing advice and direction to all that wish to derive advantage from his remarkable acquirements and rare sagacity." Kalamaras died in Hydra in 1823, being then about 60 years of age. He was seized with a pleurisy, and through poverty died from the want of necessary comforts and attention.

Administration. We will not dwell on the artifices he frequently employed to mislead our military leaders regarding the provisions of the constitution; nor how often he endangered its existence; nor specify all the occasions, on which enlightened and earnest patriots were compelled to withstand him to the face. We will merely mention a small proportion of his flagrantly lawless and base proceedings.

1.—To our amazement we perceive that he has been using in this island a seal called *Royal*, entirely unknown to the Government.

2.—He has issued official letters and orders with his own signature alone, in defiance of the express provisions of our Constitutional Charter.

3.—He has given portions of the public property of Crete without the knowledge of the inhabitants to foreign merchants for his own ends, having for instance given silver plate to Joannes Vlakhos, and other articles of public property to others.

4.—He has received sums of money for cargoes of oil, and retained them without giving any account. He has also received patriotic contributions for the public service without acquainting therewith the Commissaries-General of Finance, and has appropriated them, as, for instance, at Platanias, Mossaria, Lutros, and elsewhere.

5.—He has violated all legal arrangements fitted to promote order and prosperity in the island, and has sown among the inhabitants the seeds of dissension, and in particular, he has employed numberless artifices to excite the people against the Authorities, as well as against influential and honourable patriots.

6.—He has in his daily intercourse with foreigners endeavoured to dishonour and vituperate the whole Greek nation, as well as the local administration of Crete, and has incessantly and unjustly maligned the members of the Administration.

7.—He has without the knowledge of the public Authorities received from different persons absurd and illegal protests, got up by himself for the purpose of doing grievous harm to this island, besides other illegal and criminal proceedings.

Whereas we have ascertained by sad experience from the facts to which we refer, and numberless others of a similar nature, that he is destitute of the sentiments and principles indispensable in a leading public functionary, that he is void of honour and truthfulness as a man, that he has no respect for our nation, no regard for the obligation of an oath, no consideration for the Local Government, and that he is at the same time without capacity:

Whereas, moreover, he, for known purposes, has, since the 16th of May to the present day, continued to tender his resignation, and secretly circulated letters intended to mislead the unsuspecting people:

The Local Administration of this island, watching over the public interests, and desirous of preventing disastrous consequences which would arise from such proceedings if any longer permitted, hereby proclaims to the Panhellenium, and in particular to the inhabitants of this island, natives or sojourners:

That Michael Komnenos Apheutulief, hitherto Eparch-General of Crete, is hereby debarred from all interference with the affairs of this island:

That none of his proceedings, except such as were legal and constitutional, are recognized as binding:

That he will sojourn in the island as a private individual, till the arrival of a successor, to be appointed by the Central Government of Greece:

And whereas his intentions have on various occasions been manifestly criminal and dangerous in the extreme, and his proceedings towards carrying them into effect, have constituted the crime of high treason, we in behalf of our country have determined to take from him all public documents in his possession, excepting those that may be entirely personal to himself, if such be found; and have ordered that all effects and sums of money now in his possession shall be sequestrated and sealed with his seal, and that of the Administration; and that a list of all writings and effects in question shall be drawn up, and shall be signed by him, and by the principal Secretary of the Cretan Administration, and that he himself shall remain in honourable custody wherever it may be deemed proper, till the Central Government issue its orders on the subject, and that then he shall be allowed to leave the island after giving a strict account of his administration:

That no document or order issued by him from this date shall have any public authority or validity whatever in this island.

The Cretan Administration has in the meantime, adopted all necessary measures for the direction of the public affairs of this island, and has sent a deputation to the Central Government, requesting it to appoint a new Eparch-General, and grant all possible aid for the success of the national cause in Crete.

The Secretary-General of the Cretan Administration shall communicate a copy of this solemn act of dismissal and deposition to the Panhellenic Parliament, deliver another to the said Michael Komnenos Aphentulief, and shall send copies of it throughout the island to make it duly known to all the inhabitants, and the original shall be preserved in the Archives of the Cretan Administration for the ends of justice.

Sphakia, 15th November (o.s.) 1822.

NEOPHYTOS ŒCONOMOS, Secretary-General

EMMANUEL ANTONIADES, First Clerk.

(Then follow the other signatures, as in the preceding document).

The Cretan deputation arrived on the 18th of November at Hermione, to which the Central Government had retired on account of Dramales' invasion; and, after presenting their commissions to the Minister of the Interior, fully explained to him by word of mouth the state of affairs in Crete. They had a second interview with the same Minister on the 28th, urging on the attention of the Government the necessity of immediately appointing some person of character and capacity to supersede Aphentules in the Government of Crete, and proposed as a very suitable individual, Emanuel Tombazes of Hydra, leaving his appointment to the discretion of the Government. The Cretans, in proposing Tombazes were influenced by a sense of the importance of securing the aid and support of one of the Naval Islands to the Cretan cause, and they preferred Hydra on account of its pre-eminent influence in the affairs of Greece, through its superiority in wealth and naval strength.

We now return for a brief space to the state of matters in
the Eastern Provinces of Crete, where Hassan Pasha since
his arrival in Knossos about the beginning of September, had
continued to display the utmost energy and cruelty. Having
remained encamped for about 15 days near Heracleion and
the village of Tellison, he daily despatched powerful detachments of cavalry and infantry to make inroads, sometimes
into Gortyna, and sometimes into other parts, capturing and
slaughtering, without mercy, large numbers of unarmed and
helpless Christians. The rest of the insurgents, still mostly
unarmed, owing to the great want of arms in Crete, and
having but recently joined the insurrection, and therefore
still unaccustomed to warfare, were thrown into the greatest
consternation. They were, as a matter of course, obliged to
give way before the overwhelming forces of the enemy, and
from inexperience had not the foresight to fortify the strong
position of Lasiti, which they might have rendered a safe
retreat for the helpless members of their families. Such entire want of foresight was displayed not only by the insurgents of Knossos, but had unfortunately been manifested in
many other parts of Crete. In almost every part of the
island there existed retreats of difficult access, which, with a
little foresight and energy, might have been rendered impregnable, and yet were entirely overlooked. Through this
neglect many myriads were captured or perished.

The position in question, called Siti or Lasiti, is a broad,
fertile, and wooded valley, abounding in water, and surrounded by lofty and rugged mountains, having Gortyna,
Knossos, and Kherrhonesos on the north-west, and on the east
Minoa, Siteia, and Hierapytnos; and these mountains are
everywhere impassable, with the exception of two or three
very narrow and very dangerous defiles. Had the insurgents
fortified these passes with breast works, as they had plenty of
time to do, a few troops could have easily prevented the
march of the most numerous hostile force. Thus the insurgents might have, within this valley, remained in perfect
safety, and set the enemy at defiance, had they not been entirely without warlike experience, as well as unjustifiably
abandoned by their more warlike brethren in arms; and,
Hassan Pasha, instead of being enabled to cause such inex-
pressible calamities, would have failed in his enterprise here
as signally as he had failed in his attempts to suppress the
insurrection in the west.

From Knossos Hassan Pasha marched with all his forces
to the province of Kherrhonesos or Pedias, and encamped in
and around the villages of Malia and Kastelli. Here, however, about 2,000 Greeks, under the command of Anagnostes
Kuskumbes, Nicolaos Zervos, Emmanuel Lutsakos, Konstantinos Stakakes, Rusakes Khurdos, Vusomarcos and others,
were stationed around the villages Krasi, Audos, Mokhos, and
even at Kastamonissa, and prevented the enemy from advancing on Site (or Lasition), a position which the Turkish
commander was as eager to occupy, as he had been to get
possession of the strong position of Malaxa in the west. A
very obstinate engagement ensued. After a conflict which
lasted many hours, the Greeks, greatly aided by the advantageous nature of their positions, rushed on the Turkish
forces and put them to flight, killing a number of horses,
capturing flags, slaying upwards of 100 men, besides
making a number of prisoners. On the side of the Greeks,
about 15 were killed, and a considerable number, including
Vusomarcos and Georgios Critovulides, wounded.

Having failed in this attempt, Hassan Pasha resolved to
attack the Greeks from other points; and a few days after this,
suddenly encamped on the other side of the province of
Arcadia, at the site of the ancient city of Vienne, where the
present town of Viannon stands. During a stay of nearly a
month here, he continued to send out frequent detachments
of cavalry and infantry to the neighbouring mountains, who,
with unrelenting ferocity, slaughtered or captured great numbers of Greeks, and desolated the country. These atrocities
at length showed the insurgents in those parts the necessity
of seeking a safe retreat among the inaccessible mountains of
Lasition, and thus save themselves from utter destruction.
Hassan Pasha, on his part, sustained considerable loss during
his stay at Viannon, as detachments of Greeks frequently
attacked bodies of his troops in advantageous situations,
with which the latter were unacquainted, and often killed
great numbers of them. This at length compelled him to
return to Kherrhonesos and encamp on nearly the same spot
as before. He again remained there several days.

The Pasha now determined to have again recourse to artifice, and what he had not been able to accomplish in the
Western parts of Crete by promises alone, and an affectation
of kindness, he now tried to achieve here by a mixture of
severity and policy. The greater part of the Lasitiot moun-

taineers, either overwhelmed by a sense of the dangers to which they were exposed, or deceived by fallacious promises, unexpectedly presented themselves in October to Hassan, to express their regret for having taken part in the insurrection. These Hassan cunningly received with great appearance and profession of kindness, in order to make use of them in promoting his ultimate object.   The submission of these mountaineers excited the indignation of all the rest of the Cretans, who, in the same way that they regarded Sphakia as the great asylum, and its inhabitants as the champions of liberty, in the west, looked on the Lasitiots as the defenders of the national cause in the east, and counted greatly on the strength of their position, their natural valour, and their singular fleetness of foot, as fitted to be of great importance in times of danger.   The submission of the Lasitiots, however, did not produce the harm that was at first apprehended, as many of the rest of the inhabitants who had been dispersed by the presence of the enemy, were soon again collected, and were daily joined by warlike veterans from Sphakia, Kydonia, and Rethymne, and subsequently reinforced by nearly the whole of the auxiliaries.   Thus strengthened, the Lasitiots recovered courage, and the Greek forces now in these parts made frequent attacks on the enemy on different points, sometimes harassing them by sending out small parties, and sometimes by combined attacks.

Towards the end of November another squadron of the Viceroy's, consisting of about 15 vessels of war, arrived from Egypt, and besides landing provisions and warlike stores for the fortresses of Rethymne and Heracleion, brought Hassan Pasha a reinforcement of about 1500 fresh troops.   This squadron arrived in Crete and returned to Alexandria in safety, not having encountered in either voyage any Greek vessels of war.   The arrival of these supplies and reinforcements further dismayed the Cretan insurgents, as they now perceived that their enemy, or rather, the powerful enemy of all Greece, was able to transport fresh supplies and reinforcements at pleasure, and thus gradually accomplish the suppression of the Greek insurrection, and, as Lord Palmerston expressed it, "rivet for ever the fetters of the whole Greek race."

CHAPTER IV.

On the 1st of December the Central Government of
Greece, then at Hermione, appointed the Secretary-General,
N. Œconomos, *Interim* Director of the affairs of Crete
till the arrival of the Eparch-General about to be selected.
N. Œconomos immediately repaired from Sphakia to Armeni,
in Apocoronos, as a more central and convenient position for
the exercise of his functions, and, by a proclamation, acquainted the inhabitants of Crete with his appointment,
adding a communication from the Cretan deputation to the
effect that Emanuel Tombazes was to be the future Governor
of Crete, a piece of intelligence which caused great joy in
Crete, it being understood that through his influence the
island of Hydra would furnish naval assistance to the Cretan
cause. As N. Œconomos was generally respected as a worthy
man and sincere patriot, all the inhabitants of Crete readily
submitted to his authority.

Almost simultaneously with these events intelligence
reached Crete that on the 30th of November the almost impregnable fortresses of Nauplia had surrendered to the
Greek forces. Œconomos lost no time in making known
throughout Crete the joyous news, which greatly animated
the enthusiasm of the insurgents, and inspired them with a
determination to rival or surpass the exploits of their
brethren in Peloponnesus. In fact, at all times the Cretans
had their eyes fixed on their fellow-combatants in other parts
of Greece, in the spirit of noble emulation; and they had
ventured to commence the contest unaided and alone, and
their arms had often been crowned with victory, though the
advantages they had obtained were of far less permanent
importance than recent events in Peloponnesus. V. Halles
in concert with Siphacas, was now prompted to suggest a
plan for capturing the fortress of Kydonia; and owing to
the state of the fortress, and the season of the year, which
was winter, his plan was perfectly practicable, had it not

been for an apprehension of its failure through want of discipline among the troops, and of the disastrous consequences of a failure. Besides, there was no person in Creto fitted to direct such an enterprise. The late Valestras, in whom the Cretans had placed great hopes in connexion with such enterprises, on account of his military skill and experience, had, as we have already mentioned, fallen a victim to the intrigues of Aphentules. These considerations, and the want of a naval force to co-operate in the undertaking, deterred V. Halles from the attempt. Other leaders, as we shall see, attempted, about the same time, to take Hierapytnos, and would have succeeded, had not disorder and confusion, the inseparable companions of an undisciplined army, marred the enterprise.

During this period none of the Turks of Kydonia ventured to make any sallies either from the fortress of Kydonia or from Suda. Hassan Pasha had taken a large portion of them with him on removing thence to the eastern parts of the island, and others had repaired by sea to Kisamos, to escape from the plague, of which great numbers wore dying. The fortress was thus left with a very defective garrison. Œconomos, however, turned the attention of the above mentioned military chiefs in another direction, representing the expediency and necessity of driving, with all possible speed, the Turks from Kisamos and Selinon, to enable the new Governor of Creto, whose arrival was daily expected, to land and take up his abode in those parts. He, further, induced A: Panayotes to give his cordial consent to the plan, and, accordingly, preparations wore instantly commenced for an expedition to the provinces of Selinon and Kisamos. The enterprise urged by Œconomos was very judicious, and its object was to deliver nearly the whole of the inhabitants of Creto from the indescribable sufferings they had been enduring for upwards of three years, having no mart for the purchase of necessaries and the sale of their produce but Latros in Sphakia.

He, accordingly, convened, not only the above mentioned leaders, but also Rasos, M. Papadakes, Suderos. and Poloyoryakes, who were to take part in the expedition, to deliberate on the measures to be adopted to secure its success. The enterprise required circumspection and mature reflection, as the enemy about to be encountered possessed natural bravery, military skill, and strong positions, from which they had repelled previous attacks.

The importance of the enterprise was enhanced by the circumstance that the arrival of the new Governor with reinforcements would strike the enemy with greater respect if he landed at Kisamos or Selinon, than if he went to the mountainous Sphakia, which was only at the commencement of the war suitable head-quarters. Though the reasons which influenced Œconomos in urging this expedition were well founded, he would, however, had he possessed a greater amount of daring and enterprise, have employed the large army now collected in attempting to execute the project which Halles still persisted in preferring.

It was, at length decided, that the expedition to Kisamos should be carried into effect, and in January, 1823, the whole united Greek army, now so formidable as to amount to about 5,000 men, marched from the province of Kydonia on the 3rd of February, across the winter-flowing river Tavronites into Kisamos. The Turks stationed at the villages of Polemarkhi and Vucoliæ made a vigorous but unavailing resistance, for they were soon compelled to shut themselves up, and were blockaded by a detachment of Greeks; while the rest of the Greek army overran, without resistance, the whole province. Part of the dispersed Turks saved themselves with difficulty, by reaching that day some towers in the neghbourhood, while others fled in great haste to the fortresses of Kisamos and Grambusa, and others, intercepted in scattered parties in the plain, were killed. Thus, in one day, the Greeks made themselves masters of the whole province, and next morning commenced a vigorous attack on the towers still held by the enemy. Some of the towers were destroyed by mines, and all within them perished. About 300 Turks, consisting of men, women, and children, were killed in other towers, which for some time continued to hold out. About 500 other Turks, partly combatants, and partly not, were blockaded for some days in the villages of Vucoliæ and Polemarkhi. The whole of these would have perished, if the blockade had been conducted with due order, and if the besiegers had not been diverted by pursuing, for the sake of spoil, such of the besieged as attempted during the night, to effect their escape, either to the fortress of Kydonia or to that of Kisamos.

Four or five days after these events some of the military leaders met at the village called Trialonia, to deliberate how and from what point an attack could be most effectually made on the more mountainous province of Selinon, where the Turks were still more formidable, both on account of their natural valour and their strong positions. Notwithstanding the difficulties to be encountered, so numerous and so warlike were the Greek forces now assembled here, that they might have destroyed even these Turkish mountaineers, had not the greater part of the Greek army gone away from Kisamos, hastening to secure the booty they had recently obtained, and to carry provisions to their starving families, who were living in other provinces, then in a state of desolation. The remaining part of the Greek army was obliged to confine itself to the possession of Kisamos, without attempting the intended invasion of Selinon. Such are the ordinary results of the want of discipline in an army. The most favourable opportunities may be lost, if an army be not under due control, and adequately furnished with supplies by an active and provident Government.

N. Œconomos, accompanying the army, established his head-quarters at the monastery of Gonia, and thence adopted all possible measures for the security of the Province of Kisamos. He gave orders that the siege of the fortress should be instantly commenced, and gave the command of the blockading force to Manoles Protopapadakes, leader of the Skyphiots and Apocoronites, but who, on account of his youth, acted under the guidance of his uncle Polios Protopapadakes. Œconomos, further, directed Michael Mavrakes at the head of Mesoyanni,* to blockade the island of Grambusa, and appointed Martinianos Perakes and Georgios Draconianos, military leaders for Kisamos. The latter, at the head of the Kisamitæ, who had lately taken up arms, unremittingly assisted in the above mentioned blockades. Kisamos was thus added to the liberated Provinces of Crete, and the results of the expedition were officially communicated by Œconomos to the Central Government of Greece.

Œconomos, besides exhibiting such activity by land, directed his attention at the same time to the necessary measures required at sea, to hasten the accomplishment of his present aim. Considering it of the utmost importance that the Turks in the above mentioned fortresses should be blockaded by a naval force, acting in concert with the army,

* Mesoyela is a district of Kisamos, and comprehends five or six villages in the western part of that province, and situated opposite Grambusa to the east.

be made an agreement, either through the Cretan Deputation
or otherwise, for the services of two vessels of war, the
brig of Ioannes Macromuras of Hydra, and the Zambec of
Tombazes, the latter being commanded by Paraskevas
Samios, and the former by its proprietor. These naval
commanders, according to the agreement, began at once to
maintain such a blockade by sea, that all communication,
not only between the two besieged fortresses, but between
these and that of Kydonia, was at once stopped. The
expense of the vessels was defrayed by the sale of the oil
belonging to the Turks in Kisamos, that had fallen into the
hands of the Greeks. Crete possessed indeed great resources,
but it would have been necessary to have them husbanded
by administrators possessing requisite experience, and
requisite power and force, to prevent their misuse, or
their appropriation by individuals. Then only could
measures similar to those now employed against the fortress
of Kisamos, have been adopted for reducing the other
fortresses of Crete.

In the meantime the Turks in Kydonia, in attempting
to furnish supplies by sea to the blockaded fortresses, not
only failed in all their efforts, but sustained loss. The
two blockading ships sunk, with all hands on board, all
small vessels that attempted to run the blockade with
provisions and other supplies, and Macromuras destroyed one
night at the mouth of the Kisamic gulf a schooner bound for
Kisamos, with 80 soldiers and a large quantity of military
stores on board. The blockading ships, moreover, frequently
fired on the fortress of Kisamos, to the annoyance of the
besieged. Meanwhile, frequent skirmishes and successful
ambuscades daily took place between the Greeks and the
besieged under the very walls of the fortress, and with great
damage to the enemy, who now suffered at the same time
from the plague, which cut off upwards of two-thirds of the
1,800 persons that had been shut up in the fortress.

The besieged lost, besides, all hope of obtaining any
assistance from Selinon, as Michael Katheclus, at the head of
all the Inakhorii* (or Enneakhoriani), had occupied a conve-

* The district now called Ennea Khoria is a portion of Kisamos, situated
in the western part of that Province, and bordering on Selinon. It is
probable that the appellation is derived from some ancient city called
Inakhorion, as the number of the villages is not nine (ennea) but about
twenty. This district produces the finest and far-famed Cretan chestnuts

nient position for preventing all intercourse between Selinon
and the fortress of Kisamos, while Marcos Renieres, at the
head of the Rumathiani and the inhabitants of other neighbouring villages, and Manoles Kokkolakes, at the head of
Prasiani and others, were stationed in convenient positions,
keeping the Seliniot Turks in check, and protecting the
province of Kisamos, now in the possession of the Greeks.

During the interval between the Greek inroad into Kisamos
and these later events, the Turks of Kydonia had attempted
a diversion for the purpose of impeding the progress of the
Greeks. A detachment issuing from the fortress advanced
as far as Perivolia and Galatas to attack the positions of
Halles; while another detachment marched against Siphacas
in the direction of the villages of Nerocuron and Tsacalaria.
Simultaneously another body of the enemy issued from Suda
to overrun Apocoronos, in the hope of finding those parts
unprotected. All these attempts, however, entirely failed.
The first of these detachments was repulsed by V. Halles and
Petros Tsacalarianos, who had not taken part in the expedition
to Kisamos, but remained in their positions for the purpose
of making head against any inroads that might be attempted
by the Turks. The hostile body that entered Apocoronos
were driven back by Greek troops that happened to be there,
and were pursued as far as the coast, sustaining great loss.
The Turks of Rethymne simultaneously issuing from that
fortress had likewise made a hostile movement; but Strates
Deliyannakes and Manoles Rustikianos at the head of Rethymnian insurgents triumphantly repulsed them. While the
Greek arms, however, were thus successful in the west, the
national cause was to an equal extent losing ground in the
east of Crete, as Hassan Pasha had commenced to overrun
those parts with an immense force, carrying everywhere destruction and desolation, as will be seen from the sequel, and
as may be inferred from the following incident.

As Hassan Pasha's great movement had spread consternation among the inhabitants of those parts, they hastened,
by applying for assistance, to avert the impending danger.
They, accordingly, sent off two couriers with a memorial to
the Provisional Government, representing their perilous and
helpless position. The couriers reached Kisamos two or three
days after Hassan's forces had entered the Provinces in
question, and were, likewise, bearers of a private letter, with
numerous signatures, addressed to Siphacas, and dated from

Minos or Mirambelos.   Siphacas, on receiving this letter,
privately requested C. Critovulides, who was attached to him
in the capacity of adviser, to explain to him confidentially its
contents, as he was desirous not to excite the envy of other
leaders, the letter being addressed specially to him.   The
letter was as follows : "Brother Captain Siphe! from our
memorial to the Government, and from our messengers, you
will have ascertained the state of matters here.   Our situation
is most critical and alarming, and we assure you distinctly
that, if at this moment we do not receive assistance, we are
undone.   Not only will our contendings and our sacrifices
have been invain, but through the calamity impending on us,
the national cause over the whole island will be brought at
once to the brink of ruin.   We have applied to others for
assistance, but our hopes of obtaining it are specially placed
in you.   We, therefore implore you to put yourself instantly
at the head of all the followers you can muster where you are,
and hasten to our aid.   We hereby promise most solemnly
that we will recognise you as our leader, and that all the
soldiers you bring with you will be maintained by us, and
supplied with every possible comfort.   With your co-operation
and with God's help we hope to baffle the enemy, who is
slaughtering and destroying without mercy, and persisting in
his determination to exterminate thousands of our brethren
whom he has shut up in a grotto.   Zervonicolas, to our great
loss, died a few days ago; but Vuzomarcos, Suliotes, Kuscumbes and some others are moving about and using every effort
to protect us, but their force is nothing compared to that of
the enemy.   Some reinforcements of Sphakians and others
are expected, and we trust they may come before it be too
late.   Do not leave us to certain destruction, otherwise the
danger that now threatens us will soon reach where you are."

The contents of the memorial were substantially the same.
Unfortunately, however, the Government did not adopt instant measures in compliance with the prayer of the memorialists.   The good Siphakas, deeply touched at the perilous
position of his brethren, on hearing the letter read, exclaimed,
" What is to be done even yet to save them?"   " You will,"
answered Critovulides, " do a gallant and generous deed, if
you instantly run to their assistance, and, in saving them,
you will render a momentous service to our country at large."
" I agree with you," said Siphakas; " but I am most anxious
to clear Selinon of the Turks in the first place, and thus

save these parts from danger, so that, on the arrival of Tombazes, we may march in much greater force against the enemy." Œconomos also took the same view, though he lost no time in urging, by letters and messages, both Sphakians and armed insurgents of other parts, to hasten to the assistance of the suffering insurgents in the Eastern Provinces. Unfortunately, neither of these patriots was at this moment duly impressed with the fact, that the state of matters in the Eastern Provinces did not admit a moment's delay, owing to the measures of extermination that the Egyptian Commander was pursuing there. Besides, Œconomos was afraid that if Siphakas were to leave Kisamos, the Seliniot Turks would make a sudden inroad, recover the Province, and raise the blockade of the fortress, which it had cost him so great exertions to establish. Accordingly in his reply, he endeavoured merely to encourage the memorialists, by assuring them that on the arrival of the new Governor, which was daily expected, a great expedition would be instantly undertaken, that could not fail to check and intimidate the enemy. He further exhorted them to determined resistance, and informed them that he had written to many military leaders on their behalf. Œconomos at the same time urged Siphakas to repair with all the troops under his command to Inakhorion, where he could, from his vicinity to Selinon, more effectually watch the movements of the Seliniot Turks.

The worthy Siphakas immediately obeyed the orders of the Government, and lost no time in occupying the village Rogdia in the district of Inakhorion, as the most convenient position for the purpose for which he was sent. The night, however, of the last Sunday of the Carnival, while, according to custom, he was banqueting with his followers, a body of Turks from Selinon, descending on the adjacent village called Pervolakia, massacred about 50 Christians. The instant the news of this reached Rogdia, Siphakas, at the head of all the force he could muster, marched against the assailants, and, pursuing them nearly as far as Kandanos, killed some of them. After the event, he severely upbraided Katheclas for having neglected his duty, as appointed to guard those positions. This, unfortunately, was to be the last exploit of Siphakas. Over-heated in the pursuit, and having taken no precautions, he was seized with pneumonia. From Rogdia he was conveyed to Topolia, a village of

Kisamos. He died there on the 13th day of his illness, having received no medical assistance. His death was an immense loss to the Cretan cause.

Joseph Konstantudakes was a native of the village called Melidonion, in the province of Apocoronos. He was a man of great simplicity of character, and of remarkable kindness of heart. The moment he was apprized of the impending national insurrection, he joyously hailed the intended enterprize, and cordially co-operated with the leaders of the movement. From the very first he showed himself to be a brave, enterprising and undaunted warrior, his natural character, as well as his training, having made him so. Frequent achievements quietly raised him to distinction, and procured him the military rank of Pentacosiarkhos, then the highest in Crete. Though not possessing great capacity and originality, so as to be fitted to devise and to superintend operations, yet naturally brave and high-spirited, he was ever prompt in exposing himself to the greatest danger in executing the judicious and patriotic suggestions of others. Disinterested and conscientious, he ever disdained every thing dishonest and dishonourable, never deigning to interfere with the distribution of the spoils, though the troops always offered him a share specially select. It is almost unnecessary to add that he was superior to any act of extortion or oppression. He was in consequence of those qualities generally respected and beloved by his countrymen. His bodily superiority in numerous points was very remarkable. Gifted with the strength and the size of Hercules, he had great swiftness of foot, and a voice of thunder. It was in reference to those corporal endowments that his countrymen gave him the characteristic name of Siphakas, or Big Joseph. Endowed with these qualities, he has left in his country's annals, and in the hearts of all Cretans of the present and of every future generation, a memorial of glory that will never be effaced, to which his victories and his heroism entitled him. He was, when he died, about the age of 50. His death was an irreparable loss to his struggling country. His corpse was buried with the highest honours in the monastery of Gonia,' in the province of Kisamos, and accompanied to the tomb with the tears of his countrymen. Two funeral orations were delivered, the one by C. Critovulides, and the other by Panayotes Nicolaïdes, of Smyrna. Both speakers spoke in due terms of his virtues and his services.

During this period the plague was committing so much ravage among the Turks in Rethymne, as almost to threaten their utter extermination. This fearful scourge had, as we have already mentioned, been brought to Crete by the Egyptian troops. Though it cut off immense numbers in all the fortresses, and wherever Turkish inhabitants were to be found, it raged with surpassing violence in Rethymne, owing to the great numbers of persons cooped up within narrow limits and the consequent pollution of the air, on the one hand, and, on the other, to the infatuation of the Turks, who, from the idea of yielding to fate, used no precautions whatever to prevent the spread of the malady. The pestilence became so virulent that the daily number of victims was immense. Though the malady was unavoidably communicated to the Greeks, the damage it caused among them was very inconsiderable, and this difference arose from the purity of air, which the Greeks continued to enjoy in the open country, and from their more enlightened notions of divine Providence, and their judicious precautions to prevent all intercourse with persons struck with the scourge.

The Rethymnian Turks were at length compelled to leave their town almost deserted, in order to escape from this fearful domestic enemy. They encamped with their families in distinct parties, some of them outside the walls, and in the adjacent villages, but most of them at Euloyia, a position at no great distance from the fortress. They were thus, through the benefit of purer air, considerably relieved from the ravages of the plague, but were, on the other hand, exposed to attacks from the Greeks. In ordinary circumstances, physical calamities common to both sides in war, would mitigate and restrain for a time mutual animosity, but, during the Cretan war of independence, so implacable was the hatred that animated both the patriots and their oppressors, that the fearful visitation of the pestilence produced no such effect. On both sides the enemy was alternately subjected to the unrelenting vengeance of the conqueror.

The Greeks, perceiving that the Turks continued for many days to muster in the above-mentioned positions, and probably inferring that they were preparing for a hostile movement, collected about 1,000 men, consisting of Rethymnians, Kallicratiani, Lampæi, and Asphendiotæ, and before daylight one morning attacked them, burnt all the tents with

the effects they contained, killed a great number of the
Turks overtaken there, and, pursuing them as far as the
gates of the fortress, killed not a few, as daylight had not
yet arrived to facilitate their escape. Osman Pasha, the
most able of their leaders, narrowly escaped being killed or
taken. His tent was burnt with all the property it contained,
but his horses, many arms, and all articles known to be
uncontagious, were captured by the victors. During the
pursuit, many of the Turks that had remained in the fortress endeavoured to give assistance to the fugitives, the
moment they heard the noise and tumult outside the gates;
but in the sortie they suffered considerably from the incessant
canonading from the ramparts, which, during the unexpected
attack and the general confusion, was indiscriminately directed
against the armed and the unarmed, without possible distinction. The Turks that survived were thus obliged to
shut themselves up within the fortress, exposed, as before, to
the ravages of the pestilence. Only two Greeks were killed
in the pursuit.

We shall now pass to the state of matters in the Eastern
parts of Crete. Hassan Pasha, as we have already seen, had
taken the field in great force, and was threatening general
extermination. The Greeks, however, occupying many
strong mountainous positions over the country, maintained
to some extent resistance, and frequently not only repulsed
the enemy, but inflicted sometimes considerable loss. They
even had the courage to attempt the occupation of the town
of Hierapytnos, though surrounded by a large hostile force.
They were prompted to this enterprise by the hope of making
that town a safe retreat.

It is situated towards the eastern extremity of Crete.
Its southern side almost touches the isthmus that joins
Siteia to the rest of Crete. It extends over a small plain,
and is surrounded by insignificant and mouldering fortifications. To the east of it, and nearly on the sea-shore, there
is on a small hill a tower well provided with guns, and
commanding the town, which contains about 700 or 800
houses, of which scarcely the fourth part are inhabited by
Greeks.

A body of Greek troops amounting to 1500 resolved to
attack this place. The leaders were Anagnostes Kuscumbes,
Nicolas Zervos, commander of the auxiliaries, Vuzomarcos,
Panayes Mitylenæos, Konstantes Stakakes, the two Iounnes

Stiakoi, the one surnamed Macrys and the other Contos, Anagnostes Symiacos, Nicolaos Andracos,[*] and others of less note. The troops, under the command of their leaders, mustered at the village of Kritsa, whence they proceeded by night to Prina and Kalamauca, villages in the province of Hierapytnos, and situated at the distance of two hours from the town ; and there held a council of war to arrange the mode of attack. It happened, however, that a heavy rain, which continued nearly two days, prevented the execution of their plan. In the meantime, A. Symiakos and Frangios Papadakes, of Hierapytnos, forming ambuscades near Lower Village, as it is called, and Kontri, took five or six of the Turks of those parts prisoners. This event made known to the enemy the presence of the Greek force, and roused the just indignation of Zervos against Frangios as the author of this unfortunate proceeding. The Turks in the neighbouring villages instantly fled to the town, which now contained about 500 men.

Though the enemy had now become aware of the presence of a large Greek force, they did not imagine that these would make an attempt on the town, and, accordingly, they did not think it necessary to be on the alert ; but the Greeks planned and attempted the capture of the place, under the conviction that the enterprise was practicable, and aware that the town contained a great deal of rich property. They knew that the inhabitants, possessing a very fertile province, had enriched themselves by the sale of its valuable produce, and that, owing to their remote situation, their mode of life was less expensive than that of landed proprietors of many other parts of Crete. The Greek forces divided themselves into three detachments. Zervos, at the head of about 300 men, occupied the middle wall of the town, extending towards the village Kentri, while Vuzomarcos, with an adequate force, occupied Kaloyoroi, a position to the south, and Kuscumbos seized the north gate looking towards Sitcia, and stationed himself in the adjoining ruin of a mill.

Zervos succeeded in mounting upon the wall, and killed five Turks there ; but the enemy with great prudence aban-

---

[*] This is the brave Andracos, who came to Crete with Tselepes and others from Asia Minor. In a previous page we spoke by mistake of his brother Stavros Andracos, instead of himself. Nicolaos Andracos was an excellent soldier, and rendered much service to the cause. He was killed at Navarino, in Peloponnesus, in 1825, in an engagement with the Egyptians. Stavros was killed in 1826, in a tower at Amasdun, in the province of Aulopotamos.

doned the defence of every other part of the town the moment they perceived the assault, and hastened in great force to the above mentioned tower. From this position they opened an unceasing cannonade, and directed a fire of musketry against the Greeks wherever they appeared. Zervos and his followers were thus obliged to descend from the wall, and retire with the loss of 10 or 12 killed or wounded. Zervos now, sword in hand, urged his own followers and those of Symineos to occupy the adjacent store houses; and in his eagerness to save the storming party he killed one, and wounded another, for attempting to run away. In the meantime Vusomarcos and Kuscumbes had been driven back by the firing from the tower, and prevented from reaching the positions assigned them. Some of the Greeks outside the walls were killed by cannon-shot, among whom was the priest of Kritsa, a very brave and experienced warrior. The Turks, too, sustained a small loss.

All this was occasioned by want of discipline. If Frangios and Symineos had not made known the presence of the Greek force in the way already mentioned, and if the attack had been carried out according to the arrangements—if Kuscumbes and Vusomarcos had, as they might have done, attempted to storm the place simultaneously with Zervos, the Greeks would have undoubtedly carried a rich and strong town, which would have enabled them to check the movements of Hassan Pasha, who was continuing to ravage the neighbouring villages almost without opposition.

The forces which had assembled at Hierapytnos now dispersed without achieving anything, the leaders uselessly throwing on each other the blame of the failure. Five or six days afterwards, it was proposed to make a second attempt to storm the place, but the leaders could not be induced to agree to this, as distrust of each other now began to prevail, and their previous failure was by many attributed to treachery.

The following circumstance appears worth mentioning:— Kuscumbes and Zervos, having marched in company to Eastern Crete, became more intimately acquainted with each other than previously, and remained ever afterwards faithful and devoted friends. Their mutual regard was confirmed by an oath, according to the usage then prevailing among the Greeks, of adelphopœia, or mutual adoption as brothers. They accordingly deliberated and acted in concert in all their military enterprises, and were greatly and generally beloved and respected by the inhabitants of those parts. Both distinguished for their bravery and military skill, they had been both promoted to the highest military rank in Crete, that of pentacosiarkos, on account of their acknowledged abilities and merits. But the mistaken policy of Aphentules was to divide these two excellent and valuable friends; and in the month of September or October, a short time before his dismissal, he had conferred on Zervos the rank of Commander-in-chief of the Eastern provinces; and Zervos had, from the simplicity of his character, immediately accepted this promotion, while Kuscumbos was allowed to remain with the same rank as before. This cooled the ardour of the attachment which till then united the two friends. Kuscumbes* bitterly complained of the slight he had sustained; and he was quite right in blaming Aphentules for preferring the one to the other, but he was wrong in allowing his resentment to interfere with the discharge of his duty to his country as well as with his own honour and true interest.

After the events above mentioned the two leaders (Zervos and Kuscumbes) repaired in January 1823 to the harbour of Minoa or Mirabello, called Hayios Nicolaos, and went on board an European vessel, which was there taking in a cargo of oil purchased from the inhabitants of those parts; and, after receiving from this vessel a quantity of arms and ammunition, which had been sent from Lutros under the care of Anagnostes Psarudakes, set off elsewhere. Zervos, having been taken ill, remained at the village called Kænurion, and died there a few days afterwards, just at the time when Hassan Pasha was preparing to enter the province of Kherrhonesos to inflict on it the most signal calamities.

Nicolaos Zervos was a native either of Kuntura in Megaris or of Eleusis in Attica. From boyhood he had led the life of an armatolos, or armed Christian in the pay of the Turks, and resided for the most part in Asia Minor, where he had become intimately acquainted with numerous Cretans, and

* He was killed in 1824, when he was wandering about with other armed insurgents among the mountains of the eastern provinces, after Husein Bey had reduced nearly the whole of Crete. His body was brought to Kuphonesia by his comrades, and buried there. Anagnostes Kuscumbes was a native of Skyphos in Sphakia. He was a brave and skilful warrior and had proved himself likewise to be an able and judicious leader. At the time of his death he was about 40 years of age.

had, at the commencement of the insurrection, proceeded
with some of those to Crete to devote himself to the national
cause there. Zervos was a person of great bodily strength,
of tried valour, and, on account of his previous life, trained
to arms from his youth. He distinguished himself on many
occasions in Kydonia and Rethymno, as well as in the
eastern provinces, and was greatly beloved and honoured
by the Cretans. It appears, however, that this able
and valuable warrior had one blemish, to which his death
has been attributed, a tendency to excess in drinking.
When he died he was about forty years of age. His death
was greatly lamented by the Cretans, who highly honoured
his memory, and felt the greatness of his loss to the
national cause. On the other hand, Hassan Pasha was
overjoyed on hearing of the death of so daring and formidable an adversary, whom he had ever found in his path
wherever he turned.

After Hassan Pasha had, as already narrated, remained
encamped some days at Pediada, where he received fresh
supplies and reinforcements from Egypt, he found himself
ready to take the field. Having previously found himself
unable to enter Site, or Lasition, from Kastamonissa, through
the difficult defiles, called Tsalion and Kera; and being
determined to spare no effort to reduce the inhabitants of
that province, as these mountaineers afforded an asylum to
the insurgents of other parts, he resolved to take another
road. He was roused, moreover, by the events that had
just occurred at Hierapytnos, and breathed vengeance. He
was further urged to immediate action by the land blockade
of the islet called Lato or Spinalonga, situated on the same
coast and containing a fortress built by the Venetians, where
many Turks from the neighbouring provinces had taken
refuge. While Michael Mayulakes and Spyros Maniatos*
blockaded these so strictly by land, as to prevent any of
them from setting foot on shore, they were, on the side of
the sea, kept in constant alarm by the occasional appearance
of Cassian vessels, and in particular of the swift sailing
schooner of Michael Boyazes.†

* This patriot was born at Constantinople. Repairing to Crete soon after
the commencement of the war of independence, he devoted himself to the
Cretan cause with great earnestness and perseverance.

† M. Boyazes was a native of the village of Tariote, in the province of
Sitela. He had five gallant sons, who, before the commencement of the
war of independence, possessed a vessel of their own, with which they

Hassan Pasha returning with his army, which was such as we have described, to Viennos in the province of (Cretan) Arcadia, remained encamped there for about a month. Whilst he had his head-quarters here, he continued, as previously, to send out detachments into the surrounding districts. Some of these entered Gortyna, spreading universal alarm by their reckless ferocity against the lives and properties of the Christians, and, proceeding as far as the cave of the Labyrinth, attacked, but without success, the Greeks who had taken refuge there. Other detachments, advancing as far as the strong village of Sycologa, massacred about 60 Greeks incapable of resistance, and captured as many more. The Turkish cavalry succeeded in entering Lasiti through the broadest defile called Katharon, which happened to be inadequately defended, and burnt several villages. This was all the mischief they could accomplish, as the inhabitants had received notice in time to save themselves by repairing to strong positions, and the Turks themselves found it necessary to effect a speedy retreat, from the apprehension of being surrounded by the Greeks in that rugged district.

From Viennos Hassan Pasha proceeded, at the head of his whole army, to the province of Hierapytnos, passing through the village of Male, the most populous in the whole province. He remained for about twelve days encamped in the environs of the fortress of Hierapytnos. He burnt Male and all other villages in the province, capturing and slaughtering helpless Greeks that fell into his hands, and exhibiting here also the same barbarity as elsewhere. Leaving in the fortress of Hierapytnos a garrison of 500 Albanians under the command of Hussein Bey, who was also an Albanian, he marched on to carry slaughter and destruction into other districts. The Greeks, however, notwithstanding their recent sufferings and losses, mustered in great numbers, with the intention of attacking the enemy at the strong positions of Kritsa, a village of Minos, through which the Pasha intended to pass.

harrassed the Turks by sea. Subsequently they procured a Schooner, with which they made frequent cruises on the coast of Crete to the great annoyance and danger of the Turks. In 1822, they burnt with all on board a small Turkish vessel (trata) as it was coming out of Heracleion, and in 1823 they captured another vessel of the same kind off Spinalonga with 18 Turks on board, all of whom they put to death. One of his sons Papageorgios, was a distinguished warrior both at sea and on land. In 1840 he was secretly strangled or drowned by the Turks of Spinalonga where he had arrived with a small vessel of his own, under the Greek flag.

It may not be superfluous to mention that the Pasha had been greatly encouraged in his hopes of general success by the death of Zervos, which had been announced to him at Hierapytnos. The intelligence, it is said, produced ntent and universal joy in the Turkish army, who, by discharges of musketry, intimated their joy at the fall of so formidable an adversary.

Kritsa is a very large village, containing about 700 families, and is situated at the foot of the Lasithian mountains. Here Greeks, from nearly all the Eastern Provinces of Crete, assembled to make head against the Egyptian army.

Besides the leaders mentioned as having taken part in the expedition to Hierapytnos, except the heroic Nicolaos Zervos, now lost to the Greek cause, there had arrived Rusakes Khurdos with a body of Anoyani, Aulopotamites, and Knossians, Andrinos Hadjidakes with a large number of Gortynians, Manias Balesca with a small body of Sphakians, Konstantinos Sampathianos, Zaccharias Apostolakes, Georgios Kapasakales, with their usual followers. There were likewise leaders of less note from more distant provinces; and the whole of the Greek forces here mustered, formed a warlike army of upwards of 3,000 men. The Pasha, having removed his camp to the village of Kalon, in the vicinity of Minoa, began to contrive the most effective means of driving the Greek forces from the positions they occupied. Concluding that the Greeks, after the recent calamities, would not offer a very formidable resistance, and finding himself at the head of so large and efficient a force, the enterprising Pasha resolved to commence a general attack forthwith. Dividing his army into two divisions, he directed the one, consisting of about 5,000 infantry, to march through a small village called Krusa, situated on a high hill to the east of Kritsa, and at about half an hour's distance from that place, and occupy grounds in the rear of the Greek positions at Kritsa; while he himself, at the head of the cavalry, about 1,000 strong, and the rest of the infantry, was to attack the Greeks in front. Trusting to his arrangements and resources, the Pasha confidently counted on a brilliant victory, and even the entire destruction of the insurgents.

The Greeks, meanwhile, waited for the attack, not indeed without anxiety, but without despondency, trusting to the strength of their positions, in addition to their numbers and determination. They divided their forces into three detachments. One of these made a gallant stand against the Pasha himself, who rushed on them with great impetuosity at the head of the cavalry. Another received the charge of the Turkish division from Krusa. From an early hour in the morning till it was almost dark, the conflict was kept up with great obstinacy on both sides, during which both parties alternately made impetuous onsets, amidst thundering shouts. The Greeks, though far inferior in numbers, yet, favoured by their positions, drove back the enemy with great loss. Both divisions of the Turks lost numbers of their men, and the division led on by the Pasha in person, lost five superior officers of the cavalry in their repeated attempts to storm the Greek positions. Both Greeks and Turks, as night came on, began to retire from the scene of conflict, perceiving it impossible to make any advance without immense loss. During the day both parties had avoided a retreat for fear of being assailed to disadvantage by the enemy. The Pasha was thus completely disappointed in his expectations, and, accordingly, returned to his camp at Kalon after losing upwards of 150 men. The Greeks, in this action, had θ killed, and about 20 wounded. Though victorious, they abandoned their strong position at Kritsa during the night, either for want of provisions, or from the apprehension of a still more formidable attack the following day.

Hassan Pasha, on hearing that the Greeks had abandoned their positions at Kritsa, was greatly astonished, and at first suspected an ambuscade. On ascertaining, however, that they had really marched off, he despatched the whole of the cavalry about noon to burn down the village and facilitate his advance. After this, he returned to the Lower Village, where he remained encamped about 15 days. What he had not been able to accomplish by the bloody battle at Kastamonitsa, towards reducing the mountainous district of Lasition, he now effected by the destruction of Kritsa, as nothing is impracticable if pursued with judgment, perseverance, and at all hazards. On the other hand, it is painful to contemplate the lot of those, who, having it in their power to avert danger, fail to turn advantages to account, through want of foresight and experience.

Whilst Hassan Pasha remained encamped at the above mentioned village, waiting for opportunities to execute his plans, he sent out, in the meantime, the whole of his cavalry and the greater part of the infantry on various excursions. These troops again went up the country suddenly through the defile of Katharon, which would have been impossible, if the Greeks had had the foresight to station parties at suitable points of it for its defence. This measure, however, having been entirely neglected, the enemy passed the defile, and reached Lasition almost without opposition. On entering that province, they proceeded to burn and desolate all the villages, and killed a great number of Greeks, as well as captured about 400 helpless females, children, and old men. After taking possession of a large number of cattle, sheep, and beasts of burden, that had been collected there, and obtaining a great quantity of all other sorts of spoil, they returned to their camp in triumph.

All obstacles to the execution of his main enterprise being now removed, the wary and daring Albanian Pasha put his whole force in motion, and, entering the province of Minoa, (or Mirabello) by Kritsa, without resistance, burnt the villages, slaughtered great numbers of the inhabitants, captured about 1,000 Christians, and, encamping at the town of Kænurion, caused the putrid body of Nicolaos Zervos to be dug up and exposed as a mark, to be fired at by the barbarous Moslems.

The Christian inhabitants of the province were now seized with consternation, and were at a loss which way to turn for safety. They consoled themselves, however, in some degree with the hope that the Egyptian invasion would be transient, and that Greek reinforcements would hasten to their rescue. About 2,000 men, women, and children, including 300 armed insurgents, took refuge in a cave to the north, and at the foot of a hill near the village, now called Milaton, built on the site of the ancient city of Miletos. The refugees had conveyed to this cave as much of their movable property as they could. The breadth of the cave is very considerable, and it extends into the hill to a very great and unexplored length. It is entirely without any supply of water, with the exception of a small quantity, which in one part of it descends in drops.

The unfortunate refugees, who, in their extremity, sought refuge here, were cruelly disappointed. The enemy blockaded them forthwith, stationing troops over and around the entrance, and fired into it unceasingly with field-pieces day and night for the space of a fortnight. Greeks from various points now flocked to the aid of the wretched inmates of the cave. Rusos Vurdumbas reached tho spot at the head of 300 Sphakiots, as well as Georgios Suderos with a considerable number of Lampœi. These repeatedly attacked the enemy with impetuosity, and inflicted no small loss, eager to rescue the besieged. During the conflict a considerable number of the armed Greeks within the cave, tore themselves from their helpless dear ones, and joined the combatants. Had the Greek forces that had come to raise the blockade of tho cave, held their positions in the vicinity for a few days, they would, undoubtedly, have accomplishdd their object, and driven the enemy from the neighbouring district. But, unfortunately, they went off, after appropriating a large quantity of cattle, sheep, etc., and the inhabitants of Minoa were left to contend alone against a formidable hostile force. The Cretans in battle almost invariably maintained the honour of their country and forefathers; and had they, on all occasions, stood by each other to avert the common danger, they would have successfully maintained the cause of independence, notwithstanding the immense resources of their Egyptian enemy.

Hassan Pasha continued the blockade with great vigour, determined not to desist till he had effected his purpose. In the meantime, the wretched inmates of the cave, though many of them died of thirst and other privations, as well as anguish and despair, refused to surrender, knowing well with what tigers they had to deal. The armed men, still remaining in the cave, gallantly repulsed every attempt of the enemy to enter it; and devised a mode of neutralizing the effect of the cannon balls, by placing at the mouth of the cave sacks full of wool and similar materials. Meanwhile, the Pasha paid frequent visits to the cave, to urge its capture at any cost; and his perseverance was crowned with success

About the middle of February the besieged, being in great extremities for want of water, and despairing of all human aid, surrendered. The Pasha instantly slaughtered all the men that had remained, with the exception of 30, whom he selected to be conveyed in chains to the dungeons of Spinalonga, where in a few days they expired. Some of the defendants of the cave happened to be priests. These on surrending were tied to each other like so many beasts, and, by all accounts, thrown into a large fire and burnt alive. The elder women were slaughtered, many of them being, in wanton cruelty, trodden to death by Turkish horsemen; the

younger females and the boys were in herds sent as captives
to Asia, Egypt, or elsewhere. A beautiful young female, who
had become the prize of an Albanian, and was proceeding
with him to Spinalonga, resolved to prefer death to captivity
and dishonour. Accordingly, on arriving at the village of
Phurni, where there were some ponds full of water, she leaped
into one of them, and drowned herself. In addition to all
these, about 60 Greeks were killed in various encounters
from the time of the Pasha's entering the province of Minoa.
During the same period the Turks lost in that province
upwards of 300 men, 150 ot whom, it is said, were killed in
various attempts to storm the cave.

Hassan Pasha, after these bloody proceedings, left the
province of Minoa, and returned to that of Pedins. But
divine vengeance, which sooner or later overtakes the
wicked, now awaited him. After having destroyed by fire
and sword so many helpless victims, who had been compelled
to surrender, and who, in civilized warfare, would have been
treated with mercy and kindness, the Pasha was now unexpectedly and suddenly launched into eternity. Riding out
one day, he was thrown from his horse, which had taken
fright at some occurrence, and killed on the spot. His dead
body was secretly conveyed to Heracleion, lest the news of
his death should give fresh animation and confidence to the
insurgents.

The energetic and barbarous measures of Hassan Pasha had
greatly damaged the cause of independence in the Eastern
Provinces. Large bodies of insurgents no longer ventured
to appear in the plains, and the contest for freedom was no
longer maintained in those parts, except by some scattered
bands of patriots, who continued to wander about among
the mountains, waiting for more auspicious times after the
arrival of the expected Governor of Crete, who, it was
hoped, would come accompanied by naval as well as military
re-inforcements.

During these tragic events above recorded, skirmishes and
daily ambuscades occurred also in Knossos; as the Turks,
who had remained to defend Heracleion, attempted to molest
the Greeks, whilst the Greeks, who were blockading that
place, continued to harass the Turks in their turn. The
former frequently sallied from the fortress and advanced as
far as Daphnæ, Stavrukia, Vutœ, and other villages at the
distance of two hours from Heracleion, but were usually

attacked with great vigour by Knossians and Aulopotamites,
and driven back with loss. The Knossians were commanded
by Antonios Peratsakes, and Panayotes Zervudakes, and the
Aulopotamites by Th. Khurdos, ably aided by Antonios
Langianos, and Vasilios Sbocos Aulopotamites, and by G.
Yamales Krusaniotes, Ioannes Palmetes, G. Khalkias, and
other Knossians.

About the time of the fearful destruction of life at the
cave of Miletos, Khurdos had with others proceeded to
Yephyrakia at the head of about 500 men, accompanied by
most of the leaders just mentioned, as well as by Stavros
Muriotes and Nicolaos Koloverdes, officers of great bravery
and experience. All these advanced with great despatch
against the Turkish troops there, put them to flight, and
pursued them as far as the great bridge in the immediate
vicinity of the fortress. As the attack of the Greeks was
unexpected, they killed or captured about 20 of the enemy.
The Turks now sallied forth nearly three times as strong as
before, and accompanied by a body of cavalry, so that the
Greeks, obliged to retreat, were pursued as far as Gaza.
Between that position and Kavrokhorion below Servile, the
Greeks turned on their pursuers, and made a gallant stand.
Khurdos, ascending a hill with a few followers, made a most
heroic resistance. At length, however, he was surrounded
by the enemy's cavalry, and was slain, fighting undauntedly
sword in hand. About 15 other Greeks were killed in this
affair. Muriotes Yamales, and others, made the most
vigorous efforts to aid Khurdos, and after his fall to carry off
his body, but without success. They, themselves, were soon
afterwards exposed to imminent danger, being nearly surrounded by the cavalry, and only saved themselves by swiftness of foot. About 30 Turks, and several horses, were
killed in these encounters.

Thus perished Theodoros Khurdos. He was a native of
Skyphi in Sphakia, and at the time of his death about 38
years of age. Experience had rendered him an able commander, and his manners and bearing had gained him the
affection and respect of the Aulopotamites, for whose emancipation he had, as we have seen, made earnest and persevering
exertions. An unpleasant affair occurred in Aulopotamos in
connection with his brother Rusakes, which deserves to be
mentioned, although S. Tricoupi, in his History (Vol. III.

chap. 46, page 95), alludes to it merely as follows :—" About this time, a civil war was nearly lighted up among the Cretans, in consequence of the slaughter of two disorderly Sphakians in Mylopotamos," etc.

Rusakes, on the death of his brother, persisted in assuming, by force, the command of the Aulopotamites, who, though they had been attached to Theodoros for the reasons we have stated, felt the greatest aversion for Rusakes on account of the dissimilarity of his character and manners, though he, too, was a person of undoubted courage. Their aversion was specially heightened by the following circumstances. Rusakes, by unjustifiably killing a Knossian of the name of Vlastos, who was living in the village of Hayios Ioannes in Aulopotamos, had drawn upon himself nearly universal indignation, and had been obliged to retire from the place. Notwithstanding the want of popularity, Rusakes persisted in his purpose of assuming the command of the Aulopotamites, whilst they as firmly persisted in rejecting him, and unanimously chose for their leader, Antonios Longianos, a native of their own province. Many of the Sphakians, very improperly, took the part of Rusakes, though clearly in the wrong. Arrogating an unfounded right to domineer over the Aulopotamites, not merely beyond, but within the bounds of their province, they asserted their claim by outraging and maltreating suffering patriots, no less brave and meritorious than themselves. The Sphakians, unfortunately, persisted also in the following unreasonable pretensions.

As their mountainous position, and the trade of their harbour of Lutros, had given them, from the commencement of the insurrection, special importance, they had probably conceived the idea that, notwithstanding the smallness of their numbers, they could assume a predominant influence, both in civil and in military affairs all over Crete. Such a pretension could only be attributed to want of knowledge of the world. The Cretans, on engaging in the great struggle for independence, should have laid it down as a fundamental rule, that a strict adherence to impartial justice could alone maintain harmony, and secure ultimate success. Even bands of robbers, according to the common observation, require justice among their members to preserve them from internal destruction. Accordingly, the arrogant pretensions of the Sphakians produced, and that at most critical moments, mur-

murs and indignation on the part of the other patriots of Crete. The latter very naturally declared that they had taken up arms to shake off the Turkish yoke, and that, as long as they had these arms in their hands, they would submit to no yoke whatever. Many of the Aulopotamites, as well as of the insurgents of other provinces, had proved themselves worthy of military command. In consequence of all this, a commotion ensued, in which two Sphakians, as already mentioned, were killed. This deplorable event led to still more disastrous results, and irritated the Sphakians to such a degree, that they not only refused to supply the distressed Aulopotamites with ammunition, but determined even to attack them with great force, and treat them as mortal foes. Sudoros, however, and others interfered, and, by remonstrances and entreaties, fortunately succeeded in preventing the impending conflict. The mutual irritation gradually subsided, and the circumstances altogether proved that there existed among the Cretans, generally, no tendency to mar the common cause by civil war.

After the death of Theodoros Khurdos, the Turks of Heracleion began to make excursions more frequently, and with greater confidence, advancing as far as the above mentioned villages. The Greeks, however, determined to check them. With this view, they again mustered to the number of about 2,000, consisting of all the Gortynians under Michael Kurmules, with his small body of cavalry, the Anoyani, Aulopotamites, and Knossians. All these, with great ardour and unanimity, attacked the Turks on Good-Friday at Gaza. Though the enemy made a gallant resistance, the Greeks soon put them to flight, and pursued them as far as the Great Bridge, killing about 50 of them. On this occasion, Lazarakes Iordanes, who served in the small body of Greek cavalry, greatly distinguished himself, having killed, it is said, three of the enemy, with his own hand. The Turks, however, issued from the fortress in great strength, including cavalry, and compelled the Greeks to retreat to Gaza and Kalesia, where a very vigorous conflict took place, which continued to a late hour of the night. In this action a considerable number of Turks were killed, and on the side of the Greeks about 15 were killed or wounded. We now return to the state of affairs in the province of Kisamos.

The Turks in the fortress of Kisamos were suffering greatly, not only from the calamities of war, being blockaded

both by sea and by land, but by the ravages of the plague.
N. Œconomos was using the most vigorous efforts to get
possession of the place with all possible speed. For this
purpose he frequently repaired from Gonia, then the seat of
Government. and, appearing in the midst of the blockading
forces, urged both the land troops and the squadron to press
the blockade with still greater determination. He celebrated
Easter with the troops, with great pomp and geniality, in
order to prevent the Greeks, according to inveterate custom,
from dispersing, to keep the festival with their families at a
distance. The wise precautions of N. Œconomos, not only
kept the troops together, but attracted additional numbers.
On Easter-Monday the military and the naval forces were
entertained at a banquet, prepared by Œconomos at the public
expense. The troops, rising from the banquet, advanced with
great ardour to the very walls of the fortress, and offered
battle to the besieged. The challenge was accepted with
spirit, and a conflict was kept up with great obstinacy on both
sides for many hours, during which the blockading vessels
continued to fire on the enemy, of whom about 60 were slain.
The loss of the Greeks consisted in two killed, and seven
slightly wounded. Many of the Greeks greatly distinguished
themselves in this engagement, among whom may specially
be mentioned Polios Protopapadakes, who received a slight
wound on the shoulder. Nicolaos Lupes, Stephanos Glambes,
Manoles Kokolakes, Antonios Malitsevelos, Manoles Glymides,
and Mannaakes Protopapadakes.

Similar encounters continued to be of almost daily occurrence. The Turks, though they saw their destruction inevitable, sternly refused to humble themselves before assailants
whom a short time before they had regarded as their bonds-
men, and determined to bury themselves in the ruins of the
fortress rather than surrender to the insurgents Frequently
invited to capitulate on receiving security that their lives
would be spared, they proudly rejected every pacific offer,
and hurled back defiance and threatening: " Our fleet," they
said, " will soon be here, and then you will get what you
deserve." To this, the Greeks replied, " Tombazos is daily
expected. He has conquered your fleets, and he will soon
bring you to terms," and the like.

Incensed by these and similar taunts, the Greeks, about
the end of April, fell with great fury on a body of Turks
that issued from the fortress. A determined conflict took

place almost under the walls, and continued for many hours. A great number of Turks were killed. The loss, too, on the side of the Greeks was considerable, about 20 having been killed, and a great number wounded. Among the wounded was Manoles Protopapadakes, who had recently succeeded his father as pentacosiarkhos. His wound proved incurable, and he expired a few days after the engagement, and was buried with due honours in the monastery of Gonia. His death caused great and universal sorrow among the Cretans. He was scarcely 25 years of age, but had already displayed great intelligence, military capacity, and heroic valour. Two funeral orations were delivered in honour of him by the same gentlemen who had only a few days before delivered funeral orations over the remains of the heroic Siphakas.

After this, nothing of importance occurred at Kisamos, though small skirmishes and ambuscades occasionally took place. Meanwhile, the Turks were greatly and generally alarmed at the intelligence that a Hydriot was coming to direct the military operations of the Cretan insurgents. They inferred that if two Hydriot vessels were able to maintain so effective a blockade of the fortresses of Kisamos and Grambusa, now reduced to the utmost extremity, the other fortresses would be in the greatest danger, when blockaded by a large Hydriot squadron. At that period the name of Hydra struck the Turks with terror. It is clear from all this that both Greeks and Turks in Crete were aware of Tombazes' importance and approaching arrival in Crete, and S. Tricoupi is quite mistaken in saying, (vol. III, page 91) " That when Tombazes' vessels appeared in sight, both the Turks in the fortress, and the Greeks engaged in the siege, took them for a Turkish squadron, etc."

CHAPTER V.

On the 3rd of May, Emanuel Tombazes was appointed Governor-General of Crete, with the title of "Harmostes of the island of Crete." N. Œconomos the *interim* director of Cretan affairs, immediately suggested to the now functionary the extreme importance of his landing at Kisamos, in the vicinity of the blockaded fortress. Agreeably to this suggestion, Tombazes on the 19th of May, arrived in the gulf of Kisamos, with eight vessels, five of which were vessels of war, and three transports. Next day he landed under a salute of guns, and encamped almost within gunshot of the fortress, with the auxiliary force he had brought with him, consisting of about 600 men, enlisted at Nauplia, Hormione, Hydra, and Kalavria, the Harmostes having obtained from the Government a loan of 30,000 Turkish piastres, towards defraying the expense of raising them and transporting them to Crete. The Greek troops engaged in the blockade, immediately put themselves under the command of the Harmostes, who at once placed within range of the town, two mortars and two guns, of large calibre.[*] The same day, Œconomos, the Secretary-General, divested himself of the interim direction of affairs, presenting to the Harmostes a written report, drawn up by the able and accomplished G. Kalamaras, and containing a full account of the military affairs of Crete, down to that period.

The appointment of the Hydriot Tombazes was approved, not only by the Cretans, but by the Greeks in general, and hailed as an auspicious event for the cause, not merely of Crete, but of the whole Greek nation; as it was expected that the Naval Islands, that had hitherto done nothing for Crete, and had allowed the Viceroy of Egypt to transport

---

[*] S. Tricoupi, misled by erroneous information, asserts, in his History (Vol. III. page 91), that Tombazes landed fifteen guns, eight of which had been sent by the wealthy Greek Kallergus of Petersbourg, that Tombazes intended to make an immediate attack on Kydonia, that he brought with him 1,200 Romeliot soldiers, and that two Ionian vessels transported to Kydonia the Turks that had surrendered at Kisamos, amounting to 1,500 souls.

troops and stores to that island without opposition, would now, and especially the heroic Hydra, take an active part in the cause of Crete, the success of which had so important a connection with the general cause of Greek independence. Tombazes was accompanied by the excellent and most Phil-hellenic Englishman, Captain Hastings, who, in various ways, and in different parts, rendered most effective service to Greece, Stephanos Kanellos of Byzantion, George Spaniolakes, and Ioannes Latres, both of Smyrna, Nicolaos and Demetrios Kallerges, of Cretan descent, D. Christides, Kyriakos Scurtes, Stavros Sakhines, and Demetrios Kiosses of Hydra, and others, to serve under the Harmostes in various capacities. Meanwhile, the military leaders from the different provinces, including those of Sphakia, flocked with their followers to welcome and support the new Governor-General.

The task of this functionary was, owing to conflicting pretensions and rivalities among the military leaders, one of no ordinary difficulty. At this time there existed mutual distrust and aversion between the Sphakians and th einhabitants of the o ther twenty provinces of Crete, in consequence of the preponderance which the former, though so inferior in numbers, claimed over all the rest of their countrymen, and of which Tombazes had been fully apprised before he left Peloponnesus. It was generally hoped that, on the arrival of Tombazes, general order would be established, and that all dissensions would cease; and this might have been accomplished, had that functionary, agreeably to the urgent and repeated suggestions of the Cretan representatives in Peloponnesus, acted from the commencement and throughout with the strictest impartiality. So great was the prestige of this functionary on his arrival, owing, not merely to the high authority with which he was invested, but to the immense influence which Hydra then exercised in the affairs of Greece, that he could easily have restored and maintained harmony among the Cretans, had he resolved to act indiscriminately towards all with vigorous fairness and justice. Unfortunately, however, he determined, through the advice, it is said, of Scurtes, to receive the Sphakian leaders in his tent with a salute of guns, an honour which he withheld from the leaders of the other provinces, whom, moreover, he received with great coolness. This invidious and unfair distinction bestowed on the Sphakians, was regarded as a sanction to the arrogant and oppressive pretensions of those mountaineers, and increased in a very great degree the aversion already felt towards them by the other inhabitants of Crete, who, though they, at first, did not openly complain, were keenly wounded by the slight they had experienced.

The day after his arrival, the Harmostes sent the commander of the besieged fortress a written summons to surrender. The besieged, in reply, immediately despatched a deputation of prominent Turks, consisting of Eminagadakes, and Hadji Dervises Yanitsares, to wait on the Greek Harmostes. As they proceeded to his tent, they gazed with astonishment and awe on the mortars and guns, and on the troops drawn up in order, between whose ranks they had to pass. Those Turks who had hitherto despised their adversaries as a disorderly mob of insurgents, were now alarmed at the appearance of military discipline, and of the formidable force, both naval and military, now arrayed against them.

After some conversation, Tombazes gravely and resolutely addressed the deputation as follows :—" You must, forthwith, surrender the fortress. Be assured, that on surrendering, you will be transported in perfect safety, and without outrage, to any place you desire." The deputation before returning with this communication, received from the Harmostes the following distinct warning :—" To-morrow," said he, " we must have your final decision whether you mean to hold out, or to surrender. Assure the rest of the garrison, that the Government which sent me, as well as myself, is averse to all inhumanity and unjust bloodshed, and you will find that you can put confidence in my assurances and promises."

The day fixed for obtaining a reply passed over, and no communication was received. The day afterwards, the Harmostes sent the garrison the following written ultimatum. " If you do not surrender within three hours, I shall instantly order the guns and mortars to open a fire on the fortress." In these proceedings, Tombazes had the benefit of suggestions from the able and judicious Kalamaras. The Turkish deputation now returned in great haste to the Greek camp, and implored that a few days should be granted them, to enable them as they said, to get the people to consent to their surrendering the fortress. "I am a Hydriot," replied the Harmostes, with greater emphasis than before, " and I will not be trifled with. I am not a man to say one thing to-day and another to-morrow. This is the last time I shall receive a deputation from the besieged. If you do not

surrender before the hour stated, you will have to deal with
these mortars and guns, which, as you see, are already prepared for action." In fact, at the moment this was uttered,
Captain Hastings and others were standing by the mortars
and guns with lighted matches in their hands, ready to fire,
whenever the Harmostes should give the word.

The deputation went to the fortress, and soon afterwards
returned in great haste to the Greek camp, bearing a flag of
truce. They entreated the Harmostes to suspend hostilities
for that day at least, for the sake of the women and children,
and distinctly promised to evacuate the fortress on the mor-
row, after the capitulation, the term of which had been
agreed to, should be drawn up, and signed in form. In
proof of their sincerity, they proposed that the Harmostes
should detain, as hostages, the whole or whatever part he
pleased of the deputation, now consisting of five persons. The
Harmostes, however, though he consented to suspend hostilities, allowed all the members of the deputation to return, to
show he was convinced of their sincerity. He merely sent
a detachment of 30 men, consisting partly of Cretans and
partly of auxiliaries, who immediately hoisted on the fortress
the Greek flag instead of the Ottoman.

The leaders of the auxiliary corps were Demetrios Kapan-
taros of Kydonia (Hnivali in Asia Minor), Panayes of Lesvos,
Kostas Giones of Masses (Cranidi), Michael Duzinas of
Calavria (Poros), Pannyes Suliotes, Demetrios Dramalos
of Maina, Anastasios Vulgares, and Stavros Sakhines, of
Hydra. The Harmostes lost no time in appointing two
committees, the first consisting of Demetrios Kiosso of
Hydra, Nicolaos Andrulakakes of Sphakia, and Euthymios
Psaradakos of Kisamos, to take charge of all property
and effects in the fortress; and another consisting of
Duzinas and Martimianos Perakes, Cretans, supported by
a suitable military force, to maintain order during the
departure and embarkation of the Turks. At this moment,
fortune smiled on the Cretan cause.

The fortress was evacuated on the 25th of May, (o. s.),
on the following terms:—

"1.—That the fortress of Kisamos should be given up
to the Harmostes of Creto as representative of the Greek
Government, along with all its fortifications and defences,
its arsenal, with all arms therein, the magazines with all

military stores and all other effects, appertaining to the fortress.

2—That the Turks in the fortress should individually give up their arms, and go out unarmed, with the exception of ten individuals of distinction, who were to be allowed to retain their arms.

3.—That each of the Turks should be allowed to take whatever portable effects he thought proper, on proving to the Superintending Committee, that the effects in question were really his own property.

4.—The Harmostes of Crete engaged to protect the life and honour of the Turks who capitulated, as long as they remained on shore, until their embarkation on board the vessels, which were to convey them to their destination.

5.—The Harmostes further engaged to provide vessels to convey the capitulating Turks, agreeably to their request, to the fortress of Kydonia. The specified freight to be paid by the Turks immediately on their arrival at Kydonia.

6.—As a security to protect the Greeks on board of said transports from all danger of harm, either on the part of the passengers, while on board, or of these or other Turks, after their landing at Kydonia, as well as to ensure the payment of the stipulated freights, the Harmostes was to retain five Turkish hostages, selected by himself till the return of said transports to the harbour of Kisamos, and till their Commanders should declare that all stipulations had been fulfilled to their satisfaction, after which the Harmostes was to cause the said hostages to be conveyed in safety to Kydonia.

7.—The embarkation of the Turks and their effects was to commence early on the 25th of May, and the fortress was to be completely evacuated on the 26th, before sunset.

8.—The capitulation was to be signed by the Harmostes of Crete, the Turkish Governor of the fortress, and two other Turks of distinction, and one duplicate of the capitulation was to be retained by the Harmostes, and another by the Turkish Governor."

The hostages selected by the Harmostes were, besides the Governor of the fortress, H. Dervises Yanitsaris, Eminagadakes and two others. The last four presented themselves at once, and the Governor surrendered himself immediately after the evacuation of the fortress. As the whole of the Turkish garrison had persisted in their entreaties to be allowed to march forth with their arms, the Harmostes thought proper to grant their request. Accordingly 280 Turks marched out in arms. The whole number of individuals, including women and children, that left the fortress, amounted to 600 souls. All these were, without the slightest molestation or insult, conveyed in three vessels to Kydonia. The number of persons originally shut up in the fortress on the 3rd of February, when the Greeks invaded the Province of Kisamos, amounted to 1,800 souls, including 1,000 men bearing arms. Such had been, during the blockade, the loss of the enemy, partly from the ravages of the plague, and partly from the evils entailed on them by the war.

The capture of the fortress reflects great honour on the judicious and persevering efforts of Œconomos. He had adopted the most effective measures for reducing the fortress, and overcome immense difficulties, the last of which were at length surmounted by the arrival of the Harmostes. Such are the happy results of earnest and determined perseverance! The fortress of Grambusa,* then suffering greatly from famine in consequence of the blockade by sea, might have been captured soon after the fall of Kisamos, had the blockade of it been urged with the same energy and judgment as that of Kisamos. Unfortunately, however, the general direction of the affairs of Crete was no longer marked by requisite discretion, capacity, and local knowledge. In vain did the zealous and sagacious patriot Mavrokes raise his voice, earnestly and repeatedly, to point out the importance of Grambusa, from its situation, and the facility of reducing it. The naval blockade of that fortress, instead of being maintained with

---

* Grambusa, or Krambusa, is situated, not in the north-east of Crete, as Tricoupi erroneously says (Vol. III. chap. 55, p. 250), but in the western, opposite Ægileia. The island of Grambusa lies at the distance of a musket-shot from the mainland of Crete. On its elevated part towards the east is situated a strong fortress, built by the Venetians. To the north of the island, and at nearly the same distance as the mainland, is a small desert isle, now called Palæogrambusa (Old Grambusa.) Opposite these two small islands to the east is cape Kimarra, as it was anciently called. These two islands are probably what were anciently called Myla. At the Turkish conquest of Crete, in the year 1669, the Venetians retained by treaty the fortresses of Grambusa, Suda, and Spinalonga, for 30 years.

additional vigour, was neglected, and soon afterwards
entirely abandoned. This enabled such of the Turks, till
then blockaded in Grambusa, as were not required for its
defence, to repair elsewhere ; and those that remained were
further supplied with provisions, and subsequently gave
great annoyance to the insurgents. It is strange that so
experienced a naval officer as Tombazes, and especially
after the results of a naval blockade in reducing the
Peloponnesian fortresses, did not take advantage of the
opportunity to get possession of Grambusa.* He even sent
away Macrymurus, who had till then conducted the blockade by sea with remarkable vigilance and vigour, and who,
if he had been continued and duly supported in the same
service, would have soon reduced a fortress, the possession of
which would have been of immense advantage to Tombazes,
and would have furnished the Cretan patriots with a safe
retreat for their families, and a secure depot for private
effects and public stores. In a word, the capture of that
fortress would have saved all Crete from the humiliation
and the disasters produced the following year by the operations of the bold and energetic Khusein Bey. Such then
are the evils that arise from want of judgment, foresight,
and energy on the part of rulers.

After having made all necessary arrangements in regard
to the fortress, the Harmostes undertook an expedition
against the Seliniots. The province of Selinon, situated on
the western part of the southern coast of Crete, is bounded
on the south by the Libyan sea, on the east by unsubjugated
Sphakia, and on the north by Kisamos and the more mountainous parts of Kydonia. The whole surface of the province
has a great elevation above the level of the sea, and the
nearest part of it to the fortress of Kydonia, is about 11 or
12 miles distant. Its Turkish inhabitants, trained to the life
of mountaineers, were more warlike and hardy than any
of the other Turkish inhabitants of Crete, and had hitherto
triumphantly repulsed every hostile inroad into the province.
Confiding in the strength of their position and valour, they
determined, on hearing of the fall of Kisamos, to prepare
for resistance, and immediately conveyed their families,
cattle, and moveable property to Kandanos, a town in their
province, as a place of security. This town, situated on a
plain, nearly about the centre of the province, is divided
into four settlements, separated, but at small distance from

each other, and respectively called Nisaraki, Kuphalotos, Nycterianon, and Vamvacadon. They had occupied in the different settlements the strongest houses, which were surrounded like castles with walls, and they felt confident that they would be able to repulse the expected attack of the Greeks. But the plague was making fearful ravages among them, and the whole number of combatants that now remained, amounted only to about 1,000 men.

Against these the Harmostes now marched, at the head of a chosen army of 5,000 men, both he and his staff being convinced of the necessity of reducing the warlike Seliniots in their strongholds, before attempting other military operations, which would encounter great obstacles should these be left unsubdued. This view of the matter might have been very correct under other circumstances, but the attempt to reduce the Seliniots was very unwise at that moment, and speedily led to the most disastrous consequences. Tombazes was a most sincere Greek patriot, a skilful warrior, experienced in naval warfare, and a merchant of honour and integrity; he was, however, greatly deficient in experience and capacity for the general direction of military affairs. His want of foresight and judgment had already appeared in his neglecting the opportunity of reducing Grambusa. After the fall of Kisamos, the Harmostes ought not to have lost a moment in investing the fortress of Kydonia, and exhibiting himself to the besieged as a high-minded and determined Hydriot both by sea and by land, his prestige from the recent capture of Kisamos, and the noble exploits of the heroic Hydra, was such as to strike the enemy with terror, and enable Tombazes to make himself speedily master of the place, especially as the Greek troops now rallied round Tombazes, while the Egyptian forces were in the east of Crete, and left without a head owing to the death of Hassan Pasha.

Instead, however, of investing Kydonia, the Harmostes persisted in assailing the stronghold of the Seliniots, like a wasp's nest, which would not give molestation, if it had been let alone, as it was out of the way. The Seliniots were at this time suffering from the plague, and were not in a condition or a disposition to leave their homes and interfere with the Greeks at a distance. We proceed to detail the operations now directed against them.

On the 5th or 6th of June the Greek forces appeared

before Kandanos, and without delay all, but especially the
auxiliaries, commenced a furious attack on the Kandaniots,
on the western side of the place. The attack was vigorously repulsed, and the assailants were obliged to retreat
with the loss of about 30 or 40 men. Another attack was
simultaneously made by the Greeks on the other side of the
place, but was vigorously met by the besieged, who ever
pursued the assailants to some distance. About 15 were
killed and the same number wounded on both sides. Towards
sunset the conflict was suspended, the Turks returning to
their fortifications and the Greeks occupying positions around
the place. The Harmostes established his head quarters on
the south side, opposite Kuphalotos with his staff, comprehending Bastings, Scurtes, Œconomos, Papadakes and
others.

Next day a great deal of skirmishing took place on
various points, but with very small result. Meanwhile
Mutsoyannes with a small number of followers, including
Demetrius Kalliergos. repairing to a small stream near the
position of Harmostes, made a skilful attack on the enemy
at that point, and killed two or three of them. After some
skirmishing, the Turks in that position rushed upon the
small party of Greeks at the stream, who might have been
all cut to pieces, had not Tombazes, at the critical moment,
advanced against the assailants sword in hand. His staff
and immediate followers eagerly imitated his example,
the Turks were at once repulsed, and Mutsoyannes and his
party saved. The same evening, a large gun and a mortar
arrived from the schooner Terpsikhore, then lying on the
southern coast. These were immediately planted at the
position occupied by the Harmostes, and Hastings with his
Kœanidiot and Hydriot followers, instantly prepared to fire
on the town. There were many reasons for cannonading
and shelling the place, and this was expected by all the
Greek forces, as the besiegers moreover were prepared and
eager to storm the place. The whole of the enemy might
have been destroyed,[*] or compelled to surrender, had not
the Harmostes unexpectedly changed his mind owing to the
following circumstance :—

* Mr. Tricoupi says (vol. III. p. 92) that 1,500 Greeks were ordered to
storm the place, that they were repulsed, and that in an engagement which
ensued, 110 Greeks were killed and as many wounded, and that the Turks
lost 30. All this is untrue.

The Turks, on perceiving the preparations of the besiegers, were in great consternation. Their ablest leader, Kaûres of Selinon, was ill of the plague, and Aletsauses, Vedures, and Algerinos, Turks of great bravery, but far inferior to Kaures in capacity and influence, had the command in his stead. These, next morning, required an interview with the Greek leaders, which accordingly took place. Russos Vurdumbas and Poloyoryakes, after conversing with one of the Turkish commanders, communicated his proposals to Scurtes, who, having great influence over Tombazes, induced that functionary to grant the besieged a truce for two days, on condition that they should, within that period, retire under capitulation to Kydonia. Œconomos, G. Papadakes, and other leaders, full of indignation at this proposal, boldly remonstrated with Tombazes for acceding to such an arrangement in defiance of the determination which, with unanimous consent of all present, he had previously adopted. To these remonstrances he replied, that the enemy's fleet, according to authentic intelligence he had received, would speedily arrive at Suda, that the immediate evacuation of Selinon was of extreme importance, and the arrival at Kydonia of 4,000 souls from Selinon, with the plague among them, would, by increasing the scarcity of provisions, as well as by spreading the contagion, hasten the reduction of the fortress of Kydonia. The truce expired without effect, and the Harmostes again threatened to storm the place. This instantly brought a deputation from the besieged, imploring an extension of the truce. The real cause of their delay, is said, and appears to have been, their desire not to leave behind them, in the hands of his enemies, the expiring Kaures, whom they highly honoured and revered. But for this, the Turks would have naturally desired to depart with all possible haste from the place where they were suffering so much, and which they had no longer any hope of defending.

Meanwhile, however, the sagacious Seliniots were making every preparation for their safe departure. They despatched by night a swift-footed courier to Kydonia, who, evading the observation of the Greek sentinels, reached Kydonia in safety, and intimated the moment the Seliniots were to evacuate their stronghold, and asked the co-operation of the Kydonian Turks. On returning by night to Kandanoa, the courier was observed by the Greek sentinels, who fired on

him, but without effect. The unexpected report of muskets
spread alarm, and immediately produced a general discharge
of musketry throughout the Greek camp, from a belief that
the enemy intended a hostile sortie by night. At sunrise,
however, it became apparent that there was no hostile movement among the Turks, who were now seen to be collecting
their families and cattle, and who at the same time sent
back the same deputation to offer hostages, pretending to carry
the capitulation into effect. As the secret departure and return of the courier and other circumstances had reasonably
awakened the suspicions of the Greeks, the Harmostes sent
on Demetrios Kapandaros of Kydoniæ (Haivali) with the
followers he had enlisted at Nauplia, to occupy along with
V. Hales a position called Hayia, which it was necessary
for the Turks to pass, should they attempt to escape by
land.

The suspicions of the Greeks proved to be well founded;
for a little before sunset on the seventh or eighth day
after the arrival of the Greek forces at Kandanos, the
Turks set out without giving the proposed hostages, and
without completing the pending negotiations, taking with
them a great number of cattle, as well as effects and provisions, loaded on horses, mules, and asses. Tricoupi,
(vol. iii., p. 92) asserts, that the Turks were authorised to
depart by a mere private letter of Tombazes, and to take
with them a large quantity of provisions to a fortress reduced
to extremities, the fall of which the Harmostes expected to
hasten through famine, by sending to it the Turks now
besieged in Kandanos. What Tricoupi here asserts, if
at all a reality, was utterly unknown to all the Cretans.
If the Harmostes acted on this occasion, as Tricoupi alleges,
his conduct was a betrayal of his duty, from mistaken
humanity, or through the influence of fallacious suggestions.
What was intended as humanity to the Turks was cruelty
and injustice to myriads of the Christian inhabitants of
oppressed and bleeding Crete. Our own full conviction is,
that the Harmostes did not, and never said he did, act the
part Tricoupi imputes to him, and we cannot help thinking
that Tricoupi has here, as on too many other occasions,
shown a disposition to speak with bitterness and unfairness
of the Cretan patriots.

The brave and able Hastings, displeased with Tombazes'
unexpected want of judgment in the direction of military.

operations, immediately took his leave of that functionary at Selinon, and returned to Peloponnesus.

The Greek forces, indignant at the movement of the Turks, instantly pursued them; and, overtaking them at Seprona, a village of Kydonia, fell upon them there, and continued to assail them with deadly effect as far as Valsamioti; and, having surrounded them on a hill, killed about 300 men bearing arms, besides a large number of women and children. All the provisions, effects, cattle, and beasts of burden, were captured, and upwards of 1,000 persons were either made prisoners or killed. The loss of the Turks would have been more complete, had not a Turkish detachment from Kydonia come to their assistance. About 30 or 40 Greeks were killed in this affair. Kapandaros and V. Halea, however the matter is to be explained, quitted their positions instead of resolutely opposing the advance of the Turks. Next day Stamatios * of Anoya, a subordinate leader, returned with a few followers to Kandanos, and killed about 30 or 40 Turks, who were lying in a mosque, disabled by the plague from following their companions. This act of Stamatios, the Greeks universally denounced as inhuman and atrocious.

It is difficult to conjecture whence Tricoupi† derived his information regarding the occurrences at Selinon, which led him to speak of the Cretan Greeks in terms of bitterness, such as the most implacable enemy could hardly have uttered. He has given a narration of events that never occurred. He most unjustly and unfoundedly states, that the Cretan Greeks would have acted with treachery to the Turks who evacuated the fortress of Kisamos, had they not been prevented by the presence of the Harmostes. The truth is, that the Greeks, not only at the evacuation of the fortress of Kisamos, but at that of Kandanos, acted with perfect sincerity and good faith, and the only treachery intended or committed on either occasion was on the part of the Turks. The Cretans submitted implicitly and unanimously to the public decisions of the Harmostes, in connection with the evacuation of both places, though many of

---

* This Stamatios died of the plague a few days afterwards, at Skruf, a village of Kydonia on the river Platania, as he was proceeding with G. Papadakes, Œconomos, Chrysophopulos, Critovulides, and others, to the Assembly of Arcudœna. He was a very brave man, but intensely incensed against the Seliniot Turks, at whose hands he had suffered much.

† See vol. III. chap. 46, p. 93.

them regretted that the Harmostes had thought proper to re-inforce the garrison of Kydonia, by transporting thither the garrison of Kisamos, and though all of them would have blamed him if, in violation of the decision he had previously adopted publicly and by common consent, he had, as Tricoupi alleges, determined to permit the warlike Seliniot Turks to repair to Kydonia, and that too, with a supply of provisions. We are far from thinking that the Harmostes ought to have put to death persons whom the fortune of war brought into his power—that he should have imitated, for instance, the atrocity of Hassan Pasha, or the brutality of Seriph Pasha, of whom the former, in various parts of Apocoronos, and the latter in Minoa, slaughtered, or led into captivity, so many helpless victims. He might have treated the Turks who surrendered, or proposed to surrender, as the Greek authorities in Peloponnesus treated the inhabitants of the fortresses which capitulated there, safely transporting them to places specified in the capitulation, and at a distance from the seat of war. Probably the Harmostes, in acting differently to the great detriment of Crete, imagined that the Turks could appreciate his humanity and courtesy. Tricoupi, however, attributes his conduct not to unseasonable levity, but to the necessity of restraining the alleged cruelty and premeditated treachery of the Cretans, thus unfairly and rashly aspersed, for complaining of measures which, however well intended, were greatly detrimental to the Cretan cause.

The Turks who escaped were, on arriving at Kydonia, safely located in the environs of the fortress at Khalepa, Taratsos, and other villages of Kydonia, and served as a re-inforcement to the weakened garrison of Kydonia. The latter, emboldened by the presence of the Seliniot Turks, now ventured to encamp outside of the place, to escape the ravages of the plague, and soon began, in concert with the former, to meditate operations against the Kisamite insurgents in the vicinity, who had begun to harass them. They, accordingly, made a sudden attack one night on the Kisamite Greeks assembled at a hamlet near Varypetron. The Turks had received information regarding the presence and situation of the Kisamite Greeks from a Seliniot Ottoman female captive, who had made her escape the night before. The Turkish assailants killed 12 Greeks at the advanced post, and 20 others who had, on the alarm, rushed forward during the moonless night, without knowing what was the matter. The whole

of the Greeks stationed at the hamlet, and amounting to
about 300, would all have perished, as the assailants pretended to be Greeks, had not the followers of Georgios
Lupes speedily detected the fraud, and instantly dispersed.
The Turks returned to their positions without sustaining any
loss, and afterwards continued to make similar inroads, to
the great damage of the Greeks.

We have given above a faithful account of the occurrences
in Selinon. The apparent advantage of the Greeks proved
of little advantage to them, or, rather, led to reverses. They
had not yet learned to follow up success. The joy and hope
awakened by the arrival of Tombazes, his recent victory at Kissamos, the prestige of heroic Hydra, and many other favorable
circumstances,* proved but a transient glimpse. His administration soon ceased to inspire the enemy with awe or
respect, while the Greeks he had come to govern, began to
lose all confidence in his capacity and experience. The disappointment of the latter was greatly increased by the
following blunder.

Instead of instantly investing the fortress of Kydonia, and
compelling the Seliniot Turks, as well as the garrison, to
remain, as previously, within the walls, he unexpectedly, and
through the influence of Scartes and a few other exclusive
advisers, suspended all military operations, and in spite of all
the faithful suggestions, and earnest counsels he had received
in Peloponnesus, attempted to satisfy the special pretensions
of a party. On the departure of the Turks from Selinon,
the Protopapas of Sphakia, Rusos Vardumbas and a few

* Panayotes Nicolaides of Smyrna, in a pamphlet ou Crete, published in
1824, speaks of the affairs of that island at this period as follows:—" The
imposing cortege, the three vessels of war, the four transports with provisions, stores, and 700 warlike Romeliots, besides so many other sources of
prestige that accompanied the Harmostes to Crete, the full powers with
which he was invested by the Central Government of Greece to dispose of
the resources of fertile Crete, his encampment under the walls of the
fortress of Kissamos, his energetic and prompt preparation to bombard the
place, his creditable transporting of the garrison and inhabitants to Kydonia in safety, his immediate expedition against the Seliniot Turks, whom
he soon overawed and humbled, compelling them to evacuate their strongholds,—all these, added to the sincere and general respect with which the
Cretans, with the exception of the Sphakiots, honoured him before his
arrival, and the unlimited authority they conferred on him in writing—all
these circumstances, combined with the hope that Crete, after all her sufferings, was speedily to become a part of emancipated Greece, reasonably led
to the general expectation that the Harmostes would soon be enabled to
announce to the Central Government his progress in Crete in the same
triumphant terms which Cæsar employed in writing to the Roman Senate,
" I came, I saw, I conquered.' "

other Sphakians prevailing with the Harmostes to put himself under their guidance, conducted him by a rugged road among the mountains to Arcudæna, a village in the province of Rethymne, and at the foot of the Sphakian mountains. This party declared that, unless they obtained a confirmation of the special claims of Sphakia, they would no longer take part in the war, and Scartes induced the Harmostes to comply with their demands. It is necessary to state that the inhabitants of the district of Anopolis had no share in this manœuvre, but, on the contrary, strongly disapproved the conduct of the Protopapas and his associates.

Misled by the unwise counsels of individuals in his retinue, the Harmostes imagined that, by means of a General Assembly of the Cretans, he could now settle the civil and military affairs of the island, remove existing dissensions, introduce some degree of order into the financial department, so as to make the revenue nearly sufficient to meet the expense of the army, by a judicious and righteous management of the immense resources of Crete. He accordingly issued writs, summoning the provinces to send two plenipotentiaries each to the said village, and at the same time directed that these plenipotentiaries should come unarmed and without armed attendants. Œconomos, the Secretary-General, and G. Papadakes, addressed strong remonstrances to the Harmostes, representing to him that the present moment was not a time for holding political meetings, but for vigorous warlike operations against the enemy, that there already existed a Cretan constitution still in force, and sufficient for all present purposes, till the affairs of Crete should be in a state of greater tranquillity and security, and that, even if it had been necessary to convene an Assembly, Arcudæna was not a suitable place for it. They further complained that they had not been previously acquainted with the intention of the Harmostes to convoke an assembly. After having made such communications, but without effect, they, too, finally attended the assembly.

The Harmostes soon perceived the snare into which he had fallen. He saw all the other plenipotentiaries arriving unarmed, and without armed attendants, in compliance with his directions, while on the other hand the Sphakiot plenipotentiaries came accompanied by about 300 or 400 armed Sphakiots. In vain did the Harmostes as well as Scartes remonstrate with them for this open defiance of orders, to which all the

other plenipotentiaries had conformed   The Protopapas, the
main author of the whole machination, at first endeavoured
to excuse himself and his friends by alleging the existing
enmity between the Aulopotamites and the Sphakians as rendering it necessary to appear in arms at the assembly, for
their own protection ; while the real object of the Sphakians
was to urge their pretensions to exclusive possession of all
offices, both civil and military, in the island, by overawing
the assembly.   They now openly demanded that the military
commanders of every province in Crete should be Sphakiots.
This arrogant claim excited the indignation of the rest of
the Cretans.   There were natives of the other provinces, no
less capable than the very ablest of the Sphakiots to lead
respectively the forces of their native provinces, and the
proposal of forcing these to submit to the command of strangers was felt as a grievous insult, as stated by Tricoupi (vol.
iii. p. 96). In fact, the contentions thus excited nearly ended
in a disastrous conflict.   The Harmostes, to avert the danger
and remove all pretext on the part of the Sphakians, induced
the deputies of the Aulopotamites to retire from Arcadæna.
At length the Sphakian plenipotentiaries consented to sign
the following constitution, which the Harmostes had drawn
up himself, and now presented to the assembly.   These
Sphakians agreed to sign this document, on account, it
appeared, of the great concession made to them, inasmuch
as of the 16 members of the new Government, nine were
natives of Sphakia   But even this immense concession did
not satisfy these mountaineers, and they still grumbled at
the refusal of their claim to have Sphakians appointed to
the military command of every province in Crete. The
constitution was as follows :—

THE HARMOSTES OF THE ISLAND OF CRETE TO THE INHABITANTS
OF CRETE.

The Representatives of the Greek nation assembled at Astros, after
deliberating on the most suitable measures for establishing order, and promoting the general interests of Greece, and the progress of the Hellenic
struggle for independence, have thought proper, in reference to the existing
state of affairs in Crete, to send a Governor-General (Harmostes) to this
Island, to direct both the civil and the military service here for the space of
one year.   The National Government in virtue of decisions of the National
Assembly has been pleased to do me the high honour of appointing me to
the arduous functions of Harmostes of Crete, with the powers and duties
specified by the Assembled Representatives of Greece.   Entering on the
task assigned me, I have, after paying minute attention to the present state

of affairs in Crete, and after maturely deliberating on the most accurate information I have been able to procure, come to the conclusion that a settlement of the form of Local Government for Crete, in accordance with the fundamental principles of the Greek Constitution, would, under existing circumstances, greatly promote the welfare of this island. With this view, I have drawn up a form of Local Government for Crete, which will be communicated to the inhabitants accompanied with requisite orders and directions, and I shall do every thing that depends on me towards upholding and enforcing these for the general benefit of Crete.

PROVISIONAL GOVERNMENT OF GREECE.

THE HARMOSTES OF CRETE.

Form of Local Government for Crete to be enforced for the space of one year.

Of the HARMOSTES (Governor-General).

1. The Harmostes shall be Representative of the National Government of Greece throughout the island of Crete.

2. He shall be responsible for his public acts to the Central Government alone.

3. He alone will officially and directly correspond with the National Government.

4. He shall have the general superintendence and direction of the civil and military service in Crete.

5. He will propose to the National Government military promotions and rewards.

6. Whenever he takes the field in person, he shall appoint a substitute.

7. The Harmostes shall issue his orders and instructions through the medium of the competent offices.

8. When personally at the head of an expedition he shall issue orders directly so far as regards the conduct of the war.

9. He shall appoint all administrative functionaries, and change them, as the public interest may require.

OF THE HIGHER BRANCHES OF THE PUBLIC ADMINISTRATION.

10. The general Administration of Crete shall be divided into three departments, respectively conducted by :—

(a) A Home Office.

(b) A War Office.

(c) A Finance Office.

ORGANIZATION OF THESE OFFICES.

11. Each of them shall consist of Five Members, equal in power and authority, and a Secretary-General.

The Finance Office shall comprehend a Treasurer and a Treasurer's Clerk.

COMPETENCY OF THEIR RESPECTIVE OFFICES.

(A) HOME OFFICE.

This Office shall superintend and direct whatever regards—

12. The appointment and conduct of the Eparchs.

13. The registration of the inhabitants, houses, and of all private property, the topography and description of the villages, towns, &c., of the island.

14. Public Instruction.

15. Agriculture, manufactures, and trade.

15. Public hospitals.

17. Enlistment of troops.

18. Public roads, bridges, postal service, &c.

19. General police, measures, weights, and currency, harbours, public health, and everything relating to general order and public security.

20. Courts of Justice.

21. Ecclesiastical affairs.

22. The payment of public functionaries.

23. An accurate account of receipts and expenditure to be submitted monthly to the Finance Office.

(B) WAR OFFICE.

This Office shall direct and superintend whatever regards—

24. The duties and conduct of all individuals in the military service.

25. The organization of the Army.

26. The pay of the army.

27. All military movements and proceedings.

28. The building, repairing, and maintaining of fortresses, arsenals, &c.

29. The provision and management of military stores and supplies.

30. The management of military hospitals, the treatment of the wounded or sick therein, the appointment and the conduct of military physicians and surgeons.

31. The maintenance of military discipline.

32. The distribution of spoils and prize money.

33. The care and disposal of prisoners of war.

34. The Administration of the Navy.

35. The drawing up of military laws, the establishment and superintendence of Courts-martial, &c.

36. All other matters relating to the warlike service.

37. The War-Office will submit to the Finance-Office an accurate and minute monthly report of its receipts and expenditure.

(C) Finance-Office.

This Office shall superintend and direct whatever regards—

38. The statistics of Crete, comprehending a description and evaluation of property, national or private, etc.

39. The collection of all direct or indirect taxes, customs, or other public contributions.

40. The exportation and sale of such part of the public revenue as may be collected in kind.

41. The management of all state property and the disposal of the produce thereof.

42. It shall, by daily report, acquaint the Harmostes of the amount of cash in the public treasury.

43. It shall keep a general register of receipts and expenditure for all Crete.

44. It shall submit to the Harmostes a quarterly balance-sheet of receipts and expenditure.

Secretary-General.

45. The Secretary-General of each department shall regulate and superintend the internal management of the office.

46. He shall not occupy his time with the private matters of the Directors of his department.

47. He shall take part in the deliberations of the Directors, with permission to make suggestions, as well as to give information, but without a vote in their decisions.

Treasurer.

48. The Treasurer receives and takes care of all moneys transmitted to the Treasury, and cashes all written orders of the Finance-Office, and no other.

49. He keeps a general register of all receipts and disbursements.

50. He submits to the Finance-Office every day a summary account of the state of the Treasury.

51. He presents to the same office a detailed balance-sheet of the Treasury, annexing thereto written vouchers for all sums disbursed.

Rules and Regulations of the Offices.

52. The State-Offices and the Treasurer shall be always at the headquarters of the Harmostes, or his substitute.

53. The State-Offices act in virtue of written orders from the Harmostes, or his substitute, verbal communications being null and void.

54. The Directors of each office of the Administration shall have daily sittings and deliberate on the business of the day along with the Secretary-General.

55. All documents issuing from any State-Office shall be signed by all the Directors, or at least by three of them being present, and countersigned by the Secretary-General.

56. No act of any State-Office shall be valid without being endorsed by the Harmostes.

57. Each State-Office shall daily submit to the Harmostes a regular written statement of all affairs brought under its consideration.

58. No single Director shall have power to open letters addressed to the office; but these shall always be received by the Secretary-General, and opened by him in presence of the Directors, or at least in the presence of one of them.

59. No Director shall interfere with any matter of the competency of any other State-office, except that of which he is a member.

60. No Director of a State-Office shall leave the seat of Government without leave of the Harmostes on pain of immediate dismissal, and the appointment of another individual in his stead.

61. More than two Directors of one and the same State-Office shall never be simultaneously absent from the seat of Government.

62. Each State-Office shall have the superintendence and direction of all its subordinate functionaries.

63. Every charge brought against any Director of a State-Office, and relating to his public functions, shall be communicated to the Harmostes.

64. Directors or Secretaries-General accused of a State crime, or a delinquency committed in the discharge of his functions, shall be tried by a commission of three members appointed by the Harmostes. If the charge be of a serious nature, the accused functionary shall be suspended from his functions, and brought before the competent tribunal, and if acquitted, he shall resume the duties of his office.

65. All civil functionaries, before commencing their functions shall swear the following oath : " I swear in the presence of God to be faithful to the National Government of Greece, faithful to our country, and to discharge the duties of my office diligently and conscientiously."

———

PROVISIONAL GOVERNMENT OF GREECE.

THE HARMOSTES OF THE ISLAND OF CRETE.

In consideration of the present state of affairs of this island, the Harmostes has deemed it expedient to introduce a few slight changes into the form of provincial administration, ordained and enacted by the National Assembly of Astros (No. 12 of the record of enactments). The said form of Provincial Government, with the said modifications, according to which the provinces of Crete are to be administered, is hereby made known to all the inhabitants of Crete.

FORM OF ADMINISTRATION FOR THE PROVINCES OF CRETE.

1. The island of Crete shall be divided for the present into 24 Provinces, comprehending the adjacent islets belonging respectively to each.

Province.	Islets.
Heracleia	Dia,
Knossos	

Provinces.			Islets.
Tomenos		...	Gaidaronesa.
Hierapytna		...	Kuphonesa.
Pyryiotissa			
Khersonesos			
Petra			
Lasiti			
Monoprosopon	...	...	Paximadia.
Kaenurion			
Arcadia	...	...	Spina.
Sitcia	...	...	Longa.
Messara			
Malevizion			
Mirabelo			
Rethymne			
Leuka Ore (Sphakia)	...	...	Gaudos, Gandopula.
Apocoronos	...	...	Suda, Palea Suda.
Amari			
Hayios Vasileios			
Mylopotamon			
Kydonia	...	...	...	Hayios Theodoros.
Kisamos	...	...	...	Grambusa, Ponticonesos.
Selinon	...	...	...	Elaphonesos.

2. Each province shall be divided into town and village districts.

3. Each province shall have an Eparch, an Eparch's Principal Clerk, an Inspector of Revenue, an Inspector of Expenditure. The functions of Commissary of Police shall be discharged, in the inland provinces by the Eparch, and, in those of the coast, by the Captain of the port.

4. Each village shall have Demogerons (Elders) the number of whom shall be in proportion to the population, villages containing a hundred families, having one elder; those containing two hundred families, two; those containing three hundred, three; those containing four hundred, or upwards, four.

5. Towns, whether chief towns of the province or not, shall have Elders, whose number shall be on the preceding proportion to the population.

EPARCHS.

6. The Eparch shall be directly appointed by the Harmostes, but he shall not be a native or previous resident of the province, and one and the same person shall not be simultaneously Eparch of two different provinces.

7. The Eparch, as representative of the Government, shall have the general superintendence of the province.

8. He shall correspond with the Harmostes through the Home-Office.

9. It will be his duty to watch with vigilance the proceedings of all subordinate functionaries within the province.

10. He shall have an armed Police force at his disposal, greater or less, according to the extent and state of the province. The said force being composed of inhabitants of the same province, and its commander shall be proposed by the Eparch, and appointed by the Harmostes.

11. The Eparch superintends the execution of the decisions of Courts of Justice.

12. He shall support with the armed force at his disposal, the Inspectors, Elders, and the Port-Captain in the discharge of their functions.

13. He shall execute through the Inspectors and Elders the orders of the Government addressed to him, relating to the raising of troops, and shall put the troops thus raised within the province, under the orders of the commander, appointed by the Government.

SECRETARY-GENERAL.

14. The Secretary-General is appointed directly by the Harmostes.

15. He has, under the Eparch, the direction of the Eparch's office.

16. He countersigns all public documents, signed by the Eparch.

17. In the absence of the Eparch, he discharges the duties of that functionary.

INSPECTORS.

18. The Inspectors are elected from among the most respectable inhabitants of the province, by a majority of vote, in the following manner :—

(a) Each village chooses one or more electors, and the towns, whether or not chief towns, do the same, and the suffrage of each elector is appreciated according to the number of families which he represents.

(b) The electors meet in the chief town of the province, and elect the Inspectors.

(c) No election is valid unless the candidate has obtained two-thirds of the suffrages.

19. The Inspector collects the revenue of the province, and keeps an accurate account of his receipts and disbursements.

20. He is not at liberty to disburse any sum whatever, without a regular written order of the Eparch.

21. He submits through the Eparch to the Finance-Office a quarterly report of his procedure.

22. He receives through the Eparch orders addressed to him by the Finance-Office, and corresponds with the Eparch.

23. The Inspector of expenditure meets the necessary expenses of the public service for the province, receiving the sums necessary from the Inspector of revenue.

24. He keeps an accurate account of all sums received, and of all sums disbursed.

25. He submits to the Finance-Office every two months, through the Eparch, a regular account of his proceedings.

26. He receives through the Eparch orders from the Finance-Office, and corresponds with the same functionary.

HARBOUR-CAPTAIN.

27. The Harbour-Captain is appointed directly by the Harmostes, and discharges the functions of Commissary of Police.

28. He receives orders from the Home-Office through the Eparch, and corresponds with that functionary.

DEMOGERONS.

29. The Demogerons are elected by the inhabitants of the province, in the following manner :—

(a) The inhabitants of each village, as well as of the towns, including the chief town, meet and elect a Demogeron by a majority of suffrages; the respective number of Demogerons being in the proportions specified in Nos. 4 and 5.

(b) No election is valid unless each Candidate obtain two-thirds of the suffrages.

(c) The Demogerons on being elected, receive a written certificate of their regular and lawful election.

30. The Demogerons are bound to execute the lawful orders they receive from the Eparch.

31. They keep an accurate account of all sums they receive, and all sums they disburse.

32. They submit to the Eparch a monthly report of their proceedings.

33. They discharge also the functions of Justices of the Peace.

34. Eparchs found guilty of illegality in the discharge of their functions, are dismissed and punished.

35. Any Inspector, Eparch's principal Clerk, or Harbour-master, accused of illegality in the discharge of his functions, shall be suspended from his office by the Eparch, who shall appoint an *interim* successor, and submit the case to the Harmostes. These *interim* functionaries shall be selected by the Eparch from among the Demogerons.

36. Should any Demogeron be accused of illegality in the discharge of his functions, and the accusation be found by the Eparch and the Inspectors substantiated, the functionary thus convicted is dismissed, and a successor appointed conformably to No. 29.

MEETING OF THE DIRECTORS AND SECRETARIES-GENERAL OF THE THREE STATE OFFICES.

The Directors and Secretaries-General of the three State Offices hold a general meeting once a week, that is, every Thursday.

The Chairman of this general meeting shall be the oldest Director present, and one of the Secretaries-General in turn shall act as its Secretary.

At this general meeting the proceedings of the different departments are respectively reported.

The meeting deliberates and decides on all matters of their joint competency.

The decisions of the meeting are formed by a majority of votes.

The Secretaries-General, besides having the right of making suggestions and furnishing information, have each a vote in the decisions.

The meeting submits its decisions to the Harmostes, who either adopts them, or communicates written reason for rejecting them. If after mutual communications between the Harmostes and the general meeting a difference of opinion still remain, the meeting shall directly submit the affair in question for the decision of the National Parliament.

The said meeting receives petitions or other communications presented by any citizen on any subject.

None but members are admitted to the meeting.

The Harmostes may convene a general meeting of the Directors and Secretaries-General of the three State-Offices, whenever he thinks proper.

PROVISIONAL GOVERNMENT OF GREECE.

THE HARMOSTES OF THE ISLAND OF CRETE,

As a judicial establishment, is an indispensable and essential part of a form of administration for the island, and as the judicial organization recently promulgated by the National Government of Greece is, owing to existing circumstances, not yet adapted to Crete, ordains :—

(a) The following judicial organization to be forthwith submitted to the National Parliament for its approbation and sanction, shall be for the present carried into effect throughout Crete.

(b) The Home-Office shall direct and superintend the establishment of tribunals, conformably to the present organization.

E. TOMBAZES, HARMOSTES,

.... The Secretary-General.

TRIBUNALS.

1. The Justices of Peace shall decide without appeal claims not exceeding 50 piastres.

2. They take cognizance of claims exceeding that amount. But if either of the parties object to the decision, the case shall be forthwith transmitted to the competent tribunal.

3. Four tribunals of first instance and one court of appeal shall be established for the whole island.

Each of the tribunals of first instance shall consist of three members and the court of appeal shall consist of seven.

5. The judges shall be elected and appointed in the following manner:— Each province shall elect, conformably to the § ...... of the organization, three citizens of irreproachable character, not under 30 and not above 60 years of age. And three shall all repair to the seat of government, and from their number the Harmostes shall select and appoint 19, that is, as members of the Court of Appeal, and 12 as members of the four tribunals of first instance, respectively.

6. The names of the remainder shall be recorded by a special act of the Home Office, and from that list all vacancies occurring through death, deposition, or resignation, shall be filled up.

7. Each tribunal has a registrar appointed by the Harmostes.

8. In each tribunal the eldest member shall be president.

9. The seat of each of the tribunals shall be the chief town of the province, also the seat of the Eparch.

10. One of the tribunals of first instance shall be established in each of the following provinces.

(a) One in the province of Kissamos, its jurisdiction comprehending the provinces of Kissamos, Selinon, Kydonia, and Apocorohos.

(b) One in the province of Amarion, its jurisdiction comprehending the provinces of Amarion, Rethymne, Hayios Vasilios and Mylopotamos.

(c) One in the province of Sphakia, its jurisdiction comprehending that province only.

(d) One in the province of Pyryiotissa, its jurisdiction comprehending the provinces of Pyryiotissa, Messara, Monoprosopon, and Malevizlou.

11. The decisions of the tribunals of first instance in all cases in which the claim does not exceed 200 piastres, shall be without appeal.

12. Their decisions in cases in which the claim exceeds that amount, are subject to appeal before the Court of Appeal.

13. The tribunals of first instance shall decide, without appeal, criminal prosecutions of small importance.

14. They shall also take cognizance of criminal prosecutions of greater importance, but then their decisions are subject to appeal before the Superior Court, to which the whole instruction of the case shall be transmitted.

15. The seat of the Court of Appeal shall be the place where the Cretan Administration has its residence.

16. The Court of Appeal cannot take cognizance of any affair in first instance.

17. It shall decide in last resort cases subject to appeal, and already tried by a Court of first instance.

18. Cases in which the Court of Appeal shall modify or annul the decision of a tribunal of first instance may be brought before a Supreme Court of Greece.

19. No tribunal shall be competent to act unless all its members be present.

20. In the decision of cases, all tribunals shall be guided by the laws in force, according to the § 80 of the Provisional Constitution of Greece.

21. In each Court the decision shall be formed by a majority of votes.

22. Each tribunal shall transmit a monthly report of its proceedings to the Home Office.

23. The tribunals shall in the meantime be guided in their proceedings by general rules of procedure communicated to them by the Home-Office.

24. Conformably to the § 78 of the Provisional Constitution of Greece, all criminal trials shall be conducted with publicity.

25. No member of a tribunal shall take part in any case in which either of the parties is his relative.

26. Judges are irremovable except on being convicted of criminal acts.

27. The Harmostes shall appoint a Procurator-General, to prosecute before the tribunals any civil or military functionary, against whom there may be ground for instituting criminal proceedings.

28. Judges are liable to criminal prosecution for legal offences committed either in the exercise of their functions or otherwise.

29. The Procurator-General shall collect and submit to the Harmostes the evidence in the case, when it is intended to institute criminal proceedings.

30. The Harmostes suspends the accused functionary and transmits the evidence to the competent tribunal, that is, to Court of Appeal, if the accused functionary be a member of a tribunal of first instance, and to one of the tribunals of first instance, if he be a member of the Court of Appeal.

31. The tribunal, to which the evidence is submitted, shall examine it minutely and maturely, and if it find ground for further proceedings, the Harmostes shall transmit the accused functionary with all the evidence in support of the charges brought against him to the National Government of

Greece, that the accused may be tried conformably to the §...... of the Provisional Constitution of Greece.

32. All commercial difference shall be tried by arbitration and without appeal.

33. The number of arbitrators in each case shall be five, one to be appointed by the Eparch, and two by each of the parties.

In such unseasonable occupations did the Harmostes and the Cretans spend their time at this crisis.

On the 12th of July Georgios Draconianos, Ioannes Mutsakes, Georgios Lupes with their followers, and a great part of the auxiliaries, suddenly attacked and occupied the village of Taratsos, situated at a short distance from the fortress of Kydonia. Regarding the possession of that strong position as of great importance, the Turks made a sortie from the fortress, but, after a vigorous attempt to recover Taratsos, were repulsed with loss. In the number of Turks killed on this occasion was Hadji Dervises Yanitsares, one of the hostages at the surrender of Kisamos. Soon afterwards the Turks in greater force made a second attempt to recover the village; but though they brought with them several guns and maintained an obstinate conflict during the whole day, they returned at last without having accomplished their object, or made any impression on the Greeks, and with the loss, it is said, of about 170 killed, and a great number wounded. These they conveyed in boats to the fortress. The Greeks in this affair had about 20 killed or wounded.

The Turks, however, provoked at the sight of a Greek station in the immediate vicinity, devised numberless plans for attacking it. Issuing from the fortress one day they placed about 200 men in ambuscade in a ruined building between Taratsos and the village Macryteikhos, and made a few others move about openly as if in pursuit of game. The Greeks at Taratsos, on observing them, paid little attention at first to the circumstance, but, after some time, rushed forward in great numbers to attack these straggling Turks, and unawares fell into the ambuscade; and being suddenly and vigorously attacked by the Turkish detachment that had been concealed in the ruined edifice, lost 36 of the foremost. The Turks stripped the slain, and would have inflicted a still greater loss, had they not quickly abandoned the pursuit, from the apprehension of an ambuscade on the part of the

Greeks. Similar adventures continued to be of almost daily occurrence. At length the resolute Seliniot Turks, having blockaded Tarataos for three days, compelled the Greeks there to retire from their position during the night and with great peril for want of provisions. Thus the Turks were now masters of nearly the whole of the plain of Kydonia.

Meanwhile, the Turks of Rethymne also resumed a threatening attitude, the Harmostes, during all these proceedings, being exclusively occupied in framing laws for Crete. Accordingly, a large body of Turks made a sally from the fortress of Rethymne, and attacked the Greek positions in the vicinity, but were vigorously resisted, and at length repulsed by the Lampæi under Suderos, and the Rethymnians under Strates Deliyannakes and Manoles Rustikianos; and, being pursued to the very walls of the fortress, had about 30 of their number killed or made prisoners.

In the meantime the Egyptian fleet, under the command of Ismael Gibraltar, and consisting of about 50 vessels, partly ships of war and partly transports, arrived at Heracleion; and, after landing provisions, warlike stores, 3,000 fresh troops, and a new commander-in-chief of the Turkish forces in Crete, an Albanian called Khusein Bey, successor to the late Hassan Pasha, returned to Alexandria unmolested; this being the second time that an Egyptian fleet had come to Crete and returned, without even seeing a Greek ship of war. The landing of fresh troops and stores on this occasion greatly disappointed and discouraged the Cretans, who had confidently hoped that their shores would be protected by a Greek naval force, as the Central Government had undertaken the direction of Cretan affairs, and Hydra, in the person of the Harmostes, had espoused the Cretan cause. The new Turkish commander-in-chief, a person of great energy and perseverance, lost no time in preparing to take the field. Finding the Eastern Provinces almost entirely in possession of the Turks, in consequence of the calamities previously inflicted, he resolved to attack at once the insurgents still holding out in other parts of Crete.

The situation of Crete was now perilous in the extreme, and was soon to involve in equal peril the whole of Greece. The Central Government, instead of adopting instant measures to avert the storm about to burst over Peloponnesus, allowed the Cretans to struggle alone against the over-

212

whelming forces of the common enemy. Some of the Cretan Representatives* earnestly and repeatedly urged the Central Government to send to Crete a military force of about a thousand men, which, if landed on the Eastern coast of the island and in the province of Minoa, might by an opportune diversion effectively baffle the general plan of the enemy. They explained to the Government the strength of the positions specified, the eagerness of the Cretan patriots to renew the struggle the moment assistance should be sent them, and dwelt on the necessity of supporting the Cretans still in arms, as, by giving occupation to the Egyptian troops in Crete, the Central Government might prevent the impending invasion of Peloponnesus and Continental Greece. Unfortunately, however, these earnest representations and remonstrances were disregarded. The recent defeat of Dramales had inspired many Greeks in Peloponnesus with over-weening confidence, and shut their eyes to the fact that a far more formidable enemy than Dramales would invade Peloponnesus the moment he had suppressed the insurrection in Crete. Thus the Cretans, abandoned in the hour of need, were soon overpowered. The insurrection in their important island was for a time suppressed, and Crete became a convenient and safe bridge, over which the Viceroy of Egypt could send with ease and security successive armies to Peloponnesus, and other parts of Greece. The consequence was the desolation of the Peninsula, and all those calamities, which, but for the battle of Navarino, and the arrival of the French army of occupation, would have led to the ruin of the Greek cause, not to say the almost total extermination of the Grecian race.

The Harmostes after the occurrences at Arcudæna repaired to Vrysæ, a village in the province of Amarion, where he took up his residence for the purpose of superintending the execution of the new Cretan constitution, and of attempting to make head against the hostile movements of the new Egyptian Commander-in-chief. He made preparations for taking the field, but postponed his departure. In the meantime, the Pasha, more energetic and with greater military capacity and experience, commenced operations, and daily harassed the insurgents. The Harmostes summoned the Sphakians to take the field under his command,

* Such were at this time Zaccharias Practikides, Emm. Antoniades, and Demetrios Pardalakos.

but they very partially obeyed. He also summoned the armed insurgents of other provinces, but they, too, paid little or no attention to the summons, owing to the discontent* that had spread among them in consequence of what took place at Arcudæna, as well as owing to the unexpected arrival of a fresh Egyptian expedition at Heracleion. Thus the Cretan Government brought upon itself the contempt, not merely of the enemy, notwithstanding the indulgence that had been shown them, but of the Greeks also. Tombazes undoubtedly was actuated by a sincere desire of serving Crete, and through Crete the whole of Greece, but he was very far from possessing requisite judgment, capacity, and experience for his high and arduous task.

He at length succeeded in collecting an army, about 2,000 strong, from the provinces Sphakia, Rethymno, Lampe, Amarion, and Gortyna. As to the patriots of Kydonia, who might have added great and effective strength to this army, he left them in Kydonia to contend with the vindictive Seliniot and Kydonian Turks. The Harmostes appointed Rusos Vurdumbas Commander-in-chief of the Greek force, now consisting of about 3,000 men, with Georgios Suderos, Michael Kurmules, Poloyoryakes, and many other subordinate officers, leaders of divisions. The whole of the auxiliaries under Panayes Souliotes, Demetrios Kapantaros, and Panayes Mitylenæos, formed part of the array. The Harmostes, after concerting measures with all these leaders, put the army in motion about the middle of August with the intention of opposing Husein Bey, who was then encamped with about 12,000 troops, partly cavalry and partly infantry, at Hayia Varvara, a village in the plain of Gortyna, and preparing to advance into the western parts of Crete. The Greeks, though immensely inferior in numbers, boldly occupied Yeryero and Amuryelæ, strong positions at the foot of mount Ida, confident of being able to harass the enemy. But here again disasters occurred such as may always be apprehended in the movement of an army, not only undisciplined, but torn by internal jealousies and dissensions.

Two or three days before the engagement about to be described, Vurdumbas proceeded at the head of 300 of his immediate followers to Anlopotamos, to enforce his previous determination of intruding Rusakes as leader of the insurgents of that province (see page 181.) Though we must blame the

* See P. Nicolaides' pamphlet on Crete, page 14.

obstinacy of the Aulopotamites in rejecting, under the circumstances, the leader recommended to them, we must, at the same time, condemn still more strongly the arrogant determination of Vurdumbas to impose on them a leader to whom they unanimously and persistingly objected. This attempt to lord it over the province at this critical moment, so intensely incensed the Aulopotamites as to lead to a defeat, when a victory might have been achieved that would have compelled the enemy to retire, or at least impeded his advance, and would have animated the patriots all over Crete, as had been previously the case in similar emergencies, and in particular during the great expedition of Seriph Pasha, (see page 117,) as well as when the terrible Hassan Pasha invaded these same parts (see page 156).

Meanwhile the day approached on which the Greek army was to try the fortune of war in a conflict with the enemy. A Greek detachment, advancing to the immediate vicinity of the enemy's camp, killed five Turks, and, collecting a large number of cattle and beasts of burden, drove them with great speed towards the Greek positions. This naturally roused the indignation of the enemy ; and nearly the whole of their cavalry pursued the daring detachment of Greeks as far as Amuryela. Here a sharp engagement ensued, in which both parties displayed alternately remarkable impetuosity and resolution, so that the number of slain on both sides was very considerable. During the conflict a large body of Greeks, who happened to be posted on a neighbouring hill, were surrounded by the enemy's cavalry. The Greeks thus surrounded, defended themselves with great courage for a long time against the repeated charges of the cavalry ; and though parties of patriots hastened from all parts to the rescue, all their gallant endeavours proved vain. In fact the eagerness of the Greeks to save their brethren only increased the danger, as it collected around the hill reinforcements of the enemy, both cavalry and infantry. The gallant detachment on the hill consisting of about 100 men, was at length overpowered, and all cut to pieces, with the exception of about 15 or 20, who, contrary to all expectation, effected their escape. Among the slain were the following brave and experienced leaders :— Panayes Mitylenæos, who had taken part in the Cretan struggle from its commencement, and had greatly distinguished himself on numerous occasions, and Astrinos, a Cretan of Gortyna, (who must not be confounded with Hadjidakes,)

who had served and distinguished himself under Niketaras in
Peloponnesus. Night coming on put an end to the hard-
fought engagement, in which the Greeks had about 150
killed and a great number wounded, while, as it was afterwards ascertained, the enemy's killed or wounded amounted
to 500. Upwards of 100 horses were killed. Yet the victory
was on the side of the Turks. The following night the whole
Greek army dispersed, and the Harmostes, with a few followers, escaped from Yeryere with considerable difficulty and
danger, and arrived at Aulopotamos.

The day after the engagement the victorious Turks overran the plain of Gortyna, and, advancing as far as Tympakion,
carried desolation wherever they went. A detachment of
them having attacked the famous Labyrinth, was gallantly
repulsed by a number of Greeks who had taken refuge there.
The assailants sustained some loss, and, after repeated attempts
to storm the place, returned to their camp, and prepared for
a fresh expedition.

Thus was dispersed a Greek army which, from its number
and valour, might, if ably conducted, have sustained the
struggle all over Crete. The enemy, vigorously following up
the victory, advanced towards the west without opposition,
striking universal terror, burning the houses, slaughtering
or capturing the inhabitants. The Harmostes a few days
after the fatal affair of Yeryere went on board his schooner,
then lying at Good Havens (Kaloi Limenes), and repaired by
sea to the fortress of Kisamos, leaving the Egyptian commander undisturbed in his operations. Such was the result
of the first and only general engagement that the Harmostes
risked in Crete. It proved disastrous not merely by the
loss and defeat which the Greeks sustained, but mainly
by the irremediable indirect consequences to which it
led.

If the Harmostes had possessed the good sense to avoid convoking an assembly at Arcudæna, at a moment when vigorous warlike operations, and not crude legislative arrangements, were required; and if he had possessed military capacity and experience, he might easily have averted the impending dangers. If, for instance, instead of going to so remote a
point as Kisamos, he had employed all the forces and
resources at his disposal to make head against the Egyptian
commander, when that energetic leader marched from the
east towards the west of Crete, he might have so harassed

and perplexed the enemy as to baffle all his movements. Had the Harmostes subsequently repaired in person to the east, the various bodies of armed insurgents that still continued to hold out among the mountains there, would have given him a cordial and joyous reception. Besides, his appearance in those parts would have revived the courage of the insurgents generally, who had looked for his arrival as that of a deliverer. Moreover, the insurgents who had been driven to feigned submission for a time, would have again risen in arms; and there would have been collected in those parts a numerous and most efficient Greek army, supplied with provisions in the greatest abundance. In a word, had the Harmostes acted from the moment of his arrival with wisdom and vigour, he would have effected a most important diversion, and either compelled the enemy to return to head-quarters, as the Cretans had themselves repeatedly done in great emergencies, or at least, he might have saved the Cretan cause from total ruin. The mountains of Crete afford in times of danger safe retreats to enterprising patriot leaders.

If the Harmostes had been a man of experience and judgment in military affairs, he would, instead of embarking in his schooner, have ordered that vessel and any other at his disposal or within his reach to cannonade the fortress of Hierapytnos, situated on the coast, and might have carried it, owing to the wretched condition of its garrison at that moment. He might then have driven the Turks from the stronghold of Siteia, thus perplexing and alarming the enemy, and reviving the courage of the patriots. Such successes would have added a fresh prestige to the patriot arms of the west. To conquer, it is necessary to assail the enemy on all points and with unrelaxing vigour, within the bounds of possibility. We repeat that it was in the power of the Harmostes, by the exertion of an ordinary portion of vigour and judgment at this critical moment, to avert the calamities which Mehmet Ales was about to bring first on Crete and then on the whole of Greece. To the omissions, then, of the Harmostes, combined with the dissensions and irresolution of the Cretans, are to be attributed the disasters which soon afterwards befel both Crete and the rest of Greece.

Khusein Bey marched from Hayia Varvara about the beginning of October, and, as we have already stated, advancing without opposition to Panacron or Amarion, Lampe, and Rethymne, reached Kurnopatemata in Apocononos. He did not think proper to advance in the meantime beyond Halmyros, as he still apprehended attacks from the Sphakians and other armed insurgents of the western provinces. Returning without molestation, he entered Aulopotamos, and, encamping at the village of Melidonion, began to treat with his usual ferocity the Christian population within his reach. He, too, was now about to perpetrate a deed of horror equalling the most revolting atrocities of his predecessor Hassan Pasha. But, unfortunately, the Cretans had begun to view with apparent indifference the most appalling wrongs and sufferings of their brethren, if they did not occur in their own immediate neighbourhood, without reflecting, that calamities, commencing in one province, would soon reach every part of the island, if means were not adopted to avert the impending danger.

The Harmostes at this time wrote repeatedly from Kiamos to the Central Government, explaining the state of affairs in Crete, and charging the Cretans with indifference to the interest of their country and refusal to serve. He expressed the gloomiest anticipations unless the Central Government should immediately send to Crete adequate reinforcements both military and naval, to avert the arrival of another expedition from Egypt, as well as to make head against the enemy's forces already on the island. "It is in Crete," he said, "that the danger is to be met. If this island be lost, the rest of Greece may immediately expect the same fate." Notwithstanding this earnest appeal, no reinforcements were sent. The Central Government merely wrote to the communities of Hydra and Spezzia requesting them to send at least 15 vessels to Crete, to revive by their presence the courage of the patriots, and prevent them at least from utterly despairing of the cause. The shipowners* of these islands, however, replied that they had already

* It may be necessary to inform the English reader that at this period Greece had not a single national vessel, and that all the brilliant exploits of the Greeks at sea were achieved by a fleet of private merchantmen, mainly supported by the patriotic contributions of the shipowners. M. Finlay says with perfect truth, "The leading families of Hydra acquitted themselves of this duty nobly, the Condoriottes, the Tombazes, the Miaules, the Buduris, the Tsamados, the Bulgaris, spent large sums. In this way, wealthy families have been reduced to want." (See Hellenic Kingdom.) It is but fair to add that the same remark applies also to the leading families of Spezzia and of Psara. A. I.

exhausted their means in the equipping and maintenance of their vessels, and that they were unable to send the force required, without a subsidy from the Government. But the resources of the Central Government were scanty, and civil dissensions, then beginning to arise in Peloponnesus, diverted attention from the pressing claims and perilous situation of Crete. Besides the successes obtained in Peloponnesus through the overthrow of Dramales, had so elated some short-sighted patriots in Peloponnesus, as to lead them to believe that all further danger was but imaginary, and that the independence of Greece was already achieved. Consequently, in spite of all the remonstrances of the Harmostes, Crete was left to herself, and was soon after reduced by the overwhelming forces of the Viceroy of Egypt.

The patriotic cause of Crete was now daily losing ground. Three Egyptian expeditions had already arrived without encountering by sea the slightest opposition, and a fresh expedition was now expected, while there existed no prospect of assistance to the Cretans, either by land or by sea, from the Central Government. In November the Cretans beheld with dismay, and all but despair, the arrival of 12 Egyptian ships of war, which, without molestation brought an abundant supply of provisions and warlike stores, and remained at anchor in the harbour of Suda. to overawe the whole island. They received intelligence at the same time, that their representatives in Peloponnesus had earnestly and repeatedly applied to the Central Government for aid to Crete in her hour of danger, but in vain. Under such circumstances what were the Cretans to do ?

The military chiefs of some of the provinces and those, too, the most distinguished for influence and practical sagacity, now presented themselves to the Harmostes, and put into his hands a memorial, in which they stated their conviction that, unless Crete received immediate assistance, the insurgents there would soon be overpowered by the irresistible and daily increasing forces of the enemy. They added, that the Christians of Crete, if all hopes of assistance from the Greek Government were at an end, would, to save themselves from extermination, implore the protection of some neighbouring Christian power. The memorialists, therefore, entreated the Harmostes to obtain from the Central Government an immediate and distinct reply for their guidance. The Harmostes immediately forwarded

the memorial with his testimony to the genuineness of the
signatures, and at the same time stated " that the Cretan
insurgents were no longer disposed to risk their lives in the
cause of independence, but were prepared to deliver up their
island on the first emergency to England." In conclusion
he asked for reinforcements to avert such calamity.

" The loss of Crete," he added, in another communication
which he sent to the Central Government about the beginning of December "would indeed be a momentous calamity."
Nothing, however, was done to save the island. The Cretans
had not merely to contend against the warlike natives, whom
they had from the commencement of the war so heroically
combatted, but they were called upon to withstand the still
more formidable Egyptian enemy, and to expose themselves
for three whole years to disasters and the danger of extermination, in behalf of the general cause of Greece. Unaided,
with their own resources they had destroyed many thousands
of the enemy, and, having long waited for assistance in vain,
they were on the verge of despair. It was therefore no
wonder, under the circumstances, they should think of
asking the protection of powerful England. A drowning
man will grasp at anything within his reach affording the
slightest hope. As to the propriety of asking, and the
possibility of obtaining, what was contemplated, that is,
the exclusive protection of England, it may be remarked
that, at an early period of the war of independence,
the leading Peloponnesians had entered into negociations
with the Ionian Government, with a view to obtain, in case
of necessity, English protection, and that the whole Greek
nation in 1825, during the desolating incursions and atrocities of Ibrahim Pasha, when threatened with destruction,
eagerly placed itself under the exclusive protection of
England, and was thus saved from ruin. The Harmostes
was not justifiable in alleging, as Speliades in his memoirs
records "that the Cretans, in entertaining such an idea, showed
themselves to be without patriotism and without conscience.
In fact, we are disposed to think the statement of Speliades
inaccurate, and can hardly believe that Tombazes could have
uttered such an outrage against the Christians of Crete,
that had, both during the present struggle and on every
previous occasion, exhibited so striking proofs of patriotic
devotion to the cause of Greek nationality. Speliades must
either have too readily adopted erroneous information, or,

being under some prejudice against the Cretans, notwithstanding their claims to sympathy and respect for their signal services to the Greek cause, must have expressed his own views by attributing them to Tombazes. If the Cretans, by entertaining the intention in question, showed they had neither patriotism nor conscience, as Speliades asserts, the same charge applies equally to the whole nation, as the whole nation in similar circumstances determined to have recourse to the same expedient.

The Central Government, on receiving the last communication of the Harmostes, despatched D. Pardalakes, one of the representatives of Crete, and Kopas the Cephellonian, to examine the state of matters in Crete, and report. The time, however, for examining and reporting had gone by, and the urgency of the case required immediate and vigorous action, to avert the danger. Thus was the insurrection in Crete soon after suppressed, and the possession of that bulwark of Greece prompted and enabled Mechmet Ales to undertake the entire subjugation of Greece—an enterprise which he was on the point of accomplishing, when God put it into the hearts of the three great European Powers to step forward to save Greece and the Greeks from utter ruin.

Khusein Bey, having, as we have already mentioned, encamped at the village of Melidonion to pass the winter there, he continued his efforts to reduce a number of Greeks who had taken refuge in an adjacent grotto.[*] Many of the Greek inhabitants having during, former hostile incursions, saved themselves in this grotto, it was thought that it might afford refuge on the present occasion, because it was believed that the presence of the enemy would be, as previously, but temporary. Those hopes, however, now proved vain, and the refugees, amounting to 370 men, women, and children, including 30 armed insurgents, at length fell into the hands of the merciless enemy. Recollecting the slaughter or captivity that befel in previous instances refugees at Apocoronos, and at the grotto of Minoa or Mirabelo, who had surrendered, either because they could hold out no longer, or because they had been deceived by

---

[*] This grotto, of considerable depth and breadth within, and with a narrow entrance, is situated on the south side of a very rocky hill to the north-west of Melidonion. The inhabitants of Melidonion and of the adjacent villages were accustomed to convey to this grotto as a place of security agricultural produce and portable effects in times of danger.

treacherous promises, the Greeks now besieged by Khusein
Bey withstood all the efforts of the assailants for upwards
of three months. Khusein caused his troops to cannonade
and bombard the grotto without intermission, and detachments of the assailants frequently attempted to carry the
place by storm, but every attempt was baffled by the determined bravery of the 30 armed Greeks within the
grotto.

The Aulopotamites and the Knossians repeatedly implored the assistance of the insurgents of other provinces,
and the Harmostes wrote from Kisamos enforcing their
request; but the Cretans were now forgetful of the truth,
"that the fire which is consuming our neighbour's house,
will, if not extinguished, soon reach our own." Instead of
hastening to the assistance of their brethren the Cretans of
other provinces thought only of securing their own families,
and seemed to behold the sufferings of others in the common
cause with indifference. The auxiliaries and a few native
Cretans, comprehending Antonios Langianos, a few Anoyani
and others, alone went to the aid of the Aulopotamites.
The Turks were now attacked repeatedly with greater or
less effect, sometimes near Vlykhada, sometimes at the
village of Hayia, where a considerable number of the enemy
were killed, and sometimes at Margaritæ, and Hayios
Mamanta, where an impetuous onset of the Turks was
repulsed, and about 20 of the enemy killed by Langianos,
Georgios Marules, Ioannes Khamalakes, Kyriakos Sguros,
Vasilios Hayiomamites, and their followers; and where the
Turks would have sustained much greater loss, had not
the able and experienced Langianos received a serious
wound. The Albanian Turks, breathing vengeance for the
checks they had formerly experienced, now commenced
inroads in various directions. Advancing as far as the
mountainous villages of Anoya and Goniæ, they burnt
these, and captured at a position called Zamedan a great
number of women and children. They were, however,
themselves subsequently attacked by Anoyani under Slokos,
Staviales, Niotes, and Stavrules Xetrypes, and driven from
their position. The Anoyani by this movement rescued a
considerable number of the captives, and killed about 30 of
the Turks at the passage of the small river of Joniæ.

This partial success, however, was of no avail to the
Greeks besieged in the grotto, and now reduced to extremi-

ties. The ferocious Pasha in the meantime effected an aperture in the roof of the cave, through which he threw down suffocating combustibles, while he completely blocked up the entrance below with green wood and olive-stones. They all within the grotto were suffocated by the smoke in January 1824, choosing rather to submit to destruction in the grotto than surrender themselves to the enemy, from whom they had nothing to expect but instant slaughter or infamous captivity.

While Khusein was vigorously pushing his merciless operations in Aulopotamos, and the Cretan cause was sadly losing ground, a few patriots in the neighbourhood of Kydonia conceived the hope of reviving the courage of the insurgents, and made an inroad into the plain inflicting some damage on the enemy. The Harmostes, too, collecting a body of Kisamite, Seliniot, and Kydonian Greeks, attacked a detachment of Turks stationed at Varypetron, drove them from that position, and killed some of them. About the same time Keramiani under Ioannes Hales and Apocoronites under Nicolaos Konstantudakes, commenced a movement in another direction, and in various parts considerably alarmed and annoyed the enemy. All these movements, however, led to little or no result. Something of importance could have been effected, had the Turks been attacked in their head-quarters at Aulopotamos; but as this was not attempted, hostile detachments were sent forth by the Pasha wherever he thought proper, and met with no opposition.

In this state of things the attention of the insurgents was again turned to the importance and possibility of taking Grambusa by surprise. Mavrakes had often recommended an attempt to get possession of that stronghold as a point where the cause of independence might be kept alive in Crete till more auspicious times might come round. From personal knowledge he again assured Georgios Papadakes that the fortress of Grambusa might with great ease be taken by stratagem. Both he and Georgios Papadakes pressed the subject on the attention of the Harmostes, and induced him to enter into their views, convinced that if Grambusa were in possession of the insurgents, Crete would yet be saved from subjugation. The plan was forthwith communicated to all the Cretan leaders and those of the auxiliaries, and was at once unanimously and cordially approved. Within five or six days a body of about 500 men was collected, all eager to share in the enterprise. The Harmostes, gave the command of the whole force to Demetrios a Laconian, surnamed Dramales. His reason for appointing this person to head the attempt was the hope of interesting the non-Cretan patriots in the enterprise, as well as the belief that persons who had served in Peloponnesus, would from experience be more skilful than Cretans in conducting such an undertaking.

After making all the necessary preparations, the whole force passed over to the island of Grambusa in boats, during a moonless winter night, (between 11th and 12th of December,) the Harmostes following on board the Terpsichore. The assailants were conducted in the dark by Mavrakes, and succeeded in planting the scaling ladders on the walls, on the N. E. and narrowest part of the fortress. The first that mounted were the brothers Antonios and Raphael Sosanes Hydriots, and were immediately followed by Vuzomarcos and P. Suliotes (who happened to have arrived from the eastern provinces just in time to join the enterprise) and some others. On entering the fortress the assailants found a Turkish sentinel sitting by his wife in the guard-house with no apprehension of danger. The Turk, on perceiving the assailants, wrapped himself up in his cloak, and began to utter yells of amazement and despair. The sentinel was immediately killed, but the wife was spared. About 150 Greeks, including the Commander with his secretary Papamoskhos, as well as A. Panayotes and G. Papadakes, followed those who had already mounted the wall.

They thus made themselves masters of that part of the ramparts, where they ascended, and they would have soon made themselves masters of the whole of the fortress, had their movements been guided by skill and reflection. Unfortunately, however, they had attempted to take a fortress by stratagem without providing the necessary ammunition for making use of the guns they might have captured, and without previously arranging combined operations, and without even procuring more than two scaling ladders, and these were such as soon to prove useless. Want of ordinary foresight led to the failure of the enterprise and the disaster that overtook the assailants. The blame does not lie with the brave and patriotic men who eagerly consented to share in the enterprise, but with those who, having proposed and adopted the plan, neglected to provide such things as were obviously and absolutely necessary for its success. At the same time, the gallant party that mounted the walls cannot be excused for not taking advantage, vigorously and in concert, of the success they had achieved. Instead of instantly advancing, while the Turks were still asleep, to other parts of the fortress, and seizing commanding positions —instead of bursting open the gate from within while it was yet dark, and admitting the rest of the assailants, waiting for daylight to summon the garrison to surrender, they spent a great deal of time in vain by uselessly lingering on that part of the ramparts, of which they first got possession. The first assailants spared the life of the sentinel's wife with praiseworthy humanity, but thoughtlessly neglected to prevent her escape. Eluding their observation in the dark, she proceeded through paths with which she was familiar, and alarmed the garrison.

About dawn, Vuzomarkos, Raphael, and Karayannes, with a few followers, hastened to take possession of the adjacent bastion, while others went directly towards the gate; but Vuzomarkos was killed, and Karayannes wounded by shots from a neighbouring house in which part of the garrison had already posted themselves. Soon afterwards Raphael also fell, and his brother received a wound in the arm. The garrison, now posted in commanding positions, fired from all points both with musketry and guns on the assailants within the fortress. These called to their friends for assistance, and the Harmostes, sword in hand, exposed himself to imminent danger, while urging the remainder of the Greek troops to mount the walls and aid their brethren, but in vain. The troops, however, who had not yet attempted to mount the walls, began to retire towards the ships, discouraged by the sight of wounded comrades descending or let down from the ramparts, and still further alarmed at the return of Dramales, the commander of the enterprise, Papamoskhos, and others who, deserting their companions, attempted to excuse their cowardice by alleging that the guns of the enemy had made great havoc among the Greeks that had scaled the wall.

The Greeks still within the fortress continued, during the whole day, though entirely without refreshment, to defend themselves with great gallantry. Towards night A. Pan-

ayotes descended from the rampart, and urged Papadakes to
follow his example, but Papadakes refused to do so, and
bravely remained at his post to encourage the survivors, in
the hope that night might bring them some relief. The
Turks, however, watching their movements, and determined
at all hazards to destroy them, rushed upon them with impetuosity and assailed them at close quarters. Many were
killed on both sides in the desperate conflict that ensued, and
some of the Greeks attempted to save themselves by leaping
from high rocks into the sea, and were thus dashed to pieces
or drowned. G. Papadakes having leaped from the rampart
broke one of his legs, and in this condition made his way
behind a large stone, from which he continued to defend
himself with great bravery, till he received a mortal
wound.

Thus Crete lost 83 chosen warriors, including G. Papadakes, M. Vazakes, P. Souliotes, Raphael Sosanes, and the
brothers Kotsoi. Georgios Papadakes was a native of Zizipheus, a village in Apocoronos. Distinguished for ardent
patriotism and every moral excellence, he devoted all his
energies to the cause of his country, and at length offered
himself a willing sacrifice on the altar of freedom. Markos
Vazakes or Vuzomarkos a native of Askyphos in Sphakia,
and Panayes Souliotes of Constantinople, were men of great
bravery and pre-eminent military skill and experience.
Throughout the struggle for independence in Crete they had
distinguished themselves on numberless occasions, and had
been latterly the main stay and soul of the insurgents in the
Western Provinces. Raphael Sosanes of Hydra was an able
seaman, and a man of signal courage and daring. The three
Brothers Kotsoi, surnamed Politakia, had been followers of
Niketaras in Peloponnesus, and, while under him, had greatly
distinguished themselves, and, while serving in Crete under
Mitylenæos they invariably displayed the same gallantry and
patriotic zeal. The whole Turkish garrison amounted to 100
men, 25 of whom were killed in their heroic defence of the
fortress and of their families.

The failure of the attempt to take Grambusa put an end to
all hope of success to the Cretan cause for the present; and
the Harmostes announced to the Central Government on the
29th of December, that matters were becoming worse every
day. "Our attempt to get possession of Grambusa, and to
make that fortress a rallying point for the national cause in

Crete, has failed with immense loss. The inhabitants of the Eastern Provinces, abandoned to the fury of the overwhelming Egyptian army, have begun to submit. Khusein Bey remains encamped in Aulopotamos, without receiving the slightest molestation. The rest of the Cretans now look with apparent indifference on the sufferings of their brethren in the east of the island. If the Central Authorities of Greece hope to save the national cause in Crete, a naval force, as well as military reinforcements, must be sent without a moment's delay, while the insurgents of Kydonia and Rethymne still hold out. If these gallant patriots be left unaided, Crete is lost to the cause of Greek independence." Notwithstanding this earnest appeal, the Central Authorities did nothing for Crete; but in the meantime Khusein continued unremittingly his vigorous operations for the entire suppression of the insurrection throughout the island.

The Harmostes, besides applying to the Central Government, wrote to his friend Anastasios Tsamados of Hydra, requesting him to repair forthwith to Crete, for the purpose of attempting, in concert with the Harmostes, to burn the 12 Egyptian vessels of war then at anchor in the Bay of Suda. The patriotic Tsamados forthwith repaired to Crete, and arrived at Vapheus, a village in Apocoronos, about the beginning of January.

Tsamados and the Harmostes were convinced from the observations they made, and the information they received, that the Egyptian vessels in question might easily be destroyed if the necessary means were forthcoming; as Apocoronos was still in the hands of the Greeks, and the crews of the fireships might, after lighting their trains, repair in their boats to the neighbouring coast of that province. Tsamados undertook to destroy the enemy's squadron, but required, at least, 100,000 Turkish piastres to equip 10 or 12 vessels necessary for the enterprise. The Harmostes, instantly convening various leading patriots of Sphakia and other provinces, urged them to provide the requisite sum. Part of the amount having been forthwith raised partly by private contributions, and partly from public funds, it was resolved to furnish the remainder by the sale of plate belonging to monasteries. Tsamados, accompanied by Andreas Kriaras of Sphakia immediately proceeded to Hydra with the money that had been raised, and the plate that had been set apart to be pledged or sold for completing the necessary amount.

On arriving there they handed over the plate to the Hydriot authorities, who, by melting the silver and disposing of the other articles, made up the sum required to fit out the expedition. Unfortunately, however, the Hydriot authorities did not allow Tsamados to select for the enterprise the naval officers he specified, but obliged him to accept others in their stead. This circumstance frustrated the intended Cretan expedition, as Tsamados declared he could not undertake the task without the co-operation of those naval officers, in whose zeal, courage and capacity he had entire confidence. Tsamados immediately acquainted the Harmostes with the result. There existed in Hydra jealousies and dissensions among the shipowners and naval commanders of Hydra, and the party opposed to Tombazes and Tsamados not only refused to defer to their wishes in this matter, but generally thwarted the efforts of Tombazes in his Cretan Administration. It is truly deplorable that such rivalries should be allowed to prevail, even in the most critical emergencies, and, at the hour of greatest danger, mar a national cause.

In the meantime, Khusein Bey, after destroying the unfortunate Christians that were blockaded in the Grotto of Melidonion, returned to Heracleion, and made preparations to take the field again, which he forthwith did with all his forces. Entering Gortyna, he overran that province, and afterwards Panacron and Rethymne, without the slightest opposition. He dispersed the body of insurgents under Kurmules, obliging them to flee, some to the rugged heights of Ida, and some to the islets of the Good Havens. He soon dispersed and drove to the adjacent mountains the insurgents still in arms in other provinces. Some patriots were under the cruel necessity of laying down their arms, and submitting to the oppressor, to save the lives of their wives and children. Hope was still entertained that the progress of the Pasha would be checked at the defile of Halmyros; but the Harmostes had already repaired to Sphakia, and gone on board his schooner, the Terpsichore, anchored at Lutros.

Such at length was the irresistible attitude of the vigorous and resolute Khusein about the middle of February, when he appeared on the frontier of Apocoronos. From his camp at the village of Episcope in Rethymne he sent a threatening letter to the Apocoronites; but, as it appears, did not venture to pass Halmyros without overawing the warlike insurgents still in arms in Sphakia, Kydonia, and the adjacent

Q

provinces, or at least, before ascertaining the state of matters in those parts. Various insurgent leaders at this most critical moment evinced a deplorable indifference to the sufferings of their brethren, as well as to the national cause. Khussin's letter was, in substance, as follows:—

"Inhabitants of Apocoronos! I am going to enter your province with all my forces. As, however, I wish to avoid unnecessary bloodshed, I shall remain here three days, and I call upon you to present yourselves here within that period, to obtain for each individual a written protection, testifying his submission and proving his dutiful and pacific intentions. If you allow that period to elapse without laying down your arms and presenting yourselves here to obtain protection, my troops will at once march into your province, and then for whatever calamities may overtake you, you will have yourselves to blame."

The Apocoronites had, as during former inroads of the enemy, repaired to the neighbouring mountains; but, on receiving the preceding letter, many of them assembled at Vothonakia (see p. 137) to deliberate on what course they were to take. All present were, on hearing the letter read by Critovulides, overwhelmed with sorrow and dismay, under the impression that, after all their sacrifices and sufferings, the cause of independence was lost. A difference of opinion, however, prevailed; some, recollecting with tears of self-respect the victories they had achieved, spurned the idea of shameful submission, while others, far more on account of their families than of themselves, declared that further opposition would now be madness. Critovulides, aware of the sentiments they respectively entertained, addressed them as follows:—

"It ill becomes those brave patriots who, at the commencement of the struggle, took up arms, and along with the Sphakians and Kydonians heroically maintained the cause of freedom—it ill becomes them to think of disgraceful submission. Difficult and perilous as the crisis is, it would be far better to hold on at all hazards, and consult with the companions of our former contendings and victories on the measures now to be adopted in common." After various other remonstrances, he reminded them, in conclusion, that a Greek squadron, for the equipping of which the necessary funds had been already sent, would soon reach the Cretan coast.

All present resolved to follow the earnest exhortations of Critovulides, and immediately sent a deputation to Sphakia and another to Kydonia, to concert measures with the patriots there, and at the same time implored the Kydonian and Sphakian insurgents to hasten to their aid, in order to enable them to attack the Turkish army before it cleared the pass of Halmyros. The Harmostes, at the same time, sent word to Rusos Vurdumbas and Suderos, to hasten with their respective followers to Halmyros, and reminded them that the Greek squadron, which might be daily expected, would alarm the enemy and revive the courage of the patriots in Crete. But none responded to the call! After considerable delay Vurdumbas and Suderos proceeded to Skyphos, the former with 50 men and the latter with 100, and these, too, mustered with no small difficulty. But these leaders did not advance even so far as Hulicampos and Prosneron, villages of Apocoronos, where they might at least have averted the fearful slaughter of Christian brethren which soon after occurred there. The brothers Halles did not even stir from Kydonia. Halmyros was the suitable place for checking the progress of the Turkish army, in spite of all its strength and impetuosity. It was at that memorable place that the Cretans, few in number, still inexperienced in war, and with scanty resources, had been formerly able to make head against a numerous and most formidable enemy.

When the period of three days had elapsed, and none of the Apocoronites presented themselves to make their submission, the Pasha, on the fourth day, divided his troops into two detachments, and despatched them respectively in various directions. Some of these marched to the foot of the mountains of Sphakia, to which great numbers of the Christians had fled. Another body of Turkish troops proceeded to the hills of Kephaladæ, where they massacred or doomed to captivity about 400 Christians, men, women, and children. On this occasion Malatos, an influential clergyman of Zizipheus, in Apocoronos, Georgios Pharakes, a brave warrior of Phre, Ioannes, the father of Critovulides, and many others, perished; while Helene Mikhalokæna, a venerable old lady, the daughter of Hadji Nicolos, a gentleman of great wealth and eminent worth, the mother of the Antoniadæ, and many other females of various ages and ranks, were made captives, and with the exception of the first two, who were soon after

ransomed, were sent to the slave-market of Egypt, or elsewhere. At Kephaladœ the Turks met with resistance from
G. Daminos, Prinoles, and Sakires, and lost a few men.
Khusein, then, proceeded successively to Stylos, Neokhorion,
and Armeni, villages of Apocoronos, and remained in those
parts about five days.

Retribution soon overtook the Sphakian mountaineers for
their heartless indifference, with which they viewed from a
distance the dangers and destruction of their brethren in
other provinces.

It was generally expected that Khusein, after suppressing
the insurrection in Apocoronos, would at once march into
Kydonia. But, instead of doing this, he returned to the
village of Prosneron on the afternoon of the fifth day after
his inroad into Apocoronos. The surviving Apocoronites,
expecting that Khusein would again advance to the foot of
their mountains, had had the precaution to retire to positions
more mountainous and inaccesssble. Khusein, however, again
left Apocoronos about the middle of March. and, having,
after it was dark, advanced with great despatch through
the passes of Krape and Katreus, which have been rendered
ever memorable by the defeat of the Turks there in 1821,
arrived about midnight at Skyphos, a village of Sphakia,
to the amazement and consternation of the inhabitants.
Without stopping there he continued to advance during the
night, and about daybreak unexpectedly made his appearance
above the villages Kometadœ, Murion, and Anopolis, having
passed without the slightest molestation, and even without
being observed, the large woody glen of Imbros, and many
rugged positions in the province of Sphakia. His unexpected arrival spread universal confusion and dismay. Encamping at Anopolis, he instantly proceeded towards Lutros
with part of his forces, in the hope of getting possession of
that town with all the public storehouses there, which at
that time contained a large quantity both of ammunition
and provisions. But the Greeks from the shipping there
set fire to the storehouses before his arrival, and the noise of
the conflagration, re-echoed by the neighbouring mountains,
has been described by persons then on the spot as terribly
impressive and sublime. By this precaution the enemy
received a check, and the helpless inhabitants obtained a
brief respite to save themselves from destruction.

It is painful to describe the state of the unarmed and helpless Christian population, who now ran in all directions to escape from the merciless enemy. As on similar occasions, crowds repaired to Sphakia in the hope of finding safety there. The promiscuous multitude now dispersed, and, amid tears and lamentations, the nearest and dearest of friends lost sight of each other, each hastening to save himself. Confused crowds of despairing fugitives stood on the beach,* each offering whatever he had, to be taken on board some of the vessels anchored in the harbour. Other crowds were running breathless the almost inaccessible glen of Hayia Rumele, (see page 51,) or wherever the slightest hope of safety invited.†

* The Harmostes had, a short time before this, despatched his schooner to Hydra, to urge the speedy departure of the squadron for Crete; and Theodorus Xenos contributed 200 dollars, and N. Prasakakes, G. Skylizzes, Zacharias Liangs, and others also contributed other sums, to meet the expenses of the expected squadron. There were at this time in the harbour of Lutron vessels of various sizes, and among these was a French vessel belonging to Captain Castel, freighted by Th. Xenos. The greater part of the Sphakian vessels were at this critical moment without sailors, and not in a state to get under-weigh. Consequently, the fugitives crowded to the other vessels, and chiefly to the French vessel, and the multitudes that could not be received, ran towards Hayia Rumele. The French captain refused to receive any fugitives on board, and made a protest against Th. Xenos on the alleged ground that he had only provisions for his crew, and threatened, if compelled to take fugitives on board, that he would, on leaving the harbour, land them on the nearest point of the island. Th. Xenos, however, succeeded in appeasing him by promising to provide whatever provisions might be required, and from on board the French vessel directed the Cretans to a storehouse, which had been overlooked, containing a considerable quantity of biscuit belonging to his friend Georgios Giones, of Hydra. The Cretaus preferred any danger at sea to the risk of being landed on any part of the island. Accordingly, some of the most vigorous and the boldest of them, immediately volunteered to fetch the biscuit, and with the assistance of ropes suspended from the vessel, they succeeded, notwithstanding the heavy sea, in bringing on board about 40 sacks. The vessel then set sail for the opposite island of Gandos, though the storm still continued. Here Th. Xenos purchased some cattle at his own expense, and thus by his kindness and energy had the satisfaction of rescuing and conveying to the island of Melos in safety a considerable number of fugitives that might otherwise have fallen into the hands of the Turks. The inhabitants of Melos, however, refused, it is said, to permit the fugitives to land, alleging that their island was too small and poor to admit any addition to its population; but M. Brest, the French consul there, compelled the Mellans to desist from their discreditable and heartless purpose. The Cretans by their sufferings, sacrifices, and exploits, had furnished occupation to a large hostile force in Crete, which if not detained there, would have gone forth and desolated the islands of the Ægean. But their services in the common cause were now forgotten.

† A Greek schooner, belonging to Thera (Santa Irena) took about 800 of the fugitives on board, and sailed with them for that island. About daybreak the commander of the schooner found himself off Kydonia, and in the midst of hostile vessels, which, firing on him, compelled him to surrender. The Turks, taking the captain of the schooner along with Ioannes

Thousands of these wretched fugitives, hungry and half-naked, now fled, as they or others did on the 29th of August, 1821, to Hayia Rumele, where, notwithstanding the difficulty of its access to the enemy, captivity or slaughter might at any moment overtake them. The Turks in great numbers made repeated and obstinate attempts to enter the glen, but were repulsed by armed Greeks, partly Cretans, and partly auxiliaries, who, during the whole day gallantly defended the entrance, as well as the adjacent village of Aradaena, at both which places a great number of the assailants and a few of the Greeks were killed. In a narrow lane of Aradaena the Turks suddenly surrounded and killed about 10 Greeks, including the heroic Samian H. Georgios Muriotes, (see page 58 ,) and Anagnostes Manuseles of Kallicrates, both of whom had greatly distinguished themselves in many previous conflicts. The other 8 were insurgents from other provinces of Crete, and fell after a most vigorous and desperate resistance. The rest of the armed Greeks long continued a most heroic defence, till their ammunition was exhausted. They were then overpowered and slain, after having killed a great number of the enemy.

We have already traced the causes of the utter want of foresight and presence of mind displayed by the Sphakiots whenever their country was invaded; and we have stated that, in such emergencies, the inhabitants of one village did not know what was going on in the villages of their immediate vicinity, while a panic fear had possession of the

Vlastos, a Rethymnian, and two others on board of their ships, gave orders that the schooner should follow them into the harbour of Kydonia, and, by frequent firing over the schooner urged her to enter, with all possible speed. Several marines of great skill and courage, and in particular Stratulas and Andracas Pakhynakes of Sphakia, and Michael Taratsianos of Kydonia, happening to be on board, succeeded in retarding the schooner, and gradually getting her out to sea in spite of the opposition of the crew, who were concerned for the safety of the captain. These resolute Cretans confined the crew in the hold, and persisted in their determination to use every possible effort to save the fugitives. While every moment, however, expecting to be boarded and taken by force to Kydonia, they were suddenly cheered by a favorable breeze from the shore. Setting all sail they steered towards Melos, though for a considerable time they were not beyond the reach of the enemy's guns that continued to fire on them. The fugitives finding themselves out of danger, expressed boundless gratitude to Heaven, and to their gallant countrymen, Stratulas, Pakhynakes and Taratsianos. The captain and the three other individuals that had been taken on board the Turkish vessel, were put to death. I. Vlastos, before being killed, was paraded through the streets of Kydonia with a pack-saddle on his back, the Turks having ascertained that he had been appointed Eparch of Sphakia by the Harmostes.

whole population, though universally acknowledged to be
wanting neither in physical courage nor in warlike vigour.
(see page   .) Every Turkish invasion of Sphakia afforded
its brave inhabitants an opportunity of acquiring fresh military glory, and of proving themselves the trustiest champions
of Grecian liberty. The country afforded them pre-eminent
facilities for securing their families and effects, and of surprising and defeating the invaders among their rugged mountain passes. Had they turned these advantages to account,
the patriots of every other part of Crete would have eagerly
imitated their example, and the warlike ardour that would
thus have soon pervaded the whole Hellenic force in Crete,
would have led to the speedy and permanent triumph of
Cretan independence. Such a part in these emergencies
would have been acted by the heroic mountaineers of Sphakia,
had there existed a greater amount of concord and of enlightened patriotism.

After the lapse of five or six days Khusein Bey marched
next, with his whole army, against the Lampsi, and after
proceeding from their district to Rethymna, and thence to
Apocoronos, he encamped at the village of Armeni. Many
of the inhabitants of these provinces, prostrated by the recent
events in Sphakia, now feigned submission. He lost no time
in marching in great strength against the Kydonians, whom
he summoned to instant submission. To strike them with
terror, he let loose his troops on the first night of Passion-
week. These, proceeding up to the village of Therison, overrun,
before daylight, all the villages of Kerameia and the villages
of Apocoronos as far as Phré, killing or capturing about 200
Christians. The resistance Khusein henceforth encountered
in those parts was feeble and unimportant, for, the moment
he heard that a Greek force, however small, was collecting at
any point, he marched against it with the utmost despatch
and energy, and never rested till he had completely dispersed
or destroyed it.*

A report had been generally spread at this time that a
Greek fleet was daily expected on the Cretan coast, and the

---

* Khusein Bey, who had reduced Crete to these extremities, afterwards
accompanied Ibrahim Pasha to Peloponnesus, by whom he continued to be
valued and honoured as the ablest of his Moslem leaders. He headed the
troops that attacked the Greeks who had occupied the position of Kleisova,
during Ibrahim's siege of Missolonghi. Khusein on this occasion received
a wound of which he died in a few days. His loss was deeply deplored
by the Egyptian commander-in-chief.

Egyptian naval force having, it would appear, got notice of the intended expedition of Tsamados, immediately put to sea. The enemy, determined to employ every possible means to achieve the great object they had in view—the speedy and complete suppression of the Cretan insurrection, adopted the most judicious and effective measures for the purpose. While their fleet cruised on the western coast of Crete, the land forces penetrated into the more mountainous districts, with instructions to harass and afflict the inhabitants by the most brutal cruelties, so as to reduce them to despair, and compel them to instant submission. With this view night raids were incessantly undertaken in all directions, during which the most appalling massacres were perpetrated. Khusein did all this from his determination to crush whatever spirit still remained among the Kydonians, as he apprehended that, if one spark of liberty should be left unextinguished among them, the war of independence might, as previously, in spite of all he had accomplished, again burst forth into a general blaze.

In the meantime, that is, about the end of March, the expected Greek vessels arrived in Crete; and the Egyptian squadron that was cruising off Kydonia and Kisamos, immediately returned to port. The arrival of a Greek naval force greatly revived the courage of the desponding Cretans, and especially those always most determined to sustain the struggle to the last. Unfortunately, however, these Greek ships did not effect the object for which they were expected, and for which they had been invited; for instead of attacking the naval forces of the enemy, they proceeded to the harbour of Sphakia, where they found thousands of men, women, and children, who had taken refuge there. At first Tombazes proposed that none but women and children should be taken on board and conveyed to Peloponnesus or the islands. This arrangement, however, could not be rigorously enforced. The natural affection of fathers did not allow them to send away to a distance and among strangers their dear ones friendless and unprotected; besides, the proposed arrangement was frustrated by the readiness of the seamen to receive on board, with professions of a desire to deliver them from their lengthened sufferings, all the refugees without distinction. Accordingly, here and in other parts of the Cretan coast, about 10,000 souls were embarked, including about 2,000

veteran combatants, whose absence was immediately and
very perceptibly felt in Crete. The rest of the insurgents
that still continued in arms and had taken refuge in various
mountain recesses, were so discouraged, that great numbers
of them hastened to various points of the coast,* and found
means of leaving the island, while most of those that remained made their submission to the enemy. It thus

---

* PERSONAL ADVENTURES AND SUFFERINGS OF MR. C. CRITOVULIDES
IN THIS EMERGENCY.

After being an eye-witness, at Vothonakia, to the slaughter of his father
and various members of the family, who perished with a great number of
other Christians in Crete, he resolved to repair with two unmarried sisters
and four other connexions to Sphakia, in the hope of finding for them there
security and repose. He hastened his departure more especially from an
apprehension that Khusein Bey, who had advanced in the afternoon as far
as Prosneron, was meditating another fearful inroad into the district bordering on the mountains. Critovulides, however, did not venture to take
the usual route, but was under the necessity of attempting to make his way
with the helpless females under his protection over rugged mountains
almost entirely covered with snow, and that too, in the depth of winter, and
during the night.

They immediately took their departure from Vothonakia, and, sometimes
scrambling over rugged rocks, and sometimes wading to a great depth in
the snow, arrived after great hardships to the west of the village of Skyphos
before daylight, not aware that the Turks had during the same night been
marching from Prosneron in the very same direction, and had reached the
village of Skyphos about the very same moment, announcing their arrival
by their usual signal of three discharges of a field-piece. His fellow-travellers, though appalled by the announcement, felt it was useless retracing
their steps, and therefore resolved, in spite of increasing hardships and
dangers to go on. They reached, just before dawn, a fountain on the side
of a tolerably smooth path, above and to the north of the village called
Cametado of Solomon. Here they found about 40 men, women, and
children, refugees, like themselves, from other provinces. Alarmed at the
approach of Critovulides' party, whom, as it was not yet daylight, they
suspected to be enemies, they were preparing to fire, but just discovered in
time that the approaching travellers were Christians. The intelligence,
however, communicated by Critovulides of the arrival of the Turkish force
at Skyphos, spread consternation.

Though the rest of the party were desirous of stopping for a short time at
the fountain to take some refreshment and repose, Critovulides urged them
to continue their journey afraid of their being overtaken by the Turks, and
exposed to the utmost peril, as afterwards actually took place. After a brief
repast, accordingly, he pushed on with his two sisters and their four fellow-
travellers with great despatch towards Lutros before it was yet daylight.
As the sun rose over them at a place between the village of Murion and the
neighbouring glen towards Anopolis, they heard a voice addressed to them
from Murion, and enquiring where the Turks were. Scarcely had one of
the party replied, that the arrival of the Turks at Skyphos had been announced by reports of a field-piece about midnight, but that their present
position was unknown, when looking back the party beheld about 80 horsemen at a small distance behind them, while another detachment of cavalry
was just entering the village of Murion, whence the inhabitants were now
fleeing in all directions, and many of them overtaken by their pursuers
were slaughtered. The refugees that had remained at the fountain were

happened that the very Greek vessels that the Cretans had invited and paid for the express purpose of aiding them in

now either massacred or made captives, and the party of Critovulides would have undoubtedly met the same fate, had not the cavalry halted to reconnoitre the road as they suspected an ambuscade in the rugged mountain district they had now reached; but not a single armed patriot was to be found in the mountain passes of Sphakia to oppose the advance of the invaders.

Hitherto Critovulides and his fellow-travellers had been struggling to escape impending danger. All they had apprehended had now overtaken them, and they were even beset with trials and difficulties, which they had not anticipated. The 80 cavalry now advanced at a more rapid pace, while those who had entered Murion hastened to get possession of the Lutros road. The fellow-travellers of Critovulides now became bewildered and lost all presence of mind, and proceeded towards Lutros, while Critovulides, whom in the confusion they had lost sight of, suddenly found himself surrounded by the enemy. Concealing himself at first under a piece of rock, but finding he would soon be discovered there, he ran in his extremity and climbed a cypress-tree at the foot of a neighbouring hill. He now was able to see from the top of the tree the appalling sight of Turkish forces rushing upwards from all points with yells and shouts. Some of them came almost close to the cypress-tree, and several horsemen actually passed under him. For a few minutes he gave up all for lost, but soon found himself out of immediate danger, owing to the thick branches and foliage of the cypress tree, and perhaps to the impetuosity of the Turks, who, eager to reach Anopolis and Lutros, where they expected abundant booty, did not take time to examine every tree as they hurried along.

After the most unexpected deliverance he descended about twilight, and creeped along till he was at some distance from the hill. This he did from the conviction that a sentinel would be stationed on the hill for the night, because Khusein the commander-in-chief was encamped behind it to the south. After finding himself at some distance from the hill, he wandered up and down during the moonless evening till it was near midnight, in search of some path that would take him to some safe recess among the mountains. Unacquainted with the localities he proceeded till he found himself near the glen between Anopolis and Murion, and overpowered with fatigue, as well as with apprehensions of finding himself at daylight in the midst of the enemy, he resolved to attempt concealing himself within the glen.

To reach the bottom of it appeared to him, however, exceedingly difficult, if not hopeless, in the dark, but he resolved to make the attempt. Scrambling over rugged rocks, and rolling down declivities, he was bruised and torn to the imminent danger of his life. Proceeding, however, in spite of difficulties, he, at length, heard sounds from the recesses of the glen, and was soon able to distinguish female voices and children's wailings. Perceiving that Christian brethren had taken refuge here, he instantly felt hope reviving in his breast. The thought of again conversing with brethren and fellow-sufferers refreshed his heart; but, eager as he was to approach, he reflected on the danger of advancing under the circumstances, and, therefore, resolved to proceed with caution. Remaining at a distance and sheltered behind a piece of rock, he hailed the party, and informed them that he was a Greek, and briefly stated his adventures during the previous day. The party he addressed were startled at his unexpected approach, and apprehending treachery prepared some to defend themselves with arms, and some to take to flight. After repeated explanations and assurances, confirmed by a solemn oath, they consented to receive him among them for a time. We forbear recording the grievous complaints and execrations, which during

sustaining the war of independence, proved the immediate
cause of bringing the struggle to an end, at a moment when

his sojourn with these good people he heard uttered in reference to the
misconduct of the Cretan Government,[*] to which he was a member.

The refugees deemed it necessary to leave the glen before daylight for
the purpose of proceeding to a more mountainous and more secure retreat.
Critovulides requested permission to accompany them, thinking it better to
cast in his lot with them, than to be lurking next day in unknown localities
in the vicinity of the enemy. They peremptorily rejected his request
however, they took from him the small stock of money be had about him, and
now threatened to take his life. On this he addressed himself with great
emotion to one called Marcos, that appeared to be the most humane among
them, and begged to put himself under his protection, which, in fact, he
obtained. Marcos showed him a path that would take him to Apocoronas.
Thus, at length, after a series of painful anxieties, he deemed himself out
of immediate danger.

But his trials were not yet over. No sooner had he escaped from one
danger than he was overtaken by another. He proceeded with all possible
despatch before daylight along the path, pointed out to him by Marcos;
and as he advanced, he had to walk over the bodies of persons recently
slaughtered, while he heard the wailings of children, whose mothers had
been made captives, or had saved themselves by flight. About break of
day he found himself above to the north of the village Prosyalos or Khora
in Sphakia, where overpowered by fatigue he lay down to rest himself,
and immediately sunk into a profound sleep. Awaking soon after sunrise,
he began to reflect with great uneasiness on the place where he still was,
and on the singular dangers from which he had just escaped. Starting at
once to pursue his journey, he deviated a little from the beaten track to
avoid falling in with enemies. Scarcely, however, had he advanced a few
yards, when he perceived a detachment of about 50 or 60 Turks proceeding
to a neighbouring mountain for the purpose of reconnoitring. He instantly
threw himself behind a piece of rock in the midst of thick bushes, and
thus a second time escaped the observation of enemies passing quite close
to him. It fortunately happened that a fall of snow obliged the Turks
to wrap their heads in their mantles, so as to prevent them looking to the
right or left. The detachment proceeded to the destination, and as soon
as they were out of sight, Critovulides, as on the previous occasion,
climbed a cypress-tree, and continued among its branches without food the
remainder of the day, while the snow continued to fall.

As soon as it was dark, he bade adieu to the tree that had afforded him
shelter, and during the whole of the night wandered about as best he
could, trying to keep at a distance from villages and frequented roads.
Owing to the rugged and precipitous ground he had to pass over, he was
frequently obliged to leap from fearful heights, guided in the darkness
solely by the glitter of the snow, and after indescribable hardships reached
Apocoronas on the following day.

We now return to the adventures of the Critovulides' sisters and their
travelling companions. Proceeding along the road to Lutros, from which
they had for a time wandered, they continued their journey with all the
despatch that exhausted strength and overwhelming sorrow would allow.
They had, after separating from Critovulides, lost sight of the other male
relative of the party. They arrived at Lutros in company with other

---

[*] Critovulides had been appointed Secretary to the Eparch of Apocoronas, or
rather had virtually governed that province, owing to the inexperience of its
well-disposed Eparch, Andrulios Protopapadakes, and afterwards to the inefficiency
of Manuse Kunturakes, who was appointed Eparch after Protopapadakes
resignation.

the patriot cause might, through the judicious employment of this naval force, have been revived and more thoroughly consolidated than at any former period.

We cannot here pass over in silence the manner in which, during the passage, the Cretans were treated by those they had paid to come to their assistance. On Good-Friday, when at a short distance from (Monemvasia) Epidauros Limera, where the passengers were to be landed, the crews rose up tumultuously and plundered them without distinction. Thus were the poor Cretans treated by brethren, members of the same communion, and patriots engaged in the same sacred cause of independence. All this was done in spite of the efforts of most of the naval commanders to prevent it. Even the Secretary-General, N. Œconomos, was not spared, but was stripped of most of his effects, including the great seal of Crete, and a valuable snuff-box which had long been in his possession. The unfortunate refugees, after being stripped of all the money, provisions, and clothing they had been able to rescue from the wreck of their country, were landed, and coolly left to shift for themselves. Sooner or later more than two-thirds perished from hardships, sorrows, or absolute want. Tombazes was deeply afflicted at the sufferings of the Cretans, and indignant at the inhumanity of the seamen, but was utterly powerless to control the undisciplined and mutinous crews. It is said that the disgraceful pillaging commenced on board a Spezziot vessel, but was soon followed by the rest of the squadron. The same ships having landed their first victims, lost no time in returning to Crete to receive on board others. But the captain of an Ionian vessel, who

fugitives, just as that relative had succeeded in getting on board a vessel. The scene that followed was heartrending. In vain he implored the people in the ship to receive his relatives, who were standing on the beach uttering, with outstretched hands, the most piercing entreaties and lamentations. Meantime, the Turks were hastening to enter Lutros, and the wretched females would have infallibly fallen into their hands, had not the energy of despair prompted and enabled them to start along the road to Hayia Rumele, or rather, had not a few armed Greeks succeeded in blowing up the powder magazines and most of the houses in Lutros, and thus enabled the fugitives to reach the recess of Hayia Rumele.

The sufferings and dangers to which allusion has now been made, were but a small portion of the tragic occurrences in Crete during this period. It would be vain to count the number of Cretans who then fell victims to Ottoman barbarism; and most Cretans who have survived those dreadful times, could recount similar tragic scenes, through which they, their relatives and neighbours, frequently passed, during the continuance of the sanguinary war of independence.

had been an eye-witness to what had occurred at Monemvasia, gave timely warning in Crete, so that the crews of the vessels, on approaching the coast of Selinon and Sphakia were, instead of being welcomed as friends, fired on as enemies.

Of course these deplorable occurrences filled Khusein Bey with boundless delight. To his astonishment the Greek vessels, whose arrival he had so much dreaded, not only removed from Crete the flower of the insurgent forces, but had spread among the Christians of Crete universal indignation and disgust, and thus rendered him incalculable service. The result greatly encouraged him to employ fresh energy towards the complete and permanent suppression of the insurrection. At the same time he applied to M. D'Herculay, the Austrian consul at Kydonia, to aid him in promoting the submission of the Cretans, and induced him to issue the following address to all Christians in Crete who had not yet laid down their arms:—

"The undersigned, imperial, royal, and apostolic agent for the island of Crete, and living at Kydonia (Canea) hereby declare that His Excellency Khusein Bey, Commander-in-Chief of the Turkish forces in this island, authorised me on the 4th instant to make known to the leaders of the Greeks, that he is disposed to grant them a general amnesty for the past; and, moreover, that he has given me his word of honour, that none of the Greek insurgents shall be exposed to any harm or outrage whatever, and that they shall forthwith enter into the possession of their houses and of the whole of their property, and that His Excellency guarantees to them the enjoyment of their rights as lawful owners thereof. He further directed me to state that His Highness the Pasha of Egypt has authorized him to make these proposals. Accordingly, the Greek insurgents will on laying down their arms, instantly enter on the enjoyment of all their rights and privileges as faithful subjects of His Imperial Majesty. If any of the Greeks, after submission, should have reason to complain of bad faith on the part of the Turks, or the nonfulfilment of the preceding stipulations, the undersigned will proclaim to the whole world that the Turkish authorities have deceived both him and the insurgents, and will employ the whole influence of his position to obtain for himself and the Greeks the most ample satisfaction." *—Published on the coast of Suda on the 12th of April, 1824.

This apostolic agent drew up the preceding document standing on that very soil, where still lay the scattered bones of those who were slaughtered in August 1821 (see p. 46), after numerous trials, calmly preferred death to apostasy from the faith of their fathers†—that faith which the true apostles of Christ preached and sealed with their blood. Not satisfied with publishing and circulating the document, the apostolic agent, in the fervour of his zeal, ran about exhorting those Cretans who were still maintaining the struggle for their faith and their country, to submit again to their merciless oppressors.

Notwithstanding the pacific promises made through the apostolic agent, Khusein Bey continued to employ whatever could inspire terror, in order to reduce the insurgents to instant submission. The circumstances appeared favourable to his purpose. He, accordingly, invaded the provinces of Kisamos and Selinon. The inhabitants, unable to offer resistance to the overwhelming force and fury of the invaders, left in their houses a great number of females, children, and aged persons, in the hope of their remaining unmolested; but, notwithstanding their submission, they were all either put to death or made captives. Those who had been afraid to trust themselves to the discretion of the Turks, fled to the mountains and elsewhere. These were pursued on land by the Turkish soldiery, and on the seas by the Turkish vessels, which after the departure of the Greek squadron, had resumed the blockade of the western shores of Crete, and at length exterminated nearly all, either in great numbers or in detail.

About 600 men, women, and children had at this time sought refuge in the small islets called Elaphonesia,§ on the western coast of Crete, opposite the cape called Kriou Metopon (Ram's Brow). The Turkish cavalry made a furious

* See Spellades' Memoirs, Book II., page 90.

† The number of Christians massacred at Kalyvæ, a village in Apocoronos, amounted to 200, and not merely to 70, as we inadvertently stated (in page 46.) All of them were urged by the Turks to save their lives by adopting the Moslem faith, but they all preferred death, except one, who was about 70 years of age, and, at the moment, entirely overwhelmed and fainting with consternation.

§ Perhaps these are the three islets called by the ancients Musagyræ, or Musagyroi, mentioned by Pliny the Naturalist, and the Geographer Pomponius Mela.

attempt to reach these refugees. At first they were repulsed by about 40 armed Greeks on the islets, who killed a
considerable number of the enemy, and for some time
prevented them from crossing the narrow and shallow
channel which separates the islets from the mainland of
Crete. The Turkish cavalry, however, after numerous
attempts, succeeded; and, landing on the islets in great
force, commenced an indiscriminate massacre of the refugees. Their lamentations and piercing shrieks at this
moment might have melted the most savage hearts, according to a description of the fearful catastrophe given by the
crew of a small vessel that happened to be sailing by, but
which, on account of the Turkish vessels that were approaching, were unable to give any assistance to their brethren,
some of whom, leaping into the sea, in the hope of saving
themselves, were all drowned. Such was the fate of the
600 persons who had fled to these islets. Many such disasters occurred at the same period in similar localities in the
above-mentioned provinces. One in particular occurred
at Trypete in Selinon. At length, the Turks advanced as
far as the narrow glen of Hayia Rumele, but were repulsed
with loss by some armed Greeks there. But who were the
perpetrators of these massacres? Mainly the Seliniot
Turks, whom the Harmostes Tombazes had spared, and
whose alleged treatment by the Greeks the historian Tricoupi so indignantly bewails.

Similar disasters occurred about the same time at sea.
A number of small Greek vessels happened to be sailing
past the Elaphonesia with Greek families on board, and
bound for Kythera, the island of Ægileia (Cerigotto) or
Peloponnesus. These were chased and fired on by the
Turkish squadron, so that some of them were obliged to
return to the ports from which they had started, while the
schooners of Kuletoyannes and Rusos, and some other
vessels of small size, were driven on the coast of Kisamos
at Sphenarion and Amygdalokephalon. A multitude of
refugees were thus brought back to the fate from which
they had hoped to escape. The murderers who had exercised their ferocity at Elaphonesia, hastened to recommence the work of destruction, on perceiving the points at
which the vessels, thus driven back, had touched. With the
exception of a few who had strength to walk, and who had,
on landing, instantly torn themselves from their children,

wives, and aged parents, and fled to the mountains, the
helpless refugees stood exposed to the fury of their pursuers.
The men, the aged women, and the young children, were
all massacred, while the rest of the females were made captives. On this occasion the number of victims exceeded 200
including the venerable Hadji Ioannes Damberges of
Rothymne, with his wife and two children. The number of
captives equalled that of the slain. Among the captives
were the families of Andreas Phasules, Strates Deleyan-
nakes, and the parents and sisters of Markos Kaludes and
Anagnostes Papadakes (or Yeryerianos, * and many others,
The number of individuals massacred at this period in the
above-mentioned provinces, exceeded 1500; and, as we have
said, the atrocities that occurred in the provinces around
Kydonia were perpetrated mainly by those Seliniot Turks
whom Tombazes had permitted to reinforce the garrison of
Kydonia. We again revert to the outrage that S. Tricoupi
has cast on the Cretans in behalf of these same Seliniot
Turks. He seems to have received his information from
persons prejudiced against the Greek cause, and he has
omitted all mention of the atrocities we have now detailed.
Had he known, and duly taken into consideration, all the
circumstances of the case, he could not have avoided cen-
suring Tombazes for sending to Kydonia a reinforcement
about to commit such havoc on the Cretan Christians.

Such was then the state of affairs in Crete as to render
further stay of the Harmostes Tombazes useless. On the
6th of April, 1824, he addressed a parting proclamation to
the Cretans, exhorting those still in arms to continue the
struggle with fortitude, and promised that, on arriving in
Peloponnesus, he would do whatever was possible to obtain
for them from the Central Government the means of sustaining the patriotic cause. It would be, he said to them,
and indeed if so many sacrifices should have been made, and
so much Cretan blood shed, in vain. Repairing to Kaloi
Limenes (Good Havens) and there taking the amiable and
devoted Kurmules* on board of his schooner, sailed for

* Kaludes and Papadakes on this occasion threw themselves into the sea,
and, getting on board on small vessel on the beach, sailed during the
ensuing night through the enemy's squadron, and reached the island of
Ægilelos in safety

* Michael Kurmules died soon after in Hydra from affliction at the apparent ruin of the National cause in Crete. He was then about 60 years of
age. From his arrival in Hydra till his death this once wealthy owner of

Hydra, and, landing Kurmules there, he himself forthwith
proceeded to Nauplia. Unfortunately, however, Tombazes
found Peloponnesus plunged in civil war. Some of the
Government forces were suppressing the insurrection in
different provinces, while others were blockading Panos
Kolocotrones and Dumbalina of Spezzia within the fortresses
of Nauplia. Owing to the disturbed state of the country
some members of the Government were living on board
of vessels at Lerna (Myloi) while others were sojourning at
Argos. In consequence of this all the efforts of Tombazes
to obtain assistance for the Cretans proved fruitless,
though in many parts of Crete bodies of patriots still continued in arms. Notwithstanding this fresh disappointment,
many Cretans remained true to the original watch-word of
the war of independence, "*Liberty or Death,*" and, amid indescribable perils and hardships, waited in hope till brighter
days enabled them effectively to renew the glorious struggle,
as will appear in the sequel.

immense domains in Crete lived on the charity of the Tombazes family.
His fortitude and magnanimity during the struggle were beyond all praise.
Neither the destruction of his dearest friends and relatives, nor the loss of
his high position and immense property shook his devotedness to the cause.
His manners were polished and courteous in the highest degree, and his
moral sentiments and his whole deportment truly noble. He was very fond
of relating his wonderful and tragic adventures, and his mind was deeply
imbued with Christian piety.